The Food Lover's Guide
to
Best Ethnic Eating
in New York City

Robert Sietsema

A CITY & COMPANY GUIDE • NEW YORK

Some words of encouragement

The world of small ethnic eateries is a volatile one. Restaurants open and close daily. Even though the information here was verified at the time of publication, phone before you go to make sure the place is still in business. Or, if you're the impulsive sort, like me, just go. If you find your choice closed, scout around the neighborhood— ethnic restaurants tend to travel in packs, as in Flushing's Chinatown or the Colombian part of Jackson Heights. Once you've found a place, don't be deterred if you don't recognize the food or the staff doesn't speak your language. They'll probably enjoy trying their food out on you and noting your reaction. (Remember, you can always point to something that someone else is eating.)

I hope that this book will serve not only as a convenient advisory for good places to eat, but as a point of departure for your own culinary adventures. Remember, life is too short to have a bad meal.

Robert Sietsema

CONTENTS

INDEXES

INTRODUCTION

Welcome to the third, vastly expanded edition of this book. When it was first published in 1994 as *Good & Cheap Ethnic Eats Under $10 In and Around New York*, it contained 94 restaurants in 17 ethnic categories. Today the coverage has ballooned to nearly 500 places in 79 national and cultural groupings. I'm confident the current edition will serve not only as a convenient guide for good places to eat, but a point of departure for your own culinary adventures in a city that now—more than at any other time in its history—reflects the culinary tastes of the entire world.

In addition to broadening the range of restaurants offered, we've also raised the price ceiling to include moderately priced places and even a few expensive joints offering unique and fascinating dishes. You may never want to eat a full-course meal of fugu, the potentially deadly Japanese specialty that can run as high as $200, but it's nice to know where to get it if you ever do. This book will help you find a restaurant *anywhere* in the city, serving *any* kind of food, at a wide range of prices. It's arranged by cuisine, but there's also an alphabetical and geographical index at the end of the book if you want to pick a place by neighborhood.

I'd like to point out a few new features to faithful readers and newcomers alike. A star (*) preceding a restaurant's name indicates one so good that it's worth crawling there on your hands and knees from anywhere in the city. A series of words at the end of the restaurant's description indicates if the place is vegetarian or kid friendly, kosher, halal, or has outdoor dining. There are also two symbols indicating cost—[¢] for super-cheap places where you can pig out for $7.50 or less, and [$] for establishments where a meal costs $25 or more. If there's no price symbol—the case with most restaurants in the book—you can assume the tab will fall somewhere in between. I've also highlighted a few specialties from each country.

The current hot cuisines are Malaysian, Central Asian, Shanghai, Pakistani, West African, Ecuadorian, and Korean, while French bistros and their Belgian counterparts continue to multiply like empty bottles of Beaujolais nouveau. For the first time in this edition we offer Oaxacan, Armenian, Fuzhou, Guinean, Surinamese, South African, Dai, and Bulgarian, among others. Each restaurant listing, in addition to a thumbnail review, contains an address, cross street, phone number, and subway information. The travel directions don't aim to be comprehensive; indeed, a long essay would be necessary to detail the cleverest ways to approach each restaurant from various parts of town. Accordingly, only the closest stop and trains are cited, and we leave it to your transportation savvy to plot the surest approach. For the intrepid eater, a subway map and the Hagstrom Map of New York City are indispensable.

Thanks, in advance, for buying this book, and for joining me in the life-long adventure of exploring new cuisines—meeting new people and bridging cultural barriers in the process. I'd appreciate feedback on the restaurants you've tried, and on new places that you discover in your travels around the city (my e-mail address is sietsema@aol.com). I'd also like to thank the army of people who have made this book possible, from the folks at City & Company who first believed in it, to my agent Faith Hamlin, to Robert Christgau, Don Forst, Dough Simmons and all the other editors, fact checkers and proofreaders at the *Village Voice*, to Chris Nelson, Gretchen and Tracy Van Dyk, and the rest of the staff of *Down the Hatch*, and, especially, to the intrepid eaters who have accompanied me into exciting neighborhoods in all parts of New York City.

Robert Sietsema

SPECIAL FEATURES

★ PICK OF THE PACK

A & R West Indian Restaurant and Roti Shop (Trinidadian) 205
African Village (Nigerian) 78
Alsalam Restaurant & Meat Market (Lebanese/Syrian) 156
Andy's Colonial (Italian) 106
Bereket (Turkish) 210
Captain King (Cantonese) 36
Chowpatty (Indian) 90
Culpepper's (Bajan) 120
Dosa Hutt (Indian) 91
El Rincon Boricua (Puerto Rican) 152
Hallo Berlin (German) 73
Hasaki (Japanese) 124
'ino (Italian) 109
Katsuhama (Japanese) 125
Katz's (Jewish) 132
Kuruma Sushi (Japanese) 127
Kway Tiow (Thai) 200
La Esquina Criolla (Argentine) 10
Le Gigot (French) 18
Los Dos Rancheros Mexicanos (Mexican) 148
Lupa (Italian) 110
Margie's Red Rose (Soul Food) 189
Matamoros Puebla Taqueria (Mexican) 151
Meigas (Spanish) 193
Meskerem (Ethiopian) 69
Monika (Polish) 54
O Padeiro (Portuguese) 195
Old Poland Bakery and Restaurant (Polish) 55
Pearl Oyster Bar (Regional American) 174
Pearson's Texas Barbecue (Regional American) 174
Pho Cong Ly (Vietnamese) 217
Republic (International) 103
Rio Mar (Spanish) 194
Sahara (Turkish) 212
Salinas (Ecuadorian) 62
Salut (Uzbek) 34
Seabras Marrisquiera (Portuguese) 196
Sentosa (Malaysian) 142
South East Asian Cuisine (Cambodian) 218
Sripraphai (Thai) 201
Taste Good (Malaysian) 142
Toyamadel (Jamaican) 118
Usuluteco (Salvadoran) 29
Warteg Fortuna (Indonesian) 144
XO Kitchen (Hong Kong) 42
Zenon (Greek) 83

VEGETARIAN FRIENDLY

Bahar Shishkebab House (Afghani) 169
Bangal Curry (Pakistani) 94
Bereket (Turkish) 210
Cafe al Mercato (Italian) 107
Cafe Guy Pascal (French) 17
Cafe Rakka (Lebanese/Syrian) 156
Cafe Royal (Egyptian) 159
Chowpatty (Indian) 90
Dosa Hutt (Indian) 91
Fatoosh Barbecue (Lebanese/Syrian) 157
Hoomoos Asli (Israeli) 161
'ino (Italian) 109
Kazan Turkish Cuisine (Turkish) 211
La Pizza Fresca (Italian) 111
La Poême (French) 20
Laila (Lebanese/Syrian) 157
Le Pain Quotidien (Belgian) 15
Luca Lounge (Italian) 110
Madras Cafe (Indian) 92
Meskerem (Ethiopian) 69
New Madras Palace (Indian) 92
Pepe Verde (Italian) 111
Petite Abeille (Belgian) 15
Snack (Greek) 82
Ten Pell (Shanghai) 44
Thali (Indian) 93
Tiffin (Indian) 93
Vatan (Indian) 93
Valdiano (Italian) 112

OUTDOOR DINING

Caffe Volna (Russian) 178
Emerald Planet (International) 101
Little Saigon Cafe (Vietnamese) 215
Luca Lounge (Italian) 110
Markt (Belgian) 15
Mogador (Moroccan) 166
Rectangles (Israeli) 162
Republic (International) 103
Sahara (Turkish) 212
Sahara East (Egyptian) 160

KID FRIENDLY

Baku (Azerbaijani) 32
Blini Hut (Russian) 177
Brawta (Jamaican) 118
Brennan and Carr
  (Regional American) 172
Caffe Volna (Russian) 178
Casa Adela (Puerto Rican) 51
Cino's (Italian) 108
Cowgirl Hall of Fame
  (Regional American) 172
Culpepper's (Bajan) 120
Elvie's (Philippine) 145
Excellent Dumpling House
  (Cantonese) 36
Fountain Cafe (Lebanese/Syrian) 157
Gia Lam (Vietnamese) 215
In God We Trust (Ghanaian) 77
Kway Tiow (Thai) 200
L & B Spumoni Gardens (Italian) 109
Le Pain Quotidien (Belgian) 15
Los Mariachis (Mexican) 150
Louise's (Vincentian) 120
Mama's Food Shop
  (Regional American) 173
Mandoo (Korean) 136
Mie (Japanese) 127
Obaa Koryoe (Ghanaian) 78
Old Poland Bakery and Restaurant
  (Polish) 55
Pho Viet Huong (Vietnamese) 218
Republic (International) 103
Salinas (Ecuadorian) 62
Seabras Marrisquiera (Portuguese) 196
Sentosa (Malaysian) 142
Usuluteco (Salvadoran) 29
Vatan (Indian) 93

KOSHER

Bombay Kitchen (Indian) 89
D. Zion Burger (Israeli) 160
Galil (Jewish) 132
Hapina (Israeli) 161
Jay & Lloyd's (Jewish) 132
Jerusalem Steak House (Israeli) 161
Kosher Delight (Israeli) 162
New Madras Palace (Indian) 92
Pastrami Queen (Jewish) 133
Registan (Uzbek) 33
Salut (Uzbek) 34
Second Avenue Deli (Jewish) 133

HALAL

A & R West Indian Restaurant and
  Roti Shop (Trinidadian) 205
Ali's Trinidad Roti Shop
  (Trinidadian) 205
Bukhara (Pakistani) 94
Glenda's Home Cooking
  (Trinidadian) 205
Halal Indo-Pak Restaurant
  (Pakistani) 95
Swad (Pakistani) 96
Tabaq 74 (Pakistani) 97

Argentine
and Chilean

I once edited a book of 19th-century photos collected by a traveling salesman from South American junk shops. In particular, the shots of the Argentine pampas knocked me out; one depicted a rancho's fenced yard littered with mutilated carcasses, as if every time the gauchos wanted a snack they'd haunch a calf with a single machete stroke, roast it on a makeshift spit, then leave the rest to rot. That's how passionate they were about fresh beef, and that's how available it was. The 2,300-mile Andean spine that separates Chile and Argentina keeps culinary resemblance between these neighboring countries to a minimum. While Argentinean remain obsessed with the semiferal cattle first loosed on the pampas by the conquistadors, Chilcans depend on the seafood that rides the Humboldt Current. And just as Argentine cuisine revels in its Italian borrowings, Chilean dotes on Indian contributions.

ARGENTINE

Chimichurri Grill

606 Ninth Ave near 43rd St, Manhattan,
212-596-8655, subway: A, C, E to 42nd St

This meatery, named after the zingy parsley-and-garlic sauce that Argentinean spoon on their steak, offers beef flown in daily from South America. This unaged meat is mildly flavored, well-marbled with fat, and grilled medium rare with a beautiful char on the surface (although not, alas, over charcoal). If you like to fight with your meat, pick the beef short ribs; if you want butter-soft, get the filet mignon. For dessert, don't miss the lavender flan, which caused a sensation when the place opened. Since there are only eleven tables, you'd better call ahead and reserve. [$]

★ La Esquina Criolla

94-67 Corona Ave near Junction Blvd,
Corona, Queens, 718-699-5579,
subway: G, R to Elmhurst Ave

Argentine specialties

asado
short ribs

chimichurri
parsley-and-garlic sauce

churrasco
sirloin

empanadas
meat, cheese, or seafood turnovers

entraña
skirt steak

matambre
veal roll

mate
gaucho tea

Russian salad
mixed-vegetable salad with mayo

Just over the Andean hump of the Long Island Railroad lies La Esquina Criolla, where the menu is so beef-heavy everything else is peripheral. A glass counter displays large cuts of glistening freshness, and what other restaurant can you name which proudly displays a huge electric meat saw as a decorative item? Most popular is the entraña ($10.95), a grainy, dark, and flavorful skirt steak, best ordered rare. Churrasco ($9.95) is a thin sirloin that flops over the sides of the dinner plate, while the boneless bife de chorizo ($15.95) looks and tastes like porterhouse—so big that a pair of huge fellas sharing one at the next table left with a doggie bag. The steaks come on a metal platter unadorned and ungarnished, with nary a sprig of parsley to distract you from the perfectly cooked meat. Each main course comes with a starchy side dish. Most diners pick Russian salad—cubed potatoes and mixed vegetables obliterated by clouds of mayonnaise, but I prefer the fried yuca, railroad ties of fibrous delirium.

La Fusta

80-32 Baxter Ave near Ketcham St, Elmhurst, Queens, 718-429-8222,
subway: E, F, G, R to Jackson Heights/Roosevelt Ave; 7 to 74th St-Broadway

Skip the mixed grill at this queen of Argentine meateries, unless you relish its heavy component of sweetbreads and blood sausage. Instead, order individual meats, all cooked over charcoal and loaded with flavor. Especially recommended are the beef short ribs, or any of the vast selection of steaks and variety meats (calf liver alone is offered five different ways). Plenty of attention is paid to pastas, including splendid homemade potato noquis, cousins of Italian gnocchi. It's located across the street from Elmhurst Hospital, in case you overindulge.

El Gauchito

94-60 Corona Ave near Junction Blvd, Corona, Queens,
718-271-8198, subway: G, R to Elmhurst Ave

In the heart of Corona's Little Argentina, this combo parillada (South American barbecue) and meat market produces luscious grilled skirt steaks, sweetbreads, short ribs, homemade chorizo, and blood sausage, while the overcooked kidneys and oddly fatty chitins were less than impressive. The pickled tongue appetizer, bathed in an oily version of chimichurri, was so good we ordered another plate. The utilitarian dining room is flanked by ceramic tiles of Argentine heroes, with Eva Peron conspicuously absent. Wash it all down with one of the bargain reds or with a cup of mate.

My Uncle's

89-08 Queens Boulevard near Grand Ave, Elmhurst, Queens,
718-426-8080, subway: G, R to Grand Ave

What better introduction to this parillada than the mixed grill for one ($14.95)? Demonstrating a love of variety meats that puts even the French to shame, it features grainy blood sausage, flattened and slightly charred sweetbreads, tripe, allspice-scented chorizo, and short ribs, all perfectly cooked with no extraneous seasoning. Two diners would be hard-pressed to finish this plenitude. Tripe, a catch-all term, here designates the small intestines, which taste like crunchy liverwurst. For the variety-meat-challenged, the best bet is the half portion of excellent skirt steak ($9.75), which will satisfy any normal appetite. Your meat hoard comes with a choice of sides that includes decent red beans and yellow rice, forgettable french fries, and Russian salad. The best starter is a matambre. Your meal often begins with an amuse-gueule (i.e. freebie) of deep-fried rice fritters laced with ground beef or a small plate of pickled cow's tongue.

 KILLING HUNGER

One of the best starters at an Argentine restaurant is matambre ("kill hunger"), a veal breast rolled around carrots, pimento, spinach, and boiled egg, sliced crosswise and served at room temperature. It was invented as a portable lunch for travelers crossing the vastness of the pampas, who couldn't be bothered pausing long enough to shoot a cow and barbecue it.

La Porteña

74-25 37th Ave, Jackson Heights, Queens, 718-458-8111, subway: E, F, G, R to Jackson Heights/Roosevelt Ave; 7 to 74th St-Broadway

As is customary with an Argentine parillada, the grill is in the front window with an enticing display of meat nearby. The dining room is entered through a rounded arch, under which the waiters linger trolling for customers. The dining room is paneled with rustic wood and covered with gaucho mementos: spurs, lariats, bolos, animal hides, and ugly-looking knives. The waiters extend the theme, tricked out with red neckerchiefs and wide, coin-studded black belts. Pick any of the tables except for the one right under the bird cage—the electronic peeping will drive you out of your mind. Gaucho pie ($1.50)—an empanada with a braided spine and unexpectedly flaky pastry, filled with ground beef and chopped egg— is one of the best deals on the menu, but even tastier is the eggplant vinaigrette ($3.95), four thick slices pickled with garlic and oregano.

Main courses are in the $8 to $13 range and suited in size to the diner who has just dismounted after a day-long ride. A typical national dish is pork chops riojana style ($10.50). When it arrives, you'll wonder where the pig is—the two meaty chops are concealed under a blanket of fried egg, peas, pimiento, and thinly sliced ham. Around the perimeter are fine, albeit greasy, deep-fried potatoes, sliced in rounds. The whole plate is worthwhile, and even the peas taste good.

Pampa

768 Amsterdam Ave near 98th St, Manhattan, 212-865-2929, subway: 1, 2, 3, 9 to 96th St

Debuting on the lower lip of the Manhattan Valley a couple of years ago, this Argentine spot was instantly popular among neighborhood diners, who knifed their way through outsized portions of entraña (skirt steak), asado (short ribs), and filet mignon, grilled precisely to order. Kidneys, tripe, and blood sausage are also offered, but you may want to opt for the pastas, including homemade noquis, pasta dumplings the Italians call gnocchi, sauced with tucco, a delicious combination of pureed tomatoes, strips of roast meat, and garlic. For starters, the fried corn empanadas can't be beat, or pick one of the unexpected Peruvian appetizers.

Sur

232 Smith St near Butler St, Brooklyn, 718-875-1716, subway: F, G to Bergen St

Joining a burgeoning restaurant scene along Smith Street in Carroll Gardens, this Argentine newcomer focuses exclusively on beef. The skirt steak is the most righteous, tender and richly textured, done to perfection on the gas-fired grill. The mixed grill for two includes blood and Italian sausages, skirt steak, sweetbreads, and dual racks of chewy short ribs, served with perfunctory bowls of salad and mashed potatoes and an appropriately zingy chimichurri sauce. But don't miss some of Brooklyn's best french fries, or the dulce de leche (caramel) crepes for dessert.

CHILEAN

El Arrayan

**91-06 43rd Ave at Lamont Ave,
Elmhurst, Queens, 718-478-6245,
subway: G, R to Elmhurst Ave**

El Arrayan occupies a handsome four-story house in a neighborhood of curving small-town lanes. Its dining room is decorated with a relief map of Chile so long, it's displayed in three segments. Starters include baked empanadas ($3) filled with a tasty seafood hash, and mariscal ($9.50), a ceviche of clams, baby shrimp, and gooey mussels that is not for everyone. Best of all, though, is locos mayo ($14), a stonehenge of abalone ("locos" refers to particularly large specimens), each obelisk surmounted by a pig's tail of glistening yellow mayonnaise. The gray flesh is chewy and almost chickeny, and the quantity of gastropod at this price is astonishing—even in Chinatown $30 buys only a small dose.

*Chilean
specialties*

color
*mixture of oil, garlic,
and paprika*

empanadas
*meat, cheese, or seafood
turnovers*

humitas
corn kernel tamales

locos
outsize abalone

pastel de choclo
*corn-topped meat
casserole*

Russian salad
*mixed-vegetable salad
with mayo*

Reflecting Chile's Indian heritage, pastel de choclo ($9.50) casseroles ground meat, chicken, and raisins, topped with crushed corn and sugar—a real find for the sweet tooth. Guatita ($7.50), which bathes a big plate of tripe in a cilantro-dominated "color" (the mixture of oil, garlic, and paprika that's the basis of many dishes), is one of the best renditions of cow stomach I've tasted recently. Though not on the menu, giant tamales studded with corn kernels ("humitas") are generally available.

Pomaire

**371 W. 46th St near 9th Ave, Manhattan,
212-456-3055, subway: A, C, E to 42nd St**

Not far from the capital of Santiago, Pomaire is a quiet Chilean village that is famous for its pottery, and the restaurant evokes the town with a great display of it. First, the waiter brings homemade bread, butter, and a small clay pot of salsa with a tiny spoon. It's delicious and can be smeared with butter or, even better, the red salsa tasting of onion, garlic, and cilantro, all married by olive oil. From the Special Menu: eight entrees that come with salad, dessert, and coffee for $12.95. I went for pastel de choclo y ensalada chilena, a casserole based on corn puree that contains ground beef, chopped chicken, sliced egg, pitted black olive, and onions baked in a brown crock with sugar sprinkled on top. Pollo arvejard, turned out to be a large half chicken with a nondescript sauce and lots of boiled peas and carrots—wholesome but not exotic. Also available is a special lunch with several entree choices, priced around $8. The regular menu is heavy with seafood, some of it actually imported from Chile.

Belgian and French

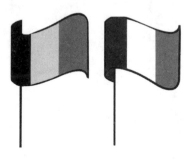

French restaurants—from those slinging haute cuisine with its truffles, foie gras, and fancy wines, to modest bistros where you pay little more than diner prices—have been around in New York for the better part of the last century. In fact, French cuisine inspired the city's first real restaurant back in 1831, when the Swiss Delmonico brothers founded their self-named dining establishment. By contrast, Belgian food is a local fad of recent vintage, probably started by Petite Abeille, a soup-and-sandwich cafe whose original location served the culinary needs of shoppers along the refurbished Ladies Mile—even though the pricier Cafe de Bruxelles had been around for two decades.

If you're accustomed to the garlicky assertiveness of French, Belgian may strike you as pallid, with its milky stews and barely-seasoned seafood. Nevertheless, these places are extremely useful if, for example, you're entertaining garlic-hating relatives from the Midwest, or you're coming off a bout of the stomach flu. Where the two cuisines meet is in the appreciation of fresh mussels and crispy french fries. Available in most Belgian and French establishments, moules frites is reasonably priced, comes in several variations, and needs no appetizer or dessert to feel like a full meal.

BELGIAN

Markt

**401 W 14th St at 9th Ave, Manhattan,
212-727-3314, subway: A, C, E to 14th St**

Listing dishes in Flemish and French, the handsome
wood-clad Markt starts strong with and appetizer of luikdr
salade/salade liégoise ($7.50), a delectable improvement
on German potato salad combining green beans, potatoes, sauteed onions, and crumbled bacon in a vinegar
dressing. Also dependable are garnaalkroketten ($9),
oblong fritters suspending North Sea gray shrimp in an
oozy puree of cheese and potatoes. But good as the
starters are, the menu stumbles badly on main courses.
One of a family of classic Belgian stews called waterzooi,
mer du nord ($19) reunites a halibut filet with its poaching
liquid, adding zucchini, fennel, potatoes, and a touch of cream. Though it made a brave picture, little flavor was coaxed out of the ingredients. A lamb shank cooked in an intriguing sauce thickened
with Leffe brown ale was hard as a subway seat, while a skate wing in pallid black butter generated
no sour twang. The very juicy steak frites ($17.50) turned out to be the best entree. Sit at the bar for
a very good moules frites and a glass of Belgian beer like Duvel or Hoegaarden. [$, outdoor dining]

Belgian specialties

flammande
prune-and-beef stew

fritessaus
mayo for fries

moules frites
mussels and french fries

stoemp
vegetable hash

waterzooi
fish or chicken stew

Le Pain Quotidien

**1131 Madison Ave near 84th St, Manhattan, 212-327-4900, subway: 4, 5, 6 to
86th St / 833 Lexington Ave near 63rd St, Manhattan, 212-755-5810,
subway: B, Q to Lexington Ave / 100 Grand St near Mercer St, Manhattan,
212-625-9009, subway: N, R to Prince St**

This Belgian eat-in bakery is the perfect pit stop after a gallery cruise on either the Museum
Mile or in Soho, offering sandwiches like brie with pecans, smoked salmon sprinkled with
green onions and dill, and jambon de Paris sided by three pots of mustard with fantastically
different flavors. The soup of the day is also worth considering—a meat-free white bean on a
recent occasion loaded with diverse vegetables. Other highlights included a creamy lemon tart
with ground nuts in the crust, and dark and rich hot cocoa. Singles dig the huge communal
table in front, while their parents grow fatter in the rear. A pricier French-leaning dinner menu
has been added in Soho. [kid friendly, vegetarian friendly]

Petite Abeille

**107 W 18th St near 6th Ave, Manhattan,
212-604-9350, subway: F to 14th St**

This tiny Belgian cafe sports an odd logo—a stingerless female bee with human legs and a
bouffant hairdo, just the thing to get you in the mood for the modestly priced, European-flaired

food. Sandwiches include prosciutto, mozzarella, and basil, grilled vegetables, and spicy tuna salad. But more particularly Belgian are the quiches and the selection of stews. Try waterzooi, made with chicken and vegetables in a white gravy, which tastes like a pot pie sans the crust. The place also doubles as a coffee bar, with pastries and Belgian chocolates.

Three newer branches expand on the formula. The more ambitious Meat Market rendition (400 West 14th St, 212-727-1505) is also the best, offering a waterzooi de poissons ($11.95) that delivers a roundhouse punch of salmon, monkfish, snapper, baby clams, and mussels in a creamy tidal pool, the shredded carrots and leeks waving like seaweed. Other delights included flammande, a thick brown stew dotted with prunes masking the bitterness of the beer that serves as beef tenderizer, and stoemp ($9.75), a raucous mash of potatoes and carrots sided with fennel sausages and doused with pan gravy. The West Village version (466 Hudson St, 212-741-6494) has a similar, but slightly smaller menu, although the outdoor tables are some of the most hotly contested in that al-fresco-crazy region. Never tried the new Tribeca branch (134 West Broadway, Manhattan, 212-791-1360), but I'm sure it's fine. [vegetarian friendly]

🍽 TWICE FRIED FRIES

Food fads battle to see who can dominate the city's smaller shopfronts. Lately, stuffed pretzels, fresh-squeezed juice, chicken wings, and wraps have been vying for attention, but, for me, the most interesting fast food has been Belgian fries—the regular coffee shop product won't do anymore. It used to be that you'd have to enjoy these twice-fried beauties at Cafe de Bruxelles (118 Greenwich Ave, 212-206-1830), sitting at the bar and washing them down with overpriced, monk-made beer. Now a half-dozen fry stalls have hit town, offering a big cone in the $3 range with a bewildering variety of sauces, of which a mayo-type fritessaus is the most traditional. Arguing about which is the best has monopolized the conversation of fry addicts for the last year.

Pommes Frites Authentic Belgian Fries (123 Second Ave, 212-674-1234, and their new location: 727 7th Ave, 212-664-0064) was the first, followed by Le Frite Kote (148 W 4th St, 212-979-2616), where the fries are slightly better, the sauces slightly worse. Newcomer B. Frites (1657 Broadway, 212-767-0858), uses a creamier potato and cultivates an atmosphere like a chemistry lab. The fries are not quite as good at Pomme-Pomme (191 E. Houston St., 646-602-8140), but the "hot ajvar," a Turkish-leaning red-pepper dip, rocks hardest of all among exotic sauces for fries. Unfortunately, this new place has discovered that the fryers can also be used for falafel, fritters, onion rings, etc., so your fries are likely to be contaminated by phantom flavors.

FRENCH

À Table

171 Lafayette St near Adelphi St,
Brooklyn, 718-935-9121,
subway: D, N, Q, R to DeKalb Ave

How many French bistros can Fort Greene absorb? This is my favorite so far, a purveyor of bistro classics with a twist, like the haricots verts slicked with vinaigrette and topped with capered chicken livers which come singed on the outside, warm and pink in the middle; or a roasted chicken breast on mashed potatoes improved with a ratatouille whose orange-colored juice makes the plate glow. Though it took too long to arrive, we enjoyed the steak with cube fries, although the lamb served with a stuffed tomato left us unimpressed.

Bouchon

41 Greenwich Ave near 10th St, Manhattan,
212-255-5972, subway: A, B, C, E, D, F, Q
to W 4th St

Ignore the surly service at this new West Village bistro and wine bar, and go for the solid French peasant food, such as the towering braised loin of veal with root vegetables, and the rib-eye mired in hearty red-wine gravy that's only a little too sweet. An exception to the culinary focus is a pair of skate wings browned to crispness and served in a delicious sauce featuring ginger, soy sauce, and two types of sesame seeds. The cozy subterranean room, and the profusion of reasonably priced wines by bottle, glass, and carafe, makes this a great date spot.

Cafe Guy Pascal

1231 Madison Ave near 90th St, Manhattan,
212-831-2340, subway: 4, 5, 6 to 86th St

Charmingly, the waiter corrected the menu's French as he took our order at this new salon de thé, which specializes in largish sandwiches and unusual salads. The Niçois (leave off the "e" due to sandwich gender) piles a good quantity of white tuna on a sourdough roll with chopped egg, lettuce, and tomato dressed with a delicious shallot vinaigrette—no mayo! And though the "Henri Bendel salad" of spinach, roasted red peppers, smoked turkey, bleu cheese, mango, and pear sounded a bit weird, it proved the perfect coda to the Hudson River School show at the nearby National Academy of Design. Be prepared to blow $20 (including tax and tip) on a modest meal of the highest quality. [vegetarian friendly]

French specialties

crepes
thin pancakes folded around a filling

croque monsieur
toasted ham-and-cheese sandwich

moules frites
mussels and french fries

steak frites
steak upstaged by crisp french fries

duck confit
leg and thigh cooked in its own fat

gigot
leg of lamb

bouillabaisse
Marseille's fish stew

pissaladière
caramelized onion tart

Chez Brigitte

77 Greenwich Ave near Bank St, Manhattan,
212-929-6736, subway: 1, 2, 3, 9 to 14th St

Every rule has an exception, and the exception to "There's no such thing as cheap French food" is Chez Brigitte. This ancient and minuscule lunch counter serves up Gallic peasant food unencumbered by cream or nouvelle cuisine, such as a luscious Provençale omelet flecked with fresh herbs and oozing ratatouille. Also recommended are any of the daily roasts— Monday it's leg of lamb, served with gravy, potatoes, steamed vegetables, and petit pois. Avoid the heroes, which are cheap, but meager in the extreme. [¢]

Chez Oskar

211 DeKalb Ave near Adelphi St, Brooklyn,
718-852-6250, subway: D, Q, N, M, R to DeKalb Ave

Neighborhoods don't come any cuter than Fort Greene, and this self-consciously bohemian bistro is a good addition to the local African-Cambodian-Italian-Soul Food culinary scene. Start with assiette de charcuterie, a worthy plate of sweet and hot dry sausages complemented with a thicket of lettuce and tomatoes and a firkin of duck liver pâté that goes great with the sourdough peasant bread. Three can share. Then move on to the marvelous, fork-tender steak au poivre, or the poached cod under a toupee of olive puree. Portions are huge, so a light sorbet is your only option for dessert.

Les Deux Gamins

170 Waverly Pl on Sheridan Sq, Manhattan,
212-807-7047, subway: 1, 9 to Christopher St

A cute and comfortable French bistro from the Old School, priced considerably below par, with fine steak frites, roast chicken, penne with basil, croque monsieur, and a salad made from mesclun and smoked duck breast that has a texture reminiscent of prosciutto. I can still taste a special appetizer of mussels steamed with saffron and shallots, the broth fortified with a dash of cream. Look out the window and see the 170-year-old Northern Dispensary, where Edgar Allen Poe was treated for a headache—with opium, of course.

This bistro has morphed into a chain, wherein quality and cheap pricing seems generally consistent between branches. Other locations (called Le Gamin): 1 Main St, Brooklyn, 718-722-3010; 183 Ninth Ave, Manhattan, 212-243-8864; 536 E 5th St, Manhattan, 212-254-8409; 50 MacDougal St, Manhattan, 212-254-8409.

★ Le Gigot

18 Cornelia St near W 4th St, Manhattan,
627-3737, subway: A, B, C, D, E, F, Q to W 4th St

This French bistro distinguishes itself not only by its charming dining room, but with a menu more ambitious than its dozen or so West Village compatriots. Try the duck confit served on a

◉ EAST VILLAGE BISTROS

Nowadays, you can't throw a stone in the East Village without breaking the window of a bistro. The menus are similar, and the decor seems to have been purchased from the same junk shop in an obscure corner of Paris. Like they used to say about the Indian restaurants on 6th Street—the food must be pumped from a central kitchen. Depend on these places to be filled with hipsters chain-smoking in contravention of the antismoking laws, and to be open way into the wee hours of the evening.

My current fave is Resto Léon (351 E 12th St, 212-375-8483), where dishes like a cod pot au feu curiously paired with a marrow bone, and a beef daube sided with polenta, make the menu more interesting. A stroll down Avenue B from 14th Street to Houston will yield a bumper crop of these places, most notably Casimir (103-105 Avenue B, 212-358-9683), named after a jolly cartoon dinosaur, where an entree of compressed pig feet called pied de cochon ($13) will knock your socks off, and the bouillabaise ($16) is better than you have any reason to expect. On the other side of Tompkins Square is Flea Market (131 Ave A, 212-358-9282), its decor consistent with the name, and its pricing more resolutely downscale. You can dine cheaply on omelets or burgers, or more expensively on leg of lamb or sauteed skate ($13). A few blocks downtown is Lucien (14 First Ave, 212-260-6481), which adds a welcome Provençal twist to the standard menu. Especially appreciated are the under-$10 salads, which make a nice light meal, the ample sardines ($8) grilled by the chef in full view of the patrons, and the very Gallic lapin moutarde ($16).

herbed crouton that sponges up the delicious juices and paired with leek-ribboned mashed potatoes. Against all odds, they also score with an ethereal bouillabaise—a riot of shellfish and finfish in a dense broth to which you add rouille (garlicky red-pepper paste), toasted croutons, and gruyère cheese at your discretion. [$]

Jubilee

347 E 54th St near First Ave, Manhattan, 212-888-3569, subway: E, F to Lexington Ave

The heart of the menu is Prince Edward Island mussels, offered in five variations for $9, or $13 with a choice of fries or salad. The remarkable thing, apart from the pristine freshness of the shellfish, is the quantity delivered for the price. A rough census of my bowl of "poulette" yielded 60, swamped in a cream sauce of rich chicken stock and mushrooms, perfected with a sprinkle of chives. The excellent side of lanky, well-browned fries was better for mopping the thick sauce than bread; the salad, however, was definitely not worth the $4 add-on.

The plate of five snail ravioli ($7.50) was a favorite starter—each stuffed with two gastropods and napped with a parsley-and garlic pesto—rubber wearing silk. Also fab was a gingery tartare of tuna diced with similar-hued onions and tomatoes, served in an ice-cold puck topped with avocado. Consistent with the Provençale warp of the menu is an excellent soupe de poissons ($7). Like the moules, the pricier seafood entrees are also notable for their freshness—witness the crisp-skinned roast salmon ($17.50) served on a bed of shredded fennel. The fish is cooked through, unusual these days, and the buttery chile powder sauce complements the orange flesh surprisingly well. Once again, the chef does amazing things with parsley: pompano filets are piled atop lemon fondant potatoes set in a lake of parsley juice, which adds verdant flavor without shouting down the fish.

Marquet Patisserie

15 E 13th St, Manhattan,
212-229-9313, subway: L, N, R, 4, 5, 6 to Union Sq

This reasonably priced patisserie, with its geometric raspberry barquettes, airy croissants, and brittle cat's tongue cookies, might have been transported from Paris. They also provide excellent light meals until 6 p.m., including soups, pâtés, salads, and amazing sandwiches—my fave made with rosette de lyon—a coarse and powerful salami—with lettuce on white peasant bread smeared with mustard and mayo. There's no better pit stop in the Union Square area. The carryout roast chickens are also divine, their cavities stuffed with onions and fresh herbs.

Pastis

9 Ninth Ave at Little W 12th St, Manhattan,
212-929-4844, subway: A, C, E to 14th St; L to Eighth Ave

Maybe by the time you read this, the hubbub will have died down. Pastis was the most talked-about new restaurant of the 99/00 winter season, obsessively duplicating a certain type of Parisian establishment that has no interest in the innovations of haute cuisine, offering short dishes that make good snacks with a glass of wine, sandwiches, entree salads, and heavier grandmotherly fare. Sure, you can blow a wad here, but some of the cheapest dishes are the best, including a transcendent croque monsieur ($7, lunch menu only) looking like a bread casserole layered with ham and toasted cheese, and the tiny Provençale pizza called pissaladière ($5), deliciously topped with caramelized onions, anchovies, and olives. Cheap burgers, sandwiches, and herb omelets are available anytime. It's open from 9 in the morning till very late at night; go at the most off hour you can manage. [outdoor dining]

La Poême

14 Prince St at Elizabeth St, Manhattan, 212-941-1106, subway: F to 2nd Ave

Furnished like someone's comfy living room, this Corsican-themed French cafe and bakery excels at soups. Check out the seafood chowder, which comes with finely chopped vegetables in a clear broth crammed with fish, or the even more satisfying Corsican bean soup, with humongous white beans in a rich broth with plenty of garlic and a touch of curry powder.

CREPES

Anyone who's wandered around Paris knows that the apex of its sidewalk food is crepes, prepared on a brace of griddles as you watch, drooling. The fillings are usually limited to ham, gruyère, Nutella, and a handful of other ingredients, although if you wander into a full-blown crêperie on the Left Bank you'll be bewildered by 50 or 100 choices.

The Manhattan crepe revival of the '90's has largely deflated, but a number of good stalwarts remain, including Palacinka (28 Grand Street, 212-625-0362), an informal Soho dive with cheap prices right across the street from a picturesque junkyard. Crepes come with a salad; better still are the dessert versions filled with honey, baked apple, chestnut paste, or Nutella. La Crêpe de Bretagne (46 W 56th Street, 212-245-4565) captures the flavor of a Brittany farmhouse. Well, almost. You'll find culinary valhalla in the dessert crepe stuffed with apples, topped with ice cream, and flamed with Calvados. Nothing haute here, although bistro favorites like steak frites and coq au vin are available. If you don't mind standing, there's a window called Crepes to Go at 90 W 3rd St associated with a bar that affects a raffish air, Shade (214 Sullivan St, 212-982-6275). Pick any three items for $4, from a list that includes gorgonzola, smoked salmon, prosciutto, roasted garlic, spinach, and mushrooms. Finally, there's newcomer Rue des Crêpes (104 8th Ave, 212-242-9900), with an interior made to look like a hokey Parisian street scene, and a flexible menu that encourages you snack or assemble a complete meal. Avold anything featuring the dull white bean puree (such as the merguez sausage crepe), in favor of the savory soups or any of the dessert crepes.

Many of the baked goods make nice light meals, like the empanada-shaped pie of sweet potatoes that comes with a small salad. In mid-afternoon, the quiches fly out of the open kitchen like clockwork—grab a slice before they cool. [vegetarian friendly]

Le Singe Vert

160 7th Ave near 18th St, Manhattan, 212-366-4100, subway: 1, 9 to 18th St

This bistro, whose name means "the green monkey," was actually filled with French people one recent evening. Best starters include gazpacho served with a plate of diced vegetables for mixing in, prosciutto and melon nestled in a basket of fried potatoes, and sinister black raviolis bulging with crab. The shell steak wears a delicious pat of garlicky herb butter on its breast, though it's difficult to get the staff to cook the meat beyond a slight sear on the outside. The entree list includes plenty of seafood, with Catalan and Provençal flourishes.

Brazilian, Colombian, and Venezuelan

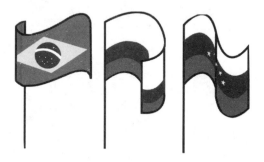

Walk in the vicinity of Roosevelt Avenue between 74th and 108th Streets, and you'll pass half the Colombian restaurants in the city. The food is supercheap, with plenty of rib-sticking snacks like tamales and empanadas; meal-size soups that seem to cover all the food groups in a single, well-seasoned bowl; and outsize entrees with the same meat-and-potatoes attitude as the American Midwest—only yellow rice is substituted for potatoes. Though Colombian restaurants are numerous, the patronage is often limited to Colombians.

By contrast, the rarer Brazilian restaurants often attract crowds of non-Brazilians, especially the rodizios—all-you-can-eat palaces featuring gauchos brandishing swords of meat and running every which way. Rodizios inflamed the imaginations and expanded the waistbands of 90's New Yorkers fleeing 80's health consciousness. But African, Portuguese, and Indian influences make the less meaty parts of the menu far more interesting. But then, it's a rare individual who can resist smoldering hunks of flesh. No reason to include Venezuela in this section, except it's right next door to the other two.

BRAZILIAN

Bêco Azul

19 W 46th St near 5th Ave, Manhattan, 212-840-9304, subway: N, R to 49th St

Putting its Little Brazil neighbors to shame, Bêco Azul offers an unusually broad range of Brazilian cooking, with an emphasis on the rustic. A chalkboard advertising carne seca com abobora ($12.95) lured us inside. It turned out to be a fragrant stew of funky sun-dried beef with chunks of pumpkin that imparted a lively color and hint of sweetness. Complemented with masses of shredded onions and a touch of palm oil, it hinted at the African Influence in the cooking of Brazil.

Brazilian specialties

pão de queijo
cheese-stuffed breadlets

feijoada
meat and black bean stew

vatapá
African fish stew

muqueca
shrimp in coconut milk

bolinhos de bacalhau
salt-cod fritters

My favorite of the cafe's regional styles is cozinha mineira, proletarian fare from the landlocked state of Minas Gerais. A mining boom in the 18th century spawned a gold rush ethos and, as in California, cornmeal was the preferred starch. Feijao tropeira ($10.95), or "mule driver's beans," binds red beans, Portuguese sausage, and cornmeal together with egg, resulting in a lumpy mush tweaked with a heady dose of garlic—totally irresistible. Other remarkable mineira specialties include a pleasantly slimy fricassee of chicken and okra poured over corn pone, and an even better oxtail stew heaped with watercress—some wilts, some remains crisp. Both dishes are served in overflowing portions for $12.95.

Cabana Carioca

123 W 45th St near 7th Ave, Manhattan, 212-581-8088, subway: 1, 2, 3, 7, 9, N, R to Times Sq

This venerable institution famous for its lunch buffet is among my fave Brazilian dives, though it emphasizes the European-leaning aspects of the national menu. The ground floor dining room—warmly lit and decorated with colorful murals, hanging wicker baskets, and exposed brick—offers a $10.95 spread that features 22 items on a serve yourself steamtable. Best is a salt cod, onion, and potato casserole, with buttery kale a close second. Feijoada, the national dish of Brazil, suffers from being underdone and insufficiently gluey. Other offerings are roast pork with gravy, baked chicken, fried calamari, cold shrimp salad, red beans, french-fried potato rounds, and potato salad with ham. If you can make it that far, there's a terrific crème caramel.

Hike to the third floor and find a $5.45 buffet. With only eight selections, this steamtable is a pale shadow of the downstairs installation. Still, the wonderful salt cod casserole is there, and so too is the good roast chicken. I cast my vote for upstairs.

⏍⃝⃒ MEAT ORGIES

The rodizio is something of a utopian concept, proposing that you eat your fill of as many meats as the restaurant can muster. Giant rodizios Green Field (108-01 Northern Blvd, Corona, Queens, 718-672-5202), and Master Grill (34-09 College Point Blvd, College Point, Queens, 718-762-0300) were founded by Korean immigrants from Rio. They caused a hubbub in the 90's, and Manhattan reviewers dutifully made pilgrimages to write about them. Nothing quite matches the sight of a charcoal grill as long as a large yacht across the humongous dining room. Skewers arrive in dizzying profusion: lamb, veal, chicken, turkey cubes wrapped in bacon, Italian sausage, three kinds of steak, kidney, and a grisly impalement of 50 chicken hearts. The anti-meat buffet is just an afterthought.

If you want to blow a bigger wad by staying in Manhattan, avoid the island's first rodizio, Riodizio, in favor of the much better Churrascaria Plataforma (316 W 49th St, 212-245-0505), where the all-you-can-eat is $32.95 ($26.95 at lunch). The meat is good, appetizers and desserts are included, and you can probably make one meal last the entire day. The exotic buffet is loaded with salads and Brazilian dishes of high quality.

Astoria has always had a handful of Brazilian churrascarias that go rodizio on the weekends and sometimes in the evenings. Basically, there needs to be a quorum of diners before they crank up the meat volume. Churrascaria Girassol (33-18 28th Ave, Astoria, 718-545-8250) charges a modest $14, which includes a bare-bones-but-good salad bar and an all-you-can-eat selection of meat. First place goes to the well-browned chicken, with brisket as runner-up. If you want to economize further, both meats are included in the $10 mixed skewer. Their feijoada is one of the city's best. Samba & Sabor (25-10 33rd Street, Astoria, 718-956-6755) is spectacularly located beneath the gleaming elevated Astoria Boulevard station, which waits for you like a spaceship at the conclusion of your meal.

Delícia

322 W 11th St near Greenwich St, Manhattan
212-242-2002, subway: 1, 2, 3, 9 to 14th St

Few baked goods in the world attain the ecstatic heights of pão de queijo ($3.50), the golf-ball-shaped Brazilian cheese bread served piping hot. While the outside is brown and crisp, inside the cheese melds with the yeast dough to create a taffy-like consistency that many dream about. Also typically Brazilian are the finger-shaped codfish fritters known as bolinho de bacalhau ($3.50). While Europeans wash salt cod meticulously to remove the salinity, the Brazilians appreciate the taste of the sea that the dried fish imparts to the fritter, which is so toothsome, you don't need sauce.

The cook makes a fine rendition of shrimp muqueca, an African-inspired concoction that finds the crustaceans swimming in a heavenly sauce of coconut milk and tomato. Her way with meat is showcased by a delicious entree of spice-rubbed roast pork ($12) that's topped with a vinegary relish of tomatoes and green onions. But foremost among the meat-bearing entrees is feijoada ($14). In its inky depths lurk pork ribs with the meat falling off the bone, intensely smoky ham hocks, and sausages—a symphony of oink bound together by black beans. This is a dish that the devil reserves for his own dinner.

COLOMBIAN

Costal Colombiana

21-20 35th Ave at 42nd St, Long Island City, Queens, 718-706-0663, subway: G or R to Steinway St

Costal Colombiana offers a broad selection of fish, beef, and chicken dishes, plus a pair of special stews each day (medium bowl, $4; large, $5). My medium order of the tripe stew called mondongo came in a cereal-bowl size portion. The broth—green with cilantro, smelling intensely of garlic—contained ragged pieces of tripe and an equal number of chunks of good pork. Potatoes, peas, carrots, and rice filled out the bowl. The pork prevented the tripe from becoming tiresome. The chorizo appetizer ($3.50) brought me one large, garlicky sausage, garnished with onion, tomato, and lettuce, plus an arepa. Arepas are small cakes made from cornmeal mush cooked on a grill, which leaves charred hash marks on the top and bottom. Hard as rocks outside, arepas are white and fluffy inside. [¢]

Colombian specialties

arepa
grilled corn cake

mondongo
tripe stew

sancocho
hearty pork or chicken soup

tamale
meal in a banana leaf

Rincon Colombiano

106-20 Corona Ave, Corona, Queens, 718-393-1060, subway: 7 to 111th St

For a huge, cheap meal keep your eye on the daily special soups: Sunday it's sancocho de gallina, a cilantro-accented chicken broth crammed with potatoes, yuca, and plantain, sided with an even bigger plate of fricassee chicken, rice, and salad, all for $5.50. Also featured are outsize Colombian tamales wrapped in banana leaves and stuffed with meat and vegetables, shrimp in creole sauce, fried pork chops with rice and excellent beans, and, of course, arepas, the rotund white corn cakes that are a national signature. For dessert, the Lemon Ice King of Corona is visible just down the block. [¢]

VENEZUELAN

Flor's Kitchen

149 1st Ave near 9th St, Manhattan,
212-387-8949, subway: L to 1st Ave

Probably the only Venezuelan in town, this 5-table joint is so small there's barely enough room for all the rave reviews plastered in the front window. I guess the food lives up to the notices, although Venezuelan cuisine is not exciting enough to send you running to the travel agent. As in Colombia, arepas are a big part of the kitchen, in this case light and fluffy and pleasingly crusty despite the paleness of the exterior. The arepas are split in half and stuffed with a variety of fillings including reina pepiada, a chicken salad stuck together with avocado. Averaging $9, the entrees run to things like pabellon, a sweet version of Cuban ropa viejo, and grilled kingfish steak sided with salad and rice.

Central American

I wish I could say there were plenty of Honduran, Panamanian, and Costa Rican restaurants in town—but there aren't. Instead, we have to content ourselves with a slew of Salvadoran (so many, in fact, that we can afford to be picky about our pupusas), and a single, glorious Guatemalan. The latter cuisine demonstrates its similarity to Mexican by reinterpreting familiar notions like enchilada and taco, while partaking of pan-Central American standards like salpicón, a crunchy salad of meat and vegetables zapped with a vinegary relish.

The heart of Salvadoran cooking is the pupusa, a grilled white masa cake that remains light despite its filling of cheese or ground pork. One of the world's great fast foods, it's a million times better than a Whopper, and cheaper, too. An enormous range of quality exists among Salvadoran cafes, and many of the undesirable places buy their pupusas readymade—and frozen solid. Accordingly, run from an unfamiliar Salvadoran unless you hear the slap-slap-slap of pupusas being made fresh.

GUATEMALAN

Xelaju

87-52 168th St near Hillside Ave, Jamaica, Queens, 718-657-5407, subway: F to 169th St

This unpretentious Guatemalan eatery has a comfortable dining room with handwoven tableclothes with Mayan motifs, and a wreath made from worry dolls. The food resembles Mexican in some ways, but the differences make it well worth a pilgrimage. Especially recommended is salpicón, a cold salad of pork, radishes, and tomatoes dressed with lemon juice and flavored with fresh mint, and the amazing plate of three tacos, like Mexican flautas—tortillas wrapped around a filing of smooshed chicken and masa, deep fried and dusted with cheese. [¢]

Guatemalan specialties

enchilada
fried tortilla with topping

longaniza
spicy sausage

pollo con crema
chicken in sour cream sauce

revolcado
pork head stew

salpicón
meat salad

taco
stuffed, rolled, and fried tortilla

SALVADORAN

Los Chorros

46 Fifth Ave near Flatbush Ave, Brooklyn, 718-230-5365, subway: 2, 3 to Bergen St

This serviceable Salvadoran on the frontier of Park Slope offers the usual Central American specialties: cheese or bean-stuffed papusas, satisfying soups crammed with vegetables and laced with cilantro and spaghetti, and comida tipico entrees of roast chicken, liver and onions, and pepper steak. The most satisfying snack is a chicken enchilada that looks like a Mexican tostada. On Fridays only there's atol de elote, a sweet puree of fresh corn described on the menu as "oatmeal of corn." [¢]

El Comal Pupuseria

148-62 Hillside Ave, Jamaica, Queens, 718-291-1340, subway: F to Sutphin Blvd

Of course, if you want really serious pupusas, go to a pupusería. You'll find more than one on Hillside Avenue in Jamaica, Queens. El Comal is a boxy lunch counter with a big griddle as its centerpiece, whereon pupusas are fried. Choices are cheese or bean, or a combination ($1 each). The pupusas are larger than average, made from a dough more stiff and pita-like than usual. The hairnetted countergal flings a pair on the griddle as you order, and with a great show of dexterity, flips them again and again, patting them with the spatula after every flip. The pureed bean interior is ramified with tiny fibers of pork that gives the pupusa a porkerific crunch. On the side is a tart cabbage slaw inundated with hot sauce. The pupusas and slaw are laid reverently on a piece of tissue in a shallow plastic basket. Other offerings at El Comal include biftek encebollado, yuca con chicharrón, tamales, Salvadoran enchiladas, conch and shrimp ceviche, and a variety of meal-sized soups. Sopa de res ($4) comes in a white bowl and contains oxtail, yuca, chayote, green beans, red peppers, zucchini, and potatoes in a light broth redolent of onions, green peppers, and garlic. [¢]

Izalco

64-05 Roosevelt Ave, Woodside, Queens,
718-533-8373, subway: G, R to 65th St

On the menu cover, an erupting volcano named Izalco eclipses the Manhattan skyline. The dining room is no less dazzling: an armadillo faces off against an iguana on a red-tile roof as a stuffed bullfrog drags his butt out of the way. Worth checking out are the three varieties of Salvadoran tamales ($2.50), the tastiest of which is sal, bursting with pork, potato, garbanzos, and green olives, all wrapped in a banana leaf, and bathed in a mild chile sauce. The towering Salvadoran enchilada showcases a diminutive tortilla (thick like a pupusa), deep fried and topped with beef and potatoes concealed by a light snowfall of crumbly cheese and a slice of boiled egg.

Most Salvadoran pupuserias limit themselves to a menu of masa-based snacks and jumbo soups. Izalco expands on this menu by offering meat and seafood entrees, and a number of huge omnibus platters called Izalqueños, priced at $9.95. One features salpicón, which is also enjoyed in Guatemala, making it something of a Central American staple. It comes with a logjam of buttery, perfectly cooked rice, meaty-tasting refried beans, sliced avocado, salad, and a plate of those tiny tortillas. You'll be taking half of it home.

★ Usuluteco

4017 Fifth Ave near 40th St, Brooklyn,
718-436-8025, subway: B, M, N, R to 36th St

Stuffed with cheese or pork, hand-patted, then cooked to speckled brownness on the griddle, pupusas are one of the great comfort foods. These uniquely Salvadoran masa pancakes get their name from a Nahuatl Indian expression meaning "swollen tortilla." At Sunset Park's Usuluteco, queso is best, oozing ropes of white cheese flecked with green loroco flowers, rescued from mellowness by curtido, a zany cabbage relish flavored with oregano and tinted beet-juice pink. Slit the pupusa ($1.25) and insert the slaw. Bet you can't eat just one.

Salvadoran specialties

pupusa
stuffed masa cake

salpicón
cold meat and radish salad

curtido
pink vinegar relish

yuca con chicharrón
fried pork and manioc

tamale de elote
sweet tamale studded with corn kernels

At two on weekday afternoons the restaurant floods with campesinos, who sit singly taking their afternoon bowl of soup with a pupusa or two. The chicken soup ($4) is particularly good, boldly flavored with garlic and cilantro, bustling with carrot, potato, chayote, and stray strands of spaghetti. Another popular dish is yuca frita con chicharrón ($6), a national passion featuring chunks of pork rubbed with garlic and fried to a concentrated porkinesss, tossed with yuca cooked like french fries, cloud-fluffy in the middle. [¢, kid friendly]

Central Asian

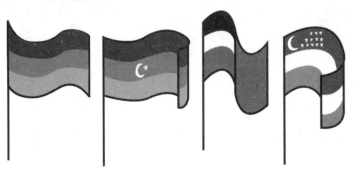

The new prevalence of Uzebek, Georgian, and Azerbaijani restaurants was one of the big food stories of the last decade. Always good cheap places to score shish kebabs, usually grilled over charcoal, each revealed new dishes unfamiliar to most New Yorkers. In particular, the Georgian use of nuts and pomegranates, and their superior renditions of chicken tabaka—the world's best fried chicken—made me want to go again and again.

The Uzbeks have established themselves as the best kosher joints in town, as long as you don't order the syrupy wine. And Azerbaijani restauranteurs accommodatingly serve a pan-Russian menu, in addition to their own secret vices of kufta-bozbash meatballs and horseradish-heaped tongue. And, hey, there's one restaurant from Soviet Armenia mentioned here, and I leave it to your investigations to reconstruct its culinary relationship to the East European version of Armenian food.

ARMENIAN

Yerevan

**47-57 41st St near Greenpoint Ave,
Long Island City, Queens,
718-784-4651, subway: 7 to 46th St**

The meal ends on an up note. I ask the host if he has any desserts. He gives me a quizzical look, and says "Turkish coffee?" which seems like a weird name for it, given the Armenian animosity toward Turks. I ask again about dessert, and finally a look of recognition passes over his knit brows like a cloud torn from the sun by a stiff breeze. He reappears with a lovely wooden tray with generous handfuls of walnuts, pecans, and cashews, and a few foil-wrapped Russian candy bars. Armenian dessert.

Armenian specialties

borek
red pepper tuffed with cheese

khinkali
large meat-stuffed dumpling

kufta
giant beef meatballs

manti
lamb ravioli

sujukh
spicy sausage

The main courses featured a pair of very long ground-beef kebabs ($8.50), light, buttery, and moist. They lay on a bed of basmati rice dusted with dried dill, topped with big arcs of onion littered with flat-leaf parsley, enough for two hungry diners. Another entree was charmingly titled "home specialties:" chicken, mushrooms, pickles, kashkaval cheese, seasoned sauce. What they don't tell you is that these ingredients are rather repulsively mixed together.

Khinkali ($1.25) arrived with the appetizers, a huge dumpling shaped like a round coin purse with a pucker on top, made of thick dough and stuffed with ground meat. Dusted with finely ground black pepper and bathed in butter, three would make a fine entree. Other appetizers were equally as good, especially a borek ($2.50) made by breading a long red pepper stuffed with feta and frying the heck out of it.

AZERBAIJANI

Sarmish

**1162 Coney Island Ave near Ave H, Brooklyn,
718-421-4119, subway: D, Q to Ave H**

Ditmas Park boasts dozens of cafes from the Caucusus. Sarmish is the newest and one of the best, offering fare from Azerbaijan. Kebabs are succulent, charcoal flamed, and bargain priced at $1.50 each (pick the pork). Soups like rassolnik are also dependable, combining lamb, barley, and vegetables in a dilled tomato broth. Also enjoy standards like fist-sized lamb dumplings called manti, looks-like-it-was-run-over-by-a-truck chicken tabaka, and rounds of grilled eggplant dressed with enough garlic to liquefy your innards. Then go elsewhere for coffee and dessert.

Baku

2718 Coney Island Ave near Ave Y, Brooklyn, 718-615-0700, subway: D to Neck Rd

A sign above the smoked-glass window offers Russian and Turkish food, and the same rack of synthesizers and amplifiers that grace so many restaurants in Brighton Beach serves to confirm the Russian part. Extended families occupy several long tables, and children run wild, or sprawl on the carpet fiddling with plastic portfolios of color markers. On the walls are paintings of mosques from Baku, the capital of Azerbaijan, including the 13th-century fortress of Bad-Kube.

Azerbaijani specialties

manti
meat dumplings

rassolnik
lamb-and-barley soup

pelmeni
tiny meat ravioli

kufta-bozbash
meatball soup

vareniki
potato potstickers

What's "Red Lobia with Nuts"? A well-endowed foe of Conan the Barbarian? It turns out to be a bowl of kidney beans in a slurry of pureed walnuts with enough raw garlic to make your hair stand on end. Another impressive starter is tongue stuffed with garlic ($5.75), a plate of thinly sliced pink meat featuring a wad of powerful horseradish relish on the side—do-it-yourself stuffing. Skip anything with caviar in it. For soups, pick kufta-bozbash ($5.90), a huge porcupine meatball of ground lamb and rice towering over potatoes and chickpeas in a thin consommé delightfully scented with cilantro and garlic. Dumpling lovers shouldn't miss potato vareniki, envelopes of noodle dough stuffed with potatoes and obscured by a mantle of crisp brown onions. [kid friendly]

GEORGIAN

Tblisi

811 Kings Highway near E 9th St, Brooklyn, 718-382-6485, subway: D, Q to Kings Highway

Welcome Tblisi, offering the nut-stuffed, fruit-sauced, herb-rife, and grilled glories of Georgia. The narrow room sports a wraparound mural in a quasi-Impressionist style depicting peasants in conical fur hats toasting each other, and a neat row of trees climbing the flanks of a mountain, from which the archangel Michael ascends.

Georgian specialties

chicken tabaka
flattened garlic chicken

lobbio
kidney bean salad

chikhirtma
yolk-thickened chicken consommé

khachapouri
cheese bread

lulya
ground lamb kebabs

The novelty of Georgian cooking is apparent as you begin your meal with a handful of cold dishes. Satsivi ($8.99) smothers chicken pieces in a puree of crushed walnuts, garlic, fenugreek seed, and onions sauteed just long enough to give the sauce its golden hue. Constructed like Japanese maki, cabbage rolls ($5.99) are even more delicious, the pickled wrapper crisp and the ground-walnut filling amplified with loads of cilantro and raw garlic.

Hot soups are also popular, including Central Asian standards like harcho and hashi, in addition to the uniquely Georgian chikhirtma ("chicken with eggs soup," $3.50), an impossibly rich broth thickened with egg yolks and zapped, once again, with cilantro and garlic. But the best starter is khachapuri ($5.99), a round flat loaf of bread stuffed with white cheese and eggs beaten together. The best main is chakapuli ($9.99), a casserole of lamb chunks cooked to tenderness with herbs that retain an intense green color. King of kebabs is lulya ($8.99), a pair of lamb forcemeat cylinders laced with onion, perfectly flamed and served on a bed of glistening fries.

UZBEK

Eastern Feast

1001 Brighton Beach Ave at Coney Island Ave, Brooklyn, 718-934-9608, subway: D, Q to Brighton Beach

Uzbek specialties

chalokhoch
lamb chop

hasib
rice-and-blood sausage

Korean carrots
garlicky shredded salad

lagman
lamb-and-noodle soup

pilaf
lamb and rice

Like the parasite in Alien, Eastern Feast insinuated itself in the belly of Mrs. Stahl's Knishes awhile back. A charcoal grill—whose fragrant smoke was more effective than any sign—was installed in the front window; a table with round loaves of nigella-seed bread was trundled into the public thorough-fare, and a sign was added to the facade with the evasive misspelling Medittereanian Food. Though the eatery is a modest one (Mrs. Stahl's remains open), the Uzbek food is some of the best in town. A glass case holds raw brochettes of pork, lamb, beef, chile-rubbed chicken and, if you're lucky, sweetbreads. Order a kebab ($2.50), and the white-smocked griller tosses it on the fire. The fuel is irregular chunks of hardwood charcoal that sizzle and shoot smoke as the meat drips. Lamb is the best, the tender meat cooked rare and offered on a bed of salad spattered with white vinegar, with a toasted pita on top.

For those accustomed to paying an inflated $20 or more for the Uzbek national dish of pilaf in Forest Hills or Rego Park, the price tag at Eastern Feast comes as a relief ($4). It's the most expensive thing on the menu, a plate of glistening rice woven with shredded carrots and green onions. There's an overwhelming presence of cumin. On top are chopped green onions and a generous portion of lamb. [¢]

Registan

65-37 99th St, Rego Park, Queens, 718-459-1638, subway: G, R to 63rd Dr

The short menu at Registan, whose staff comes from Bukhara, is bizarrely inexpensive: soups, served in big bowls, are $3, and easily make a lunch (add one of the huge salads to make dinner). Pelmeny is a wonton soup with a lighter broth and even more vegetables than lagman—almost health food. When I say vegetables, you can automatically assume I principally mean carrots, which are soul food in Uzbekistan. Half the dishes on the menu feature them in one form or another. Best are Korean carrots, raw and shredded in a salad, mounded on a huge plate like Big Bird's nest, dressed with oil and crushed raw garlic. The rest of the menu consists of kebabs (kefta, lamb, chicken, beef, liver, and sweetbreads) and french fries. Kebabs are priced at only $1.50 or $2 apiece, each with four large pieces of meat. Most of the patrons were scarfing them with their fingers. The faces of the patrons were a feast in themselves, with a stunning array of features and skin tones. [¢, kid friendly]

★ Salut

63-42 108th Street, Forest Hills, Queens,
718-275-6860, subway: E, F, G, R to Forest Hills/71st Ave

Salut is a kosher cafe offering food from Uzbekistan, where the ancient cities of Bukhara, Samarkand, and Tashkent harbored communities of Jewish silk traders for a millennium. The fluorescently-lit dining room is baited with the requisite chandelier and big-screen TV, on which a Soviet Michael Jackson clone in a Thriller costume cavorts on a pulsating stage. But what drew us inside was the unmistakable perfume of meat grilling on real charcoal.

Soon a plate smeared with babaganoush ($2.50) appeared, a strong odor of garlic and grilled eggplant wafting upward. Richly underscored with toasted sesame, it was one of the best babas I'd ever eaten, served with wedges of warm bread hacked from a turban-shaped loaf. The soup called lagman was mind-blowing, the bowl so heaped with cubed vegetables and lamb that no liquid was visible. Underneath lurked homemade noodles, no doubt related to those Marco Polo observed Samarkanders preparing in 1272. As you might expect from a Silk Road cafe, salads were rife with international references. Armenian pickled cabbage ($1.99), thick slabs of a purple head soaked in strong vinegar, left a violet puddle on the plate. Korean carrots ($3) had a wonderful tart edge—shreds flecked with garlic and cayenne that reflected the chandelier's light. It disappeared in a flash, leaving us to wonder yet again if this oft-seen dish is named after the nation or the local vegetable stand.

As for the shish kebabs, the "chicken with bone" rocked hardest, the crisp skin intact around smoky flesh, the bone adding flavor. Khorovak, amorphous morsels of sweetbreads, were nearly as good. Mostly bargain-priced at $2.25 or less, kebabs also included the mysteriously named "beef (special cuts)," which were flavorful but tough. More expensive was lamb chalokhoch ($3.50), a goldmine for bone-gnawers. Our multi-course pig-out for three came to about $40 including glasses of ghastly kosher wine, but you could dine spectacularly for under $8 with lagman, babaganoush, and a single kebab. [¢, kid friendly]

Chinese

Chinatowns in Manhattan, Queens, and Brooklyn are booming. Not just with more restaurants and better restaurants, but with more choices than Baskin Robbins, at a price range that goes as low as $1 for a light meal. Not only do we have the the old-hat-by-now Sichuan, Hunan, and Cantonese, but now we can boast Fuzhou, Dai, Hong Kong, Hainanese, Taiwanese, and Teochew, not to mention at least a couple of Chinese-Malaysian hybrids (see Malaysian). And don't think for a minute that authentic, cheap, and tasty Chinese is only found in Flushing. For a real change of pace, check out the developing Chinatown in Brooklyn's Homecrest, ranging along Ave U on either side of the D train. Cantonese eateries used to be the cheapest, but they were undersold by the Vietnamese, who, in turn, were undersold by the Malaysians. Now the Fujianese (from Fuzhou) have taken over. A hearty meal of three dishes selected from the steam table over rice will set you back $2.75 in most places. Another bonus is that most Fujians will serve you a soup appetizer free of charge, since that's their idea of how a meal is structured. Only the Cantonese are bigger soup fanatics.

CANTONESE

★ Captain King

82-39 Broadway near Britton Ave, Elmhurst, Queens, 718-429-2828, subway: G, R to Elmhurst Ave

Recently arrived, this bargain Chinese has already garnered raves. Choose any three main dishes from a list of 59 for $16.95 (each additional $5), and rice and soup are furnished gratis. Our faves on a brisk winter afternoon included a Taiwanese chicken pungent with basil, and preserved pork with garlic greens—the savory meat tasting like it had just emerged from the smoker. Shaped like fingers rather than pincushions, the pan-fried dumplings were memorably crisp and fresh; another "don't miss" is the chive-and-egg-stuffed fried buns. [¢]

Cantonese specialties

black bean sauce
fermented black beans

congee
rice gruel

dim sum
steamed dumplings

rice cake
box-shaped rice noodles

three precious ingredients
pork, chicken, and egg over rice

Congee Village

100 Allen St near Delancey St, Manhattan, 212-941-1818, subway: F to Delancey St

Their specialty is the rib-sticking rice gruel called congee, offered in 29 variations including such diverse choices as "pork heart and meat ball" and "parsley and sliced fish." Go as a group and you can order it buffet style, with the add-ons offered in bowls to be passed around. The balance of the menu is Cantonese, with some Malaysian elements like a wonderful dish of skewered shrimp (eat them shell and all) sprinkled with briny spice powder, and steamed rice dishes presented in cylindrical bamboo vessels, flavored with ingredients like eel and salt-preserved duck.

Excellent Dumpling House

111 Lafayette St near Canal St, Manhattan, 212-219-2333, subway: J, M, N, R, Z, 6 to Canal St

This small restaurant has much in its favor, especially at the cheaper end of the menu. Fresh-tasting scallion pancakes are lighter and less greasy than the usual sodden version. At $1.50 an order, they're a bargain. Rice cakes turn out to be culinary wonders, fried with garlic, green onions, and a choice of meats. The Shanghai fried rice ($5) happily unites many of the fish and meat ingredients normally found in carryout Chinese food. Another outstanding dish is the forbidding-sounding sliced fish and sour cabbage: fresh hunks of cod battered, deep-fried, and then wok-fried with tangy strands of pickled sweet-and-sour cabbage and other greens. Avoid the "sizzling" dishes. Not only are they higher priced, they're cloaked in a close approximation of bottled French dressing. [¢, kid friendly]

Fried Dumpling

99 Allen St near Delancey, Manhattan,
212-941-9975, subway: F to Delancey St

When it comes to eating out, how cheap is cheap? Check out Fried Dumpling, one of the new dollar Chinese eateries, where a Washington gets you five wonderful dumplings stuffed with a savory pork filling and fried on one side like gyoza; or four pork buns shaped like bread igloos; or a bowl of thin gruel studded with mung beans that pleads to be fortified with the chile and vinegar sauces on the table. Ranging from 50 cents to $2.50, other selections include hot-and-sour soup, vegetarian potstickers, and, best of all, a sandwich of aromatic star-anise beef on a homemade sesame flatbroad. [¢]

Natural Restaurant

88 Allen St near Stanton St, 212-966-1326, subway: F to Delancey St

Who could resist the conch with yellow chives? The wok furnishes the smoky flavor, and a fermented shrimp sauce adds salty highlights. Everything we sampled at this no-frills Chinese was fresh and perfectly seasoned, including baby octopus with black bean sauce, ostrich (like thin-sliced beef only tenderer) with scallions and ginger, and chicken lo mein made with noodles firmer and narrower than usual. Best of all was the salt and pepper soft-shell crab: big, meaty, two to an order, and strewn with shredded jalapeno and orange rind.

N.Y. Noodle Town

28 Bowery near Canal St, Manhattan,
212-349-0923, subway: B, D, Q to Grand St

With admirable economy, the name describes this place's raison d'être: noodles fried, souped, and steamed by every method available. My favorites are the Cantonese-style wide noodles, China's answer to Italian fettuccine. Order the seafood-and-vegetable version and be amazed by the quantities of squid, cuttlefish, octopus, scallops, and shrimp, interspersed with carrots and broccoli rabe. Even the humble lo mein excel, abundantly sauced and smoky from the wok. Non-noodle recommendations include roast suckling pig over rice, steamed water spinach, and any of the dishes cradled in an edible taro basket. [¢]

Sun Hop Shing Tea House

21 Mott St at Mosco St, Manhattan,
212-267-2729, subway: J, M, N, R Z, 6 to Canal St

Most people prefer to eat dim sum, the teahouse dumplings of China, at restaurants where the dining rooms are as big as football fields and where total strangers are seated cheek-by-jowl at huge tables. As the carts go 'round the room, the plates of dumplings become progressively colder and more dried out. I prefer this tiny place with ten tables, where the distance from the kitchen to the front door is only about 30 feet. After each cart passes, the plates that are not purchased are stacked in a glass-fronted steam case. Still, they're best when they come right from the kitchen. An excellent plate here is fried taro, lacy cakes made of shredded taro root, with a nutty sweetness and crunchy exterior. Another eye-opener is the bean curd stuffed with a mixture of pork, ginger, and green onion. And don't miss the bean curd skin roll—pork filling in a thin, rubbery wrapper. It's one of the most successful bean curd delivery systems ever invented. [¢]

Wong Kee

113-117 Mott St near Hester St, Manhattan,
212-226-9018, subway: J, M, N, R Z, 6 to Canal St

It is an axiom that all eateries have at least one great dish. In some Chinese restaurants, it's written in Chinese on a strip of pink paper hanging on the wall. At Wong Kee, the great dish is on the small "coffee shop" menu usually not offered to non-Asian customers. You have to ask for this menu when you sit down, and you'd better not ask for it after 6 P.M. The dish called three precious ingredients over rice ($4.65) makes an excellent late lunch or early supper. The three ingredients—sweet anise-baked pork, sliced steamed chicken, and a cold fried egg—are artfully arranged on a heaping plate of rice with the brown sauce that is poured over most Chinese barbecue. On the very top is a salty green condiment thick with green onions and fresh ginger. Do not accept the dish if the green stuff is not present. The combination of flavors is devastating. [¢]

DAI

Dai Jia Lou

19 E 48th St near 5th Ave, Manhattan,
212-230-1922, subway: B, D, F, Q to
Rockefeller Center

Half of the 50 ethnic minorities in the People's Republic of China live in Yunnan province, pushed into the mountains by successive waves of Mongol and Chinese invaders. Ethnically related to the Thai, the Dai tribe dominates the southernmost region of Xishuangbanna, directly across the border from Burma and Laos. Their Southeast-Asian-influenced cuisine has become a favorite all over China via a chain of theme restaurants in a dozen cities.

Dai specialties

black chicken
small, black-skinned, with medicinal properties

mango beef
tart beef with mango served in fruit shell

shrimp soong
shrimp with yellow chives

Shrimp soong ($7.50) is the perfect introduction to a meal: an oblong plate of diced shrimp, garlic, and yellow chives anointed with oil. The mixture is wrapped, Vietnamese style, in lettuce leaves. More adventurous eaters shouldn't miss the tiny clay pot of modestly named "steamed chicken soup with Chinese tonic" ($3.95). This spectacular nostrum is a virtual catalog of unusual ingredients, from pieces of miniature black chicken—the midnight skin and bones of which contrast arrestingly with its white flesh—to dried red lichees, to medicinal-tasting pseudo-ginseng. Also don't miss mango beef ($16.95), a sticky stew of meat and green fruit spiked with vinegar and served in a mango shell.

FUZHOU

American East Fuzhou Restaurant

54 East Broadway near Pike St, Manhattan, 212-226-0969, subway: F to East Broadway

Though Shanghai restaurants get the lion's share of attention, Fuzhou establishments have been multiplying at an equal rate—there are two brand-new ones on this stretch of East Broadway. Order anything with "foo chow sauce" to get dishes braised in hong zao, a red paste of rice-wine lees with a subtle and intriguing flavor. We ordered rabbit done this way, and the dish came larded with pieces of pork to make up for the leanness of the bunny. Sautéed snow pea shoots dotted with caramelized cloves of garlic were another favorite at our table.

Fu Chow Restaurant

84 Eldridge St near Grand St, Manhattan, 212-343-3905, subway: B, D, Q to Grand St

Obscurely located near a shop that specializes in rat poison, Fu Chow has a large dining room decorated with a smiling-babies bas-relief. As I sat looking out at the tumbledown tenements across the street, restaurant employees kept sneaking up behind me and screaming in Chinese at the top of their lungs. At first I thought they were being playful, until I realized that a PVC pipe sticking out of the floor was their intercom to the basement kitchen.

The standard combo of three dishes over rice is ($3) also includes a bowl of pearly broth bobbing with mussels. As an added refinement, the three dishes are served on a separate plate from the rice. My choices on a recent day included a sumptuous fried kingfish steak moistened with a sweet-and-vinegary chile solution, surprisingly good green peanuts braised with tiny chunks of pork, and a generous heap of chewy lotus root. [¢]

Spring Boy Fuzhou Food

81 Allen St near Broome St, Manhattan, 212-625-0001, subway: B, D, Q to Grand St

Chinatown's new frontier embraces the blocks around Grand Street east of Roosevelt Park, a region still dotted with discount lingerie merchants and purveyors of Judaica. This area is

🍽 **FURTHER FUZHOU**

Hey, I can't keep track of all the Fuzhou places opening around town. I hear about so many that I could devote every meal to the subject. As far as I know, there's no such thing as upscale Fuzhou. Here are a couple of additional places I've visited, after the enthusiastic recommendations of friends: Kam Wong (5405 8th Ave, Brooklyn, 718-851-3535), and Good Good Taste (13A Market St, Manhattan, 212-385-9220).

home to many new Chinese restaurants; the smallest and most obscure are lunch counters hawking the fare of Fuzhou, the industrial capital of Fujian. Halfway between Shanghai and Canton, this coastal province (formerly known as Fukien or Hokkien) produces the country's most prized soy sauce. The lunch counter favors slow braising over stir-frying, deploying soy sauce, sugar, vinegar, and hong zao—a red paste of rice-wine lees—to create dishes of unexpected lightness and subtlety. Spring Boy Fuzhou Food is a microscopic establishment with a menu featuring memorable dishes like tortoise sauteed with vegetables ($5), rabbit cooked in hong zao ($8), the poetic "boneless duck hand with conch" ($8), and a supernally good platter of three butterfish braised in sweet soy sauce ($6). [¢]

HONG KONG

C & F Restaurant

171 Hester St near Mott St, Manhattan, 212-343-2623, subway: J, M, N, R, Z, 6 to Canal St

Hong Kong soaked up the regional cuisines of China like a sponge, then turned to England, Southeast Asia, and the U.S. for further inspiration. To savor Hong Kong's complexities, start with a salad of julienned jellyfish dressed with sesame oil and tossed with Vietnamese vegetables, or choose any of the comforting congees. Next try baked salt-and-pepper shrimp—to be eaten without removing the crunchy shells—or the Malaysian-influenced pork with pickled vegetables over rice. Wake up early and check out the wacky breakfasts, like a Spam-and-egg sandwich washed down with Horlicks.

Hong Kong specialties

congee
rice gruel

Horlicks
hot malt beverage

Spam
potted meat product

tong shui
medicinal dessert soups

XO
fiery condiment

Hong Kong Seafood

40-48 Main St near 44th Ave, Flushing, Queens,
718-961-3302, subway: 7 to Flushing/Main St

You can spend a little or a lot here. Chinese barbecue over rice is available at low prices, as are soups, dim sum, and bakery products. The dim sum appetizer for two ($5.50) offers four pieces each of steamed shrimp dumplings and pleasantly crunchy steamed wontons with pork and water chestnuts. All of the Chinese families dining around us were enjoying a bean curd appetizer, which consisted of a huge mound of fried bean curd squares with several unexpected sauces: one combines anchovies and red wine vinegar, another is mustard based, the third a fiery red chile paste. Of the higher priced entrees, the best was squid with sour vegetables ($7.75) in a semisweet brown sauce with red and green bell peppers and hunks of pickled cabbage. Even more tender were the silky slices of stir-fried conch ($13.95) in a briny garlic sauce.

Ping's

20 East Broadway near Catherine St, Manhattan, 212-965-0808,
subway: B, D, Q to Grand St
83-09 Queens Blvd near Goldsmith St, Elmhurst, Queens,
718-396-1238, subway: G, R to Grand Ave

Named after its celebrity Hong Kong chef, Ping's serves innovative pan-Pacific chow out of a smallish storefront on East Broadway and a larger, newer space in Elmhurst. Presented as a collection of color snaps, the menu includes dishes from Malaysia, Japan, Thailand, and Korea, in addition to Hong Kong-style and its cousin Cantonese, with the emphasis always on the aquatic. Seafood tanks face a prep area where, as we entered, a turtle sprawled in a tureen of steaming broth as his comrades looked on dispassionately.

Where'd they get those amazing three-bite oysters ($2 each), nearly eight inches in length and not on the menu? Get them steamed or raw, with a delicious black bean sauce reeking of garlic or, even better, with a vaguely Malaysian concoction called XO—a smoky, incinerating relish in which bits of bacon, dried shrimp, and pickled chile are bound together with bean thread. The non-Chinese dishes can get pretty zany. Delicate Korean beef rolls ($12.95) came arrayed in spokes, stuffed with silky enoki mushrooms. Some of the wildest offerings, however, are pure inventions, like seafood soup tai chi ($13.95). Spectacularly configured as a yin-yang, the soup's dark side is a swirl of pureed greens, while the light side is a ghostly hodge-podge of crab and other former seagoers. The dots are evoked by carrot-hued crab coral. Altogether, it's one of the most appealing dishes I've eaten all year, easily sharable by three or four. [$]

Sweet-N-Tart Restaurant

20 Mott St near Chatham Sq, Manhattan,
212-964-0380, subway: J, M, N, R Z, 6 to Canal St

This expanded version of a tiny cafe up the street (at 76 Mott St, 212, 334-8088) and its more substantial Flushing location (at 136-11 38th Ave, Queens, 718-661-3380) offers informal Hong Kong coffee shop fare on three hopping levels: Chinese hipsters pick the pastel-colored basement, while

ᴵ◯ᴵ HOLDING UP THE MIRROR

Hong Kong rivals New York in cosmopolitan allure, and you won't be surprised when I tell you that the city boasts ethnic restaurants that specialize in American and European food, jiggered for Chinese tastes. Of course, many of the Hong Kong coffee shops sell a handful of American and English dishes featuring Spam and Velveeta, but ABC American Cooking (41-13 Kissena Boulevard, Flushing, 718-461-1313) goes for it whole hog, with an entire menu and premises devoted to what it believes is authentic Western cooking. A few of the dishes, like escargot bourginoise [sic], improve on the original, but most—like pork chops with fruit sauce and tofu-stuffed trout—taste like airline food, and seem like a species of culinary revenge. The dramatic dining room features a stunning full-wall transparency of Hong Kong harbor, while the vaulted ceiling is a galaxy of tiny twinkling lights. It's worth a visit, especially if you also plan to eat somewhere else in downtown Flushing.

the fogies end up on the third level. Choose among a startling array of dim sum, from excellent Shanghai soup dumplings, to iffy "Italian spring rolls" oozing mozzarella, to a salad of iceberg lettuce, shrimp, and diced papaya served in the hollowed-out fruit shell. Favorite bigger feeds—invariably soups, noodles, or rice dishes—include crystal fried rice, deliciously tossing shrimp, vermicelli, and rice with little clouds of egg white. For dessert visit the tong shui menu of salutary fruit-based beverages, puddings, and soups. Note: this is one of the few places that serve dim sum into the evening.

★ XO Kitchen

**148 Hester St near Bowery, Manhattan,
212-965-8645, subway: B, D, Q to Grand St**

Clad in a checked gingham scarf, the waitress trips across a rustic bridge to deliver the casserole, doffing the lid with a flourish to reveal the well-browned, Midwestern style chicken-and-mushroom casserole. But "baked chicken kew with portagal sauce" ($5.95) is the latest in Hong Kong diner food found at XO Kitchen. The lush green mussels ($4.95) carpeted with chopped garlic and broiled on the half shell are more Gallic; ditto the escargot delivered in its own shell and garnished with a sprig of parsley. And the pan-fried dumplings ($3.95) are Japanese gyoza, rendered in a homemade, vegetable-laced version that puts their frozen counterparts to shame. Whatever their origin, the gooey rice-starch pancakes ($3.95), rolled up like a rug and crisply fried top and bottom, are just plain wonderful.

If you're not Chinese, the waiter will warn you off the Hong Kong lo mein. "Too dry," he says—but these gossamer noodles, steamed rather than stir fried, are the perfect starch fix for those who dread the high correlation between Chinese restaurants and grease. The best of the eight lo mein are braised black mushroom ($3.75) and beef mussel [sic] ($4.25), both of which come with a bowl of scallion-strewn broth in case extra moisture is needed. [¢]

SHANGHAI

Joe's Shanghai

9 Pell St near Bowery, Manhattan,
212-233-8888, subway: B, D, Q to Grand St.
136-21 37th Ave, Flushing, Queens,
718-539-3838, subway: 7 to Flushing/Main St

The best seats in the house are in the back—huge green communal tables where you'll be seated with extended families, couples on dates, and singles loudly sucking soup. The compulsory first course—the waiters will prompt if you forget—is steamed buns, the celebrated soup dumplings of Shanghai. Other noteworthy starters included smoked fish noodle soup, with wonderful leathery pieces redolent of star anise—the fish tastes like it's been smoking since the Long March—and Shanghai yellow chive and shrimp wontons ($5.25), much perkier and chewier than the usual article.

Russia is said to have inspired the Shanghai penchant for short cold dishes, buffet style. Joe's has a typical selection—a few shared would make a meal. One is vegetarian duck($5.95), braised tofu skin with a sharp smoky flavor layered around shiitake mushrooms. The wildest is drunken crabs (6.45), with the meat and orange roe served inside the cracked blue shell and everything marinated in an aged wine viengar that produces a weird taste.

Shanghai specialties

drunken crabs
ceviche of crab in wine vinegar

garlic-sauteed kelp
submarine Shanghai fave

pork shoulder
mountain of meat in brown gravy

steamed buns
pork and gravy dumplings

vegetarian duck
tofu skin roll

yellow chives
seasonal Shanghai vegetable

New Green Bo

66 Bayard Str near Mott St, Manhattan,
212-625-2359, subway: J, M, N, R, Z, 6 to Canal St

With Shanghai restaurants more common than Cantonese these days, news that another has opened in Chinatown is likely to provoke a shrug. But this establishment, which hears a familial connection to defunct old-timer Say Eng Look, distinguishes itself by reproducing all the standards with superior delicacy: juicy buns crowned with an extra wad of crabmeat, for instance, or cold spiced beef more aromatic than usual. My favorite entrees make unusual use of tofu: pork sauteed with strips of floppy bean-curd skin, and okra with tofu puffs—clouds of spongy curd that soak up the soothing sauce. The decor will remind you of an operating room.

Shanghai Cuisine

89 Bayard Street at Mulberry St, Manhattan,
212-732-8988, subway: J, M, N, R, Z, 6 to Canal St

Another entry in the Shanghai stampede—this one looking more Soho than Chinatown with its brick walls and antique posters. The menu complements that of places like Joe's and Shanghai Gourmet by including many unique dishes like wine-marinated hog tongue and fried turnip cake with shrimp, in addition to the predictable soup dumplings and mock duck. Be shocked by the pork shoulder—a mountain of meat smothered in brown gravy with a forest of steamed baby bok choy on the perimeter, or enjoy the healthier bean curd skin with fermented cabbage and fresh soybeans, or the knockout Shanghai fried chicken.

Shanghai Tang

77 West Houston St at Greene St, Manhattan,
212-614-9550, subway: N, R to Prince St

Occupying an ungainly second-floor space with great views, this Flushing refugee poses the question: Is this Soho, or the new northern verge of Chinatown? The fare compares favorably with the dozen or so Shanghai joints further downtown, and features excellent soup dumplings, good ocean eel with yellow chives, and an above-average vegetarian duck appetizer, enfolded in well-bronzed bean-curd skin. The service is amiable but fumbling, but you won't care as you tuck into the excellent lion's head meatballs tinged with star anise or the crispy whole fish smothered in dark sauce.

Ten Pell

10 Pell Street near Bowery, Manhattan,
212-766-2123, subway: B, D, Q to Grand St

If you don't want to wait in line at Joe's, this alternative across the street will do just fine. It's an old-guard Shanghai place with Hunan and Sichuan for the tourists, but stick with some of the Shanghai dishes, like an assortment of cold appetizers including faux sliced duck made from vegetable substances, shredded and garlic-sauteed kelp, pickled cabbage, and spicy dried sardines. A favorite entree is "bean curd leaf with snow vegetable and beans"—masses of flavorful greens chopped fine, interlaced with bean curd skin and dotted with fresh green soy beans—a powerhouse of protein. [vegetarian friendly]

 SLURPING DUMPLINGS

Shanghai soup dumplings are puckered purses of noodle dough surrounding a filling of pork and trace amounts of crab swimming in greasy gravy. Bite into it unawares, and you'll be sprayed with molten grease—high-risk cuisine. Here's how to do it: gingerly transfer a dumpling from steamer to spoon so as not to prick the envelope and lose the soup, nip off the top, and noisily suck up the gravy inside, as Asians do with hot soup, before polishing off the pouch.

SICHUAN and HUNAN

Wu Liang Ye

**36 W 48th Street near 6th Ave,
Manhattan, 212-398-2308,
subway: B, D, F, Q to Rockefeller Center
215 E 86th St near 3rd Ave, Manhattan,
212-534-8899, subway: 4, 5, 6 to 86th St
338 Lexington Ave near 39th St, Manhattan,
212-370-9647, subway: 4, 5, 6 to Grand Central**

These branches of a Chinese restaurant chain specialize in Sichuan and serve dishes that are often significantly different from their Chinese-American counterparts. In general, go for anything on the menu with the hotness symbol beside it. The sesame noodles are a revelation, moist and tart without being gloppy. Ditto the prawns with citrus sauce, a half-dozen giant crustaceans lightly sauteed with variegated peppers and glazed with a sweet lemon sauce. For starters, skip the oversubtle soups in favor of the excellent "herbed spring bamboo shoots," or any of the dumplings. Its location in an elegant townhouse parlor and an expanded menu makes the west side branch the best. [$]

Sichuan and Hunan specialties

beef with chile sauce
thinly sliced fillet in fiery sauce

broad beans with scallion sauce
fresh lima beans

monkey mushrooms
brainy blobs from Yunnan

sesame noodles
cold sesame paste noodles

Grand Sichuan

**125 Canal St near Chrystie St, Manhattan,
212-625-9212, subway: B, D, Q to Grand St
229 9th Ave at 24th St, Manhattan,
212-620-5200, subway: C, E to 23rd St**

Sichuan bottomed out 10 years ago, as every two-bit neighborhood joint tossed chiles into its Cantonese and called it "Szechuan". To study the cuisine's more rustic aspects, there's no better place than Grand Sichuan.

One doesn't associate lima beans with Chinese food, making broad beans with scallion sauce ($4.95) one of the best starters. The photogenic legumes are cooked way beyond al dente and bathed in fragrant sesame oil flecked with green onions. Even for those who pick limas out of their frozen mixed vegetables, it's a delight. Another celebration of terrestrial flavors is beef filets with chile sauce ($9.95), thinly sliced beef pounded into submission, then long braised to further enhance tenderness. Chile oil and braising liquid swirl around the meat heap, which conceals a motherlode of sweet bok choy; wads of crushed garlic are strewn on top.

But the food has its subtleties as well. The flip side of the banquet menu claims to present the favorite delicacies, mainly Hunan, of Mao Zedong. One of the most intriguing is monkey mushrooms with three treasures ($11.95), spotlighting a variety that grows in Yunnan—brain-shaped blobs cooked with mild green loofah, shrimp, chicken breast, pork belly, and sliced bamboo. But the pièce de résistance is smoked tea duck ($12.95), successively marinated in wine, roasted in damp tea leaves, steamed, and finally fried. Here it's beautifully presented with slices of rich meat still glued to burnished skin, which is smoky like bacon.

TAIWANESE

David's Taiwanese Gourmet

84-02 Broadway near Elmhurst Ave, Queens, 718-429-4818, G, R to Elmhurst Ave

A special that the waitress assured us was her favorite dish, crab with squash ($10.95), shows the culinary contrast between Taiwan and the rest of China: while mainlanders sauté the whole crab in oil and smear it with black-bean sauce, Formosans steam and shell the crustacean and surround it with lozenges of loofah in a barely thickened broth. Located in Elmhurst on a stretch of Broadway that has become a panorama of Asian eateries, David's affects a Japanese decor: lithographs of kimono-clad women, a sushi bar, a suit of armor that seems to be made of hay, and a rustic appliance for polishing rice that virtually blocks the front door.

Taiwanese specialties

duck's tongue
small bony tongues in wine sauce

fermented bean curd
stinky but good

ginger chicken
chicken braised with star anise and holy basil

holy basil
smaller and more licoracey than European

loofah
pale green squash

oyster omelet
shellfish in egg and sweet-potato starch

But the inherent lightness of Taiwanese food doesn't mea that it doesn't pack a punch. Fermented bean curd ($4.25) looks like the plain old stuff, but the minute you bite into it, your mouth fills with a loamy barnyard taste. Holy basil, rarely encountered in Chinese restaurants, is all over the menu. One of its uses is in ginger chicken with sesame oil ($8.95), a facile description that fails to evoke this wonderful and complex dish, in which the bird is braised in soy sauce, ginger, and a spice mixture dominated by star anise. Fresh basil adds a second anise-flavored twist.

Laifood

38-18 Prince St at 39th Ave, Queens, 718-321-0653, subway: 7 to Flushing/Main St

Flushing's Chinatown is ballooning, just like Manhattan's. My favorite bulge is on the western edge, where a slew of new Taiwanese and Malaysian restaurants have opened. This region is characterized by a hill that rises, San Francisco style, from Main Street, to afford a breathtaking view of the stagnant Flushing River and the surreal blue mass of Shea Stadium, best viewed at sunset, or better yet in complete darkness. At the corner of Prince and 39th is Laifood, a Taiwanese restaurant with a handsome bilevel dining area. Because the island of Taiwan has been colonized by the Portuguese, occupied by the Japanese, and endured successive waves of immigration from mainland China, Taiwanese food is a rich hodgepodge of influences. The bill of fare is a menu-reader's delight, filled with inscrutable entries like "tasty duck tongue," "intestine, pig blood with sour mustard," and "crispy smelled bean curd"—suggesting that other noses have enjoyed it before your own. But maybe smelly is what's really meant, since the bean curd appetizer ($4.95) comes smothered in preserved black beans, fermented cabbage, and Vietnamese-style hot sauce, vying with each other for stinkiness. We wolfed it right down. Another amazing appetizer is oyster pancake, but our hands-down favorite was rice sausage—thick slices of sausage arrayed in two rows, stuffed with sticky rice studded with brine-soaked peanuts and dried shrimp. It comes with a bowl of oily amber dipping sauce enlivened with cilantro. The thirty appetizers were so good that we could have stopped there and been perfectly happy.

Natives from the Midwest, or you're coming off a bout of the stomach flu. Where the two cuisines meet is in the appreciation of fresh mussels and crispy french fries. Available in most Belgian and French establishments, moules frites is reasonably priced, comes in several variations, and needs no appetizer or dessert to feel like a full meal.

TEOCHEW

Sun Golden Island Restaurant

**1 Elizabeth St at Bayard St, Manhattan,
212-274-8787, subway: J, M, N, R, Z, 6 to Canal St**

Until a few years ago, this restaurant was one of the only places in New York where you could find Teochew cooking, a subtly spiced variation on Cantonese with an emphasis on seafood and noodle dishes. Skip the appetizers and go right to the entrees. Crab is the best deal of all. Crab with chingens sauce ($8.95) is a good-sized plate of four hacked-up Dungeness crabs (enough for two people) with a briny sauce of ginger and black beans. Try the house specialty, fried e-fu noodles Chiu Chow style ($7.95)—a nest of thin, deep-fried noodles with white sugar and wine vinegar poured on top. Unusual? You bet!

🍽 BLOODY ANGLE

Doyers is now an insignificant byway but around 1900, this crooked street joined with Mott and Pell to constitute the entirety of Manhattan's Chinatown. In those days, the tongs held sway over a Chinese population estimated at less than 10,000. As the On Leongs and Hip Sings vied for supremacy in gambling, opium, and prostitution, the oblique curve in Doyers became a notorious place of ambush by tong members bizarrely clad in chain mail and wielding hatchets and pistols, earning it the sobriquet "Bloody Angle." Several underground passages led from the curve to Mott and Pell, and made for the speedy escape of assassins. Nowadays, the street plays host to Vietnamese, Malaysian, and Cantonese restaurants, as well as the Chinatown post office, and the loudest noise to be heard is not the clash of hatchets, but the dropping of the mailbags from the postal truck.

Cuban, Dominican, and Puerto Rican

The food of the Latin Caribbean has long been dominated by Cuban cooking, and Puerto Rican and Dominican restaurants usually offer Cuban dishes like pernil, arroz con pollo, and the miraculous Cuban sandwich. Puerto Rico has some world-class dishes, but you're more likely to find them in homes than in restaurants. Dominicans, on the other hand, are avid restaurateurs. They're also the great chameleons of the Caribbean restaurant scene, often making their restaurants resemble Cuban, Puerto Rican, Galician, or Spanish establishments. One tip-off that a place is Dominican is a neon sign advertising seafood in the front window.

CUBAN

Havana Chelsea Luncheonette

190 8th Ave near 19th St, Manhattan, 212-243-9421, subway: C, E to 23rd St

This Cuban greasy spoon has a refrigerator case with a window on the street, so you can look in at all the good stuff: flan and coconut pudding, big ceramic bowls of octopus salad and salt cod salad, and slices of pork waiting to be incorporated into the best-selling Cuban sandwich. Made on Italian loaves with layers of roast pork, boiled ham, Swiss cheese, and pickles, the sandwiches are placed into a two-surface hot press that toasts, melts, smashes, crisps, and generally anneals the sandwich, to the benefit of the bread and the fillings. Cuban sandwiches come in two sizes—mediano ($3.50) and grande ($4.50), which could be called "humongo." Pulpo salad ($6.00), made with rubbery chunks of octopus, onion, green pepper, celery, and pimiento—all marinated in oil and vinegar—is also highly recommended. Yuca ($3) is another estimable offering, the starchy root vegetable boiled to a consistency just short of mushiness. Make sure you get the garlic sauce called mojo that makes this dish great. [¢]

Cuban specialties

alcapurrias
meat-stuffed plantain fritters

biftek encebollado
steak 'n' onions

Cuban sandwich
ham and cheese toasted in a sandwich press

flan
pudding with burnt-sugar glaze

mofongo
mashed plantain with gravy

Moors and Christians
black beans and rice

pernil
garlic coated roast pork

pulpo
octopus salad

yuca con mojo
tuber with garlic sauce

tostones
twice-fried plantains

National Cafe

210 1st Ave bet. 12th & 13th Sts, Manhattan, 212-473-9354, subway: L to 1st Ave

The corner of 13th Street and 1st Avenue is the epicenter of East Village good eats, including at the National Cafe, a Cuban joint run by a family of women who make excellent pork roast, fricasseed chicken, black beans, and yellow rice. It's one of the best places to eat in the East Village, but don't everybody go at once. There are only three tables and a few counter stools. Carryout, however, is always an option. Mofongo (a mashed plantain concoction) is made to order. [¢]

¡O¡ CUBAN CHINESE

Fleeing Fidel, Cuban Chinese immigrants hit New York in the early '60s. This unique subgroup was brought to the Caribbean before World War I to work in the sugarcane fields. They became Cuban in every respect but race: they spoke Spanish, dressed in guayaberas, and mastered the art of Cuban cooking. Plenty of the 5,000 who came to New York opened restaurants, especially on Chelsea's 8th Avenue, on the Upper West Side of Manhattan, and along the Grand Concourse in the Bronx. The best in Chelsea was Sam Chinita (recently closed), which occupied a shiny old diner on 8th Avenue. While there used to be eight along this strip, now there's only one—La Chinita (166 8th Ave, 212-633-1791). As at any Cuban-Chinese restaurant, ignore the Chinese side of the menu, which contains bland Cantonese dishes imperfectly remembered from the 1920s, and go straight to the Cuban side, where you'll find the food that the Cuban Chinese themselves prefer to eat. These dishes are prepared with gusto, and can be judged on an equal footing with the slightly different versions found in regular Cuban restaurants.

DOMINICAN

Dalquis Restaurant

318 W 36th St near 8th Ave, Manhattan, 212-502-5363, subway: A, C, E to 34th St

The lunch counter in this storefront runs along one wall and ends in a steam table with eight or so main dishes. The steamtable entrees—oxtail, pork chops, two kinds of chicken, beefsteak, and codfish salad—are in the $6 to $8 range and include mounds of rice and beans. Try the codfish salad—three generous spoonfuls of salt cod, green olives, chopped tomato, green pepper, and Spanish onion dressed with vinegar and olive oil. Chicken baked with garlic and black pepper and strewn with raw onions is also good. [¢]

Lechonera Sandy

2261 2nd Ave at E 116th St, Manhattan, 212-348-8654, subway: 6 to 116th St

The name of this East Harlem standby says it all—pig, pig, and more pig. Start with cuchifritos, the family of fried snacks that fester in the window at most places. Here they're incredibly fresh: codfish fritters, stuffed potatoes, blood sausage, and alcapurrias—torpedoes of mashed plantain filled with ground meat. But don't miss the signature pork roast, drenched with garlic and sided with crunchy skin, or mofongo, a fried mound of mashed plantains with the richest garlic gravy you've ever tasted. The menu at this excellent restaurant is rounded out with seafood, soups, and fruit shakes. [¢]

El Mambi

558 W 181st St near Audubon Ave, Manhattan,
212-568-8321, subway: A to 181st St

You're lucky if it's Wednesday, 'cause then you can order salcocho ($3): a rich stew of oxtail and chicken thickened with pureed calabaza—the Caribbean pumpkin—which flecks the mellow brown gravy with tiny dots of orange. Flavors of garlic and cilantro predominate, and hunks of yuca, carrots, and potatoes complete the picture. I'd say this was the best lunchtime bowl of soup I've had in a long time. Save the rounds of toast to mop up the bottom of the bowl. As is the custom in Hispano-Caribbean restaurants, each day of the week has its own menu, although sandwiches and salads of octopus and salt cod are always available. In the front of the cafe, the swiveling red stools are so close to the counter that only the diminutive fit. There's also a dining room in the back, but you're likely to be given a more elaborate and expensive menu. The solution: order at the counter, then sit in the back. As I left the restaurant, three women under the awning were having an enthusiastic conversation about how to remove a curse from a friend and transfer the curse to its originator. [¢]

PUERTO RICAN

Alex Bar B.Q.

356 Broadway at Hewes St, Brooklyn,
no published phone, subway: M to Hewes St

Located on a grimy stretch of Broadway eclipsed by the elevated tracks, this rickety premises produces some of the city's best roast pork, known as lechon. This is emphatically not Cuban pernil, but a distinctly Puerto Rican dish, most often dispensed in the home country out of shacks by the side of the road. The skin's most important—burnished deep brown and crispy, with a delectable layer of fat underneath to shield the flesh and keep it dripping with juices. Since Alex cooks the whole pig, ribs and variety parts are also available by the plate or by the pound, along with a comically small list of sides including rice and beans and yuca. [¢]

Casa Adela

66 Ave C near 5th St, Manhattan,
212-473-1882, subway: F to 2nd Ave

The $2.50 bowl of chicken soup may be the cheapest complete meal in the East Village: a drumstick in a clear, tomato-tinged broth jumpin' with cumin, green pepper, and oregano, anchored by big hunks of carrot and potato. The surprise additional component: spaghetti, for a double carbo charge. Other choices include pork roast and biftek encebollado, a razor-thin piece of meat quick-cooked with onion, so the onion stays triumphantly firm, deliciously finished with a dash of vinegar that generates an impromptu gravy. But Friday is the day to make the scene, when a special menu offers Puerto Rican standards of cod and octopus salads, escabeched fish, and cod stew. Don't miss the tostones, crisp and light despite the lard component. They just might be the best in the city. [¢, kid friendly]

★ El Rincon Boricua

**158 E 119th Street near 3rd Ave, Manhattan,
212-534-9400, subway: 6 to 116th St**

Located in the neighborhood known as El Barrio—which is rapidly becoming a Mexican quarter—this microscopic lunch counter is Puerto Rican and proud of it. Marvel at the roast baby pig in the window, then go in and have a plate. Carefully preserved and attached, the deep brown skin has a crackly texture and no coating of garlic, and the meat is rich and silky. Using a scissors, the counterguy carefully snips pieces from several parts of the animal and serves them up with boiled plantain, white rice, and red beans—you'll swear it's the best $6.50 you ever spent. [¢]

La Taza de Oro

**96 8th Ave near 15th St, Manhattan,
212-243-9946, subway: A, C, E to 14th St**

New York's most venerable Puerto Rican restaurant also happens to be one of the best food deals in town—each entree comes with a giant plate of rice and beans that could happily make a meal in itself. Recommended main dishes include a thick fricassee of goat and potatoes (add a shot of vinegar from the bottle on the table), a cold salad of shredded salt cod with onions and plenty of garlic, and deep-fried pork chops, two to a plate. If you want something lighter, try the avocado salad. There's a different menu for each day of the week. [¢]

Eastern European

Wander around Greenpoint, Williamsburg, or the East Village and you're likely to stumble on a Polish cafe with little in the way of decor, but great prices when it comes to gravied hunks of meat and mashed potatoes. Hats off to the Poles for some of the best cheap food in the universe. A full meal, including two sides and a couple of scoops of potatoes will set you back only $4. This type of food is best eaten in cold weather. If it's summer, go instead for one of the cooling soups, like cucumber or beet, both laced with sour cream and fresh dill.

Though the Poles dominate the Eastern European dining landscape, it's worth seeking out Hungarian, Bosnian, Bulgarian, Czech, and Slovak restaurants, all influenced by the cooking of Turkey and the Austro-Hungarian empire. What used to be a thriving Hungarian restaurant zone on Manhattan's East Side has now dwindled to a single establishment. Though sundered, Czech and Slovak restaurants still serve a common cuisine —don't miss the behemoth dumplings.

All these countries, of course, share an admiration of paprika. Brought to Eastern Europe by Ottoman soldiers returning from India in the 18th century, paprika is really a type of chile, available in mild, medium, and hot. Since 1945, the market has sadly been dominated by a sweet form that has a sunny flavor but little heat.

POLISH

Happy End

924 Manhattan Ave at Kent St, Brooklyn, 718-383-9862, subway: G to Greenpoint Ave

The menu board reads in Polish with a chalkboard offering English as an afterthought. On my first visit, a group of us sat for ten minutes before realizing that there is no wait service. A woman of amazing girth is seen through the door of the tiny kitchen, swinging pots in every direction, assembling the dinners with deadly accuracy. A hunk of meat is deftly scooped from a deep container on the steamtable, then slung on a plate with mashed potatoes and paprika gravy. Next, identical mounds of two barely distinguishable salads are heaped on: cabbage salad and carrot-and-cabbage salad. The same presentation on every plate makes this one of the most single-minded dining places on earth—and one of the cheapest. All dinners are $4 or $5. And like it says on the menu, a free beverage is provided—orange Kool-Aid that you serve yourself from a dispenser on a card table. [¢]

Polish specialties

bigos
multimeat hunter's stew

flaczki
honeycomb tripe soup

kielbasa
garlic sausage

owocowa
cold fruit soup

pierogi
Polish raviolis

pyzy
potato dumplings

shav
sorrel soup

Little Poland

200 Second Ave near 12th St, Manhattan, 212-777-9728, subway: L to 3rd Ave

Of the half-dozen East Village Poles, this is my favorite. The soups, thirteen in all, give B & H (see Jewish) a run for its money. The list includes tripe, chicken noodle, dark bean with kielbasa, potato lamb, and a wonderfully tart, dense, and flavorful cabbage. The homemade pierogi are also available in multiple variations, deep fried to a golden brown and served with sour cream. And though the entree prices hover near $9, this sum includes so much food that you're probably better off sharing. I especially liked the plate-eclipsing veal cutlet, much thicker than the usual wienerschnitzel, the tender meat annealed with a stout coating of crumbs that forced me to reach for the knife. Feeling particularly ravenous? Pick the combo platter that includes four pierogi of your choice, stuffed cabbage, kielbasa, and bigos. [¢]

★ Monika

643 5th Ave near 20th St, Brooklyn, 718-788-6930, subway: M, N, R to 25th St

Monika is found on the edge of Greenwood Cemetery in Brooklyn's Sunset Park, in an Eastern European mini-neighborhood. Monika is a shoebox of a place with only five tables, each smothered by a white plastic tablecloth further defended by Plexiglas. Tiny lamps and the small scale of the room make you feel like you're in a dollhouse, but the size of the portions transports you to Land of the Giants.

The menu offers 17 soups; luckily, most are light enough to take up little stomach space. Cold borscht ($1.50) turns out to be a sweet vegetarian consommé colored and flavored by beets, but not containing any. A potato or boiled egg is provided at no extra charge in case you require solid matter. Most of the hot soups are similarly light, like krupnik ($1.10), a barley pottage seething with fresh dill. The only soup that could conceivably serve as an entree is flaczki ($2.60), piled with tender honeycomb tripe in a garlicky orange broth. Gird your loins, 'cause here come the entrees. Meat choices run to pork chops, pork hocks, kielbasa, veal cutlet, baked chicken, and a beef goulash served plain or Hungarian-style with potato pancakes. [¢]

★ Old Poland Bakery and Restaurant

190 Nassau Ave, Brooklyn, 718-349-7775, subway: G to Greenpoint Ave

This Greenpoint mainstay offers a full-course meal of entree, gravy, two scoops of potatoes, and a selection of vegetables for as little as $3.50, which gets you delicious sauteed chicken livers. For $4 you can enjoy a pair of pork shanks, boiled skin-on till the shreds of rich flesh attain a ruby hue, or a lake of lima bean stew dotted with bits of ham and kielbasa. And don't miss the excellent red-cabbage slaw. Other entrees sampled on several recent visits included long strips of tongue in a soothing white sauce, plate-eclipsing wienerschnitzel, calf liver with plenty of onions, and meatballs stuffed with finely diced vegetables. For a lighter meal try shav, a soup made with fresh sorrel in a light chicken stock. [¢, kid friendly]

Raymund's Place

124 Bedford Ave near N 10th St, Brooklyn,
718-388-4200, subway: L to Bedford Ave

When the frigid wind knifes off the East River, pop into this Polish cafe for a bowl of sour grass soup, made with strong meat stock fortified with cream. The little bits of sour grass floating on the top look like something mowed in your backyard, if you only had a backyard. A hardboiled egg is submerged, and alongside comes a loaf-shaped mass of mashed potatoes sprinkled with plenty of crumbled-up bacon. You're supposed to dump the potatoes and bacon into the soup, which turns a light meal into something much more substantial. By the way, it's delicious. An even cheaper feed is pickle soup ($1.75), which doesn't taste all that different from sour grass soup. The pickles are shredded so as to disguise their identity, so that you're spared the repulsive idea that you're mainly drinking the juice from a jar of pickles. We should have stopped with the soup, but of course we didn't. Of the ten or so dinners listed, I picked pyzy ($5). The plate came loaded with six potato dumplings, the texture somewhere between rubber and spud, stuffed with ground meat. The potatoes had been treated like a West African mash, so the outside of the dumplings was smooth and resilient. These dumplings sat in a puddle of bacon grease dotted with more crumbled bacon, and side salads were displayed on a romaine leaf. This joint has class.

BOSNIAN
and CROATIAN

Bascarsija

44-09 Broadway, Queens,
718-777-8344, subway: G, R to 46th St

To get a fresh perspective on what happened to
Yugoslavia, visit this Bosnian bar in Long Island City,
named after an ancient neighborhood in Sarajevo.
Skip the menu, most of which is permanently "not
available," and let the barkeep assemble a banquet
for you. What you'll probably get, as we did on two
occasions, is a sumptuous heap of grilled meats,
including lamb shish kebabs, veal cutlets, and
cevapcici—cylinders of savory ground meat accented with onions and cilantro. The belt-busting array is
sided with tangy cabbage slaw assembled from cab-
bages grown in the backyard garden, pitas, cubes of
mellow feta, and ivar, a sunny puree of pimentos
that's the perfect dip for the meats.

Istria Sports Club

28-09 Astoria Blvd, Queens,
718-728-3181, subway: N to Astoria/Ditmars Blvd

Founded in 1957 by immigrants from the region, Istria Sports Club has a dining area that
mimics a suburban rec room, the blond paneling lined with soccer trophies and men playing
card games—in this case tresete and briskula. But walk out back and you'll find the best
tables on a covered terrace overlooking bocce courts and a sunny vegetable garden.

There is no menu; the waiter recites the short list of dishes, pausing to describe them in Italian
to a member of our party. The thing to get is fuzi ($8), a homemade pasta made by taking
squares of dough and folding in two opposite corners, making envelopes like miniature danish.
It's sauced with chunks of veal in a light brown gravy laced with paprika and garlic. Potato
gnocchi, nearly as good, offer an agreeably earthy flavor and the same sauce. Another fine
choice is cevapcici ($8), shotgun shells of grilled beef on a bed of red onions, the meat
accompanied by a zingy dipping sauce of pureed red pepper called ivar. In happier days, this
was the national dish of Yugoslavia.

CZECH
and SLOVAK

Restaurant Milan's

**710 5th Ave near 23rd St, Brooklyn,
718-788-7384, subway: M, N, R to 25th St**

This cafe is, according to the waiter, one of only two places in town that serves Slavic dumplings—magnificent moist loaves sliced like bread and served with stews. The best main course to enjoy them is szeged goulash, chunks of tender pork in a beige sauce thickened with sour cream and awash in sauerkraut. It tastes a million times better than it sounds. Also good are pork chops Belehrad, deep fried in an egg batter and sided with vinegary purple cabbage slaw. Avoid the pudding sundae, though—canned peaches smothered with chocolate pudding and whipped cream.

Czech and Slovak specialties

false soup
vegetarian soup

kishka
rice-and-beef sausage

palacinky
dessert crepes

pork chops Belehrad
battered and fried chops

Slavic dumplings
floating loaf of white bread

szeged goulash
pork in sour cream and sauerkraut

Zlatá Praha

**28-48 31st Street, Astoria, Queens,
718-721-6422, subway: N to 30th Ave**

Zlatá Praha, which means Golden Prague, recalls the glory days of pre-Nazi and pre-socialist Bohemia, when meat was heaped in mountains and gravy flowed like the Vlatava River. The days of abundance may be gone, but the cuisine lives on in a nearly unbelievable lunch special that offers three courses and coffee for $6.95. Tripe soup makes a spectacular starter, with chewy hunks of honeycomb tripe foundering in the chocolate-brown broth. Alternately, there's a refreshingly light lentil soup flecked with vegetables, known as a "false soup" in Czech cooking because the broth isn't made with meat.

Most of the eight entrees are sided by a dumpling the size of a slow-pitch softball, dotted with caramelized onions and sliced like white bread. The tastiest is smoked pork loin, swimming in beige sauce and sided by unusually sweet sauerkraut pricked with caraway. Or pick the midnight-brown goulash, which struggles mightily to distance itself from the Hungarian product and succeeds—the tender beef cut in one-inch cubes and concealed under shredded, parsley-dusted raw onions. Islands of uncooked green pepper point like signposts toward the meat, with no potatoes or paprika in sight. The compulsory last course: sugar-dusted palacinky, crepes bulging with apricot jam and bent acutely to fit the small plate. Watch for the game festival each winter, where you can enjoy venison, pheasant, and wild boar.

BULGARIAN

416 B.C.

**416 Broadway at Canal St,
Manhattan, 212-625-0981,
subway: J, M, N, R, Z, 6 to Canal St**

A forbidding wooden door provides ingress and, after
persevering up a dusty stair, you'll arrive at a dining
room with a psychedelic Egyptian mural painted on
the ceiling. The view from the booths is spectacular,
with the hurly-burly of two great thoroughfares at
your feet. 416 B.C. bills itself as a mehanata, or "little tavern," a rugged country establishment that furnishes simple meals washed down with local wines.

If many of the dishes seem Turkish, why not?
Witness kyopolu ($3.99), a fragrant puree of roast
eggplant, red peppers, tomatoes, parsley, and garlic.
Equally desirable is "snowhite," a dip studded with
cucumbers, garlic, and walnuts that showcases 416
B.C.'s excellent homemade yogurt. If you'd rather
slurp than scoop, try tarator—a dilled and chilled
cucumber-yogurt soup with a name like a Japanese superhero. "Chicken livers—country
style" often contains hearts, gizzards, and other innards as well, cooked in about a stick of
butter and blizzarded with paprika and garlic. Bulgarians dote on ground-meat kufte and its
cumin-laced cousin kebabche, both included in the generous mixed grill ($10.99), which also
contains a couple of pork cuts, decent fries, navy-bean stew, and ajvar, a sprightly pepper
paste. But more interesting is the kavarma omelet ($13.99), an outsized egg crepe wrapped
around a delicious pork stew sweetened with peppers and onions.

Bulgarian specialties

burek
cheese-stuffed red peppers

kavarma
sweet pork stew

kebabche
*ground beef-and-lamb
kebab*

kufte
ground lamb kebab

kyopolu
Bulgarian ratatouille

lukanka
*crumbly sausage
with chubritsa,
a Bulgarian herb*

tarator
cucumber-yogurt soup

HUNGARIAN

Mocca Hungarian

**1588 2nd Ave near 83rd St, Manhattan,
212-734-6470, subway: 4, 5, 6 to 86th St**

The tin ceiling, tile floor, and rickety furniture time warp you to an earlier decade, and the
average age of the diners—seemingly around 80—will make you feel young again. Of the
ethnographic geegaws on the walls, only a well-used leather whip and pair of fur canteens
make you wonder about the staid demeanor of the patrons. I won't go into the $6.45 luncheon
special—a belt-busting four-courser that finishes with coffee and a rich dessert. But the
$13.95 dinner is also one of the city's great meal deals.

The 20 main courses present a nearly insurmountable dilemma. First eliminate the schnitzels—though nicely cooked, they're not the kind of veal people dream about. Also avoid the interesting sounding veal knuckle, a flattened, breaded mass of glistening gray gelatin. Choose instead the twin cabbage leaves stuffed with rice, pork, and veal, smothered in sauerkraut and unexpectedly bursting with flavor. The beef goulash is a triumph, the chunks resting in a gravy dark as Mexican mole, sharing the plate with miniature dumplings. But the best thing on the menu is gypsy roast, a wild ride of a dish featuring two long-boned pork chops cooked in tons of garlic and hot paprika, and deglazed with a puckering squirt of vinegar, a spicy kick in the pants.

Hungarian specialties

gypsy roast
garlic pork chops

beef goulash
dark potatoless beef stew

liptauer
cheesy bread spread

veal knuckle
avoid it

cabbage rolls
stuffed with pork, veal, and rice

Ecuadorian and Peruvian

Ecuadorian eateries are burgeoning—in Sunset Park, Woodside, Jackson Heights, Corona, and, most recently, Washington Heights. The grub is good and inexpensive, focusing on meal-sized soups and entrees served with rice, beans, and plantains. Many of these places seem forbidding to outsiders, with no menu posted in the window, although you'll receive a warm welcome when you summon enough courage to enter.

Though less numerous, Peruvian restaurants are more accessible. In both, the menu blends Andean fare, heavy on the tuberous vegetables and meat, with the seafood of the urbanized lowlands; unexpected Chinese elements fling themselves into the mix, the legacy of Asian immigration early in the century. Both Peru and Ecuador claim to have invented ceviche (so does Mexico), the dish of raw seafood "cooked" in acid that's causing a sensation in fancy Flatiron restaurants like Sushi Samba and Chicama. Try the same dish in Ecuadorian or Peruvian places and you'll be laughing all the way to the bank.

ECUADORIAN

Don Pepe

40-56 Junction Blvd, Corona, Queens,
718-396-4366, subway: 7 to Junction Blvd

Who can finish the $5 almuerzo, a fusillade of oxtail soup loaded with corn, meat, and yuca washed down with a glass of orange soda, followed by a giant plate of rice, salad, stewed lentils, and your choice of meat, poultry, or fish? On a recent afternoon I picked corvina (aka sea trout or weakfish), a couple of tasty fillets crosshatched to increase the crispy surface. This homestyle Ecuadorian cafe is located on Corona's busiest corner, and dinner promises even larger portions of the pulled pork roast called hornado, and arroz con camarones, the South American version of Chinese shrimp fried rice. [¢]

Ecuadorian specialties

arroz con camarones
yellow rice with shrimp

caldo de bola relleno
soup with giant stuffed dumpling

chifles
plantain chips

hornado
pulled pork

llapingachos
cheese-stuffed potato patties

Eva Restaurante

551 4th Ave near 16th St, Brooklyn,
718-788-9354, N, M, R to Prospect Ave

The interior of Eva's is comprehensively pink, with long mirrors, rounded on top, which make you feel like you're in an arcade. A waitress brings a menu, which has a small section devoted to pan-Latin cuisine, including pernil, chicken with rice, pescado frito, etc. Another section lists the daily soups, Monday through Sunday, with some days being favored with two soups. A small bowl is $3.50, with a meal-sized bowl priced at $7. The largest section is devoted to Ecuadorian entrees, including ceviche, but no roasted guinea pig or pig-blood soup. I went right to the soup section and ordered sopa de torreja, a big bowl of brown broth in which peregrinate pieces of what looks like Western omelet, made with peppers, onions, and potted meat. There were also pieces of stringy pot roast (good and tender), cabbage, potatoes, and a small piece of corn on the cob. The soup came with a dish of lime wedges and an astringent sauce of green chiles, onions, oil, and vinegar. The chile sauce had a potent delayed effect. The soup was absolutely delicious, and I slurped it down as Spanish reggae played in the background.

Galapagos

126 1st Ave near 7th St, Manhattan, 212-353-2955, subway: L to 1st Ave

Play Darwin and classify the odd creatures like the flightless cormorant and sea iguana that line the walls of this new upscale East Village Ecuadorian, named after the islands that inspired the theory of natural selection. For starters, pick llapingachos—mashed potato patties stuffed with gooey cheese—or chifles, fried plantain chips sided with a powerful dip of garlic and oil. Entrees include a great soup crammed with shellfish and cod, flavored with lime and cilantro; slices of roast pork loin flopped on a bed of hominy; and an onion-strewn skirt steak sided with rice and excellent beans.

La Picada Azuaya

84-19 37th Ave, Queens,
718-424-9797, subway: 7 to 82nd St/Jackson Heights

Of the ceviches, I prefer mixto ($8.75): shrimp, red snapper, purple onion, and parsley swimming in lime juice. A few chunks of yuca have been thrown in as a culinary joke—you can't distinguish them from the fish. On top are toasted kernels of field corn, a staple of the ancient Inca diet.

Forget about ordering sopas (soups) as an appetizer. These selections, priced around $6, are meals in themselves. Choices include fish, sausage, chicken, rib, and "feet cow." As at most Ecuadorians, caldo de bola relleno is the best, floating a plaintain dumpling that looks like a brown matzoh ball. The exterior has a curious spongy texture; inside is a filling of chopped egg, meat, and raisins. The combination platters are strictly for hearty diners. The bandera special ($9.50) includes ceviche, a pint of yellow rice with peas and carrots, lamb in brown gravy, and a tripe and potato stew that's unbeatable. Or select the absurdly capacious picada azualaya: deep-fried cutlets of beef, fish, and chicken strewn over a salad of avocados and tomatoes. The plate is ringed with tostones, twice-fried plantains; it also comes with a slaw of purple onions, tomatoes, and cilantro.

★ Salinas

499 5th Ave near 14th St, Brooklyn,
718-788-9263, subway: F to 4th Ave

Don't get me wrong—any day is a good day to eat at Salinas. On weekdays you can settle for seco de chivo ($6), a thick, over-rice stew with chunks of goat so big they must be carved like miniature roasts; or arroz con camarones ($10), a South American spin on Chinese fried rice featuring shrimp with diced chile peppers instead of peas. More popular among patrons, however, are the entree-sized soups ($6), laced with cilantro and garlic and heavy with vegetables and noodles. It's your choice of chicken, fish, beef, shrimp, cow heel, or caldo de salchicha, a sausage soup thickened with pig blood.

But weekends the joint really comes alive, with larger crowds scarfing portions that swell from big to mind-boggling. Llapinganchos ($14) are typical sierra fare, yam-and-cheese patties smothered in peanut sauce—a meal in themselves. But a plate the size of an automobile dashboard also cradles a mountain of well-oiled rice, a salad of tomatoes and purple onions, a wedge of avocado, a strew of lye-slaked corn called mote (aka hominy), and delicious pork ribs, cut into small pieces and deep-fried. The meat is tender and dripping with flavor. A pair of fluffy poached eggs perches on top like clouds snagged on a rainforest peak. Cuy ($30) is something of a holy grail to ethnic food enthusiasts, and this is the first Ecuadorian restaurant where I've seen it frankly offered. When it arrived, it was nobody's pet: the tailless, foot-long cuy stood on all fours in a field of boiled potatoes, burnished flanks glistening. None of the body parts had been omitted: beady eyes, tiny legs and feet, pointy snout ending in razor-sharp teeth. The taste was heavenly, with the flavor of rabbit and the texture of pigeon (notice I didn't say it tasted like chicken), with a skin was like good pork crackling, only more delicate. [¢, kid friendly]

El Taxista Ecuatoriano

206 Audubon Ave near W 176th St, Manhattan,
212-543-9160, subway: 1, 9 to 181st St

As with many Ecuadorian spots in Washington Heights, El Taxista is a combination cafe and car service. A picture of a limousine that looks like it was carved from a cake of soap adorns the top of the menu. There are gauzy red curtains at the windows, topped with black valances gathered halfway down to afford a view of the street. It being a warm day, and there being no airconditioning, most of the diners have selected tables by the open front door.

Most Ecuadorian restaurants in town specialize in the earthy fare of the sierra—pork and innards, chicken, beans, rice, pot roast, etc. Rarer are those that, like El Taxista, concentrate mainly on seafood. The menu presents over two dozen types of lime-and-chile marinated ceviche, and particular pride is taken in the conch, flown in fresh from Ecuador. Many of the ceviches incorporate potatoes and fresh corn kernels. Another specialty is bola de pescado ($6), a mash of green plantains embedded with pieces of kingfish steamed in a banana leaf, resulting in a custardy consistency and mild flavor. It came with a plate of lime wedges and an innocent-looking crock of hot sauce, chunky with carrots and onions. It was hot as hell, of course.

🍽 PET OR MEAT

For years I looked high and low in Ecuadorian eateries for the national dish—cuy, a small animal belonging to the cavey family, usually barbe-cued or deep-fried. Unfortunately, it's a relative of the domesticated guinea pig, making a juicy story for anyone intent on making fun of food that can't be found at McDonald's or Burger King. I finally located a place in Brooklyn that served it, and reviewed it secure in the knowl-edge that I had found a unique treat. Within a few weeks, New York and the New York Times had reported it as their own scoop, but with the emphasis on the "yuck." The former led with: "The fight against rats is full of surprises, and one of the biggest of all occurs every week at Salinas...". They ran a photo of the cuy sans potatoes, cradled on a wrinkled paper bag and looking like a drowned rat. Coverage of the cuy continues, most recently on a Food TV show called "Extreme Cuisine." Although the program took the same tack as the print media, this attitude shouldn't prevent adventurous diners from enjoying the dish.

PERUVIAN

Coco Roco

**392 5th Ave near 7th St, Brooklyn,
718-965-3376, subway: F to 4th Ave**

Persistent rumors that the cook had flown the coop
and this joint was sliding downhill prompted me to
make a return visit. I'm happy to report that the food is
better than ever. Coco Roco sits in a gentrifying neighborhood real estate agents call Park Slope, though it's
more Gowanus Canal. We ordered papas a la
Huancaina ($4.95), the quintessential mountain dish of
cold boiled potatoes dabbed with cheese sauce. It
announced itself with the powerful odor of habanero
peppers, but turned out to be a mild, complex medley
of chiles. A bigger surprise was a pulpo al olivio
($7.50) so artfully stacked on the plate that we feared
we'd been teleported to Gotham Bar and Grill. The
dressed tentacles formed a gray shadow on the plate,
and squiggles of multihued sauce frolicked on the perimeter.

Even though fresh seafood from South America's west coast is now touted on upscale menus,
Coco Roco sticks with domestic red snapper, clams, shrimp, and squid. The biggest crowd
pleaser is tacu-tacu con pescado ($11.95), a largish snapper fillet wrapped with sweet potato
shreds and then fried. Also praiseworthy is a skirt steak with a homemade chimichurri more
lively than I've encountered in any Argentine restaurant, and a plate of garlicky pork roast
($8.95) nicely sided with boiled sweet potatoes and sauced with a jalapeño-driven aioli.

Peruvian International Cuisines

**688 10th Ave near 49th St, Manhattan,
212-581-5814, subway: C, E to 50th St**

This 28-year-old Incan eatery, one of the few in the city, is the one most in touch with its
peasant roots. The voluminous soups make complete meals—try patasca, made with pig's
feet, tripe, hominy, and navy beans in a savory broth with the startling addition of fresh mint.
Dishes served with rice are also fab, like seco de carne, a very thick stew of beef and potatoes
pungent with cilantro. My award for weirdest dessert in town goes to mazamorra morada,
made with ground purple corn, apples, raisins, and cinnamon, with the consistency of Jell-O.

Inti Raymi

86-14 37th Ave near 87th St, Queens,
718-424-1938, subway: 7 to 90th St-Elmhurst Ave

Named for the king of the Inca gods, Inti Raymi is the king of New York Peruvian restaurants, offering a variety of dishes that reflect the culinary heritage of the Incas—potatoes, corn, hot peppers, and cheese—rather than the international Latin cuisine found in many other restaurants. Much of the food here is spicy hot. No surprise, however, since hot peppers probably originated in Peru.

Ceviche de mariscos ($10.75) contains enough shrimp, octopus, scallops, clams, conch, and fish to serve four as an appetizer. Papas a la Huancaina ($4.25) is an appetizer of cold potatoes with a spicy cheese sauce, which also come with the steak ($9.25). For organ lovers, there's anticuchos de corazón, heart shish kebabs. Aji de gallina ($5.25) is shredded chicken

⎆ CHICKEN A GO-GO

Rotisserie chickens are now as common as pigeons, and it's hard to walk a block in some neighborhoods without seeing an enticing window display. It's a foolproof dinner plan for harried workers trudging home—you don't even need utensils. In the last five years, Peruvians have made a bold attempt to dominate the market, by offering a tastier bird. What's in the spice rub is a secret, but there are many theories. I think they use Chinese five-spice powder, among other things like crushed garlic and green onions—a spicing technique learned from the Chinese immigrants who arrived in Peru in the '20s.

The original Pio Pio (62-30 Woodhaven Blvd, Queens, 718-458-0606), whose logo sports a baby chick strutting around in big clogs, is located on a road that shortcuts to Kennedy Airport. (There's another at 84-13 Northern Blvd, 718-426-1010, in Jackson Heights). The skewers are carefully swapped around in the roasting contraption by the frantic attendant, so each bird, savory coating intact, is done but not overdone. The chicken remains succulent hours later, as you eat it under the envious gaze of your fellow airplane travelers. Apart from the decent rice and beans and OK french fries (avoid the version called salchipapas, which comes strewn with hot dog slices), there's not much in the way of sides.

Sunset Park's favorite Peruvian rotisserie is Los Pollitos (5911 4th Ave, Brooklyn, 718-439-9382). In view of the fact that this area is rapidly becoming Mexican, you shouldn't be surprise that the list of sides, in addition to the usual, also includes quesadillas and tacos. Don't miss the milk-based green chile sauce, or the amazing guacamole, made on the spot in a lava-stone metate from Haas avocados.

in a spicy sauce thickened with bread. Don't miss chicha morada, a delicious fruit beverage made with pineapple and lemon, flavored with cloves, and colored with purple corn.

El Pollo

1746 1st Ave near 91st St, Manhattan,
212-996-7810, subway: 6 to 96th St

Not to be confused with El Pollo Latino, this Peruvian restaurant focuses, perhaps wisely, on chicken roasted with a secret spice formula that's so subtle it's hard to tell what's in it (half chicken: $5). All I can tell you is that the chicken is great, and cheap to boot. Given the chicken proclivity, it comes as a surprise that the restaurant also offers a wide array of Peruvian specialties, including mote—chunky hominy kernels served cold; menudencias—chicken gizzards fried and served with a righteous hot sauce; and papas a la Huancaina. A weirdness on the menu worth sampling is the peanut sauce ($2.50), which goes great with the chicken and even greater with the mote. Sometimes you can get them to give you a sample for free. [¢]

Rinconcito Peruano

803 9th Ave near 53rd St, Manhattan,
212-333-5685, subway: C, E to 50th St

This metaphoric "Little Corner of Peru" makes only a fraction of the dishes on its expansive menu each day. From the list recited by the waitress we selected tamales, surprisingly crammed with chopped egg, chicken, and a half dozen other ingredients, and papas rellenos, a pan-Latin classic of potatoes stuffed with ground meat and raisins. Don't miss the weekend breakfast combos, or the lunch specials, which include a soup, entree, rice, and beans for under $10. The baby crawling around on the floor is your guarantee of home-style food.

Ethiopian, Somalian, and South African

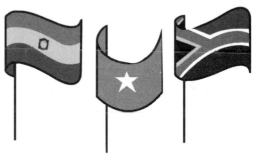

Ethiopian restaurants are common, but, unfortunately, most of them aren't any good. But at least we don't have to bow to Washington, D.C. anymore when it comes to Ethiopian—their restaurants have become bad, too. The chief pleasure of Ethiopian food is eating with your fingers, and enjoying the subtlety and piquancy of the spice mixtures that the cooking depends on.

Scoop bites with injera, a rubbery flatbread made from tef. Now cultivated in this country, tef is fantastically rich in protein and iron, brown in color, and hosts a symbiotic yeast on its surface that causes natural fermentation, producing a pleasing sourdough effect. In Ethiopia, the bread is also made with lighter grains like barley, millet, corn, rice, and sorghum. In neither Washington nor New York will you find freshly made injera these days, though a decade ago it was fairly common. In spite of that, the food is still wonderful, and quite unlike any other kind of ethnic food, bridging the gap between African and Indian. Ethiopian is also a very good bet for vegetarians.

We don't know what the tribal food of Somalia is like because every such establishment I know of has a cook who's from Yemen—a case of culinary symbiosis. Both groups demand strictly Halal meat, and get it. There's only one South African restaurant, located in trendy Fort Greene, and even though it's more expensive than it ought to be, it provides a good overview of the chow.

ETHIOPIAN

Ghenet

285 Mulberry St near Houston St, Manhattan,212-343-1888, subway: N, R to Prince St

Consistent with the increasingly upscale neighborhood, Ghenet is decorated like a bistro—yellow walls, potted palms, a long bar with elephant-sized stools, and a few tasteful framed prints. The food is carefully prepared and generally delicious; the spicing and range, however, are timid by Ethiopian standards. Like the Indians, Ethiopians make much of lentils and beans, and like the West Africans, they admire green leafy vegetables. These come together at Ghenet in the vegetarian combo ($12.95), a gorgeous food painting on the dun canvas of injera. Yemsir watt laces green lentils with berberé, the variable national spice mixture, here more reminiscent of the red chile of the American Southwest.

Ethopian specialties

azifa
tangy lentil salad

doro watt
spicy chicken and boiled eggs

gored-gored
beef in chile butter

injera
tef flatbread

kitfo
beef tartare

yebeg tibs
lamb sauteed with chile and onions

yemsir watt
green lentils with berberé spice blend

Alternatively, you can have collard greens dotted with lamb in gomen be siga ($8.75). Yebeg tibs, the hottest thing on the menu, includes bits of lamb sauteed with fresh green chiles and onions; gored-gored ($12.95) features cubes of beef awash in chile-laced butter. The tender meat is barely cooked, the way Ethiopians like it. Perversely, kitfo—a hopelessly rich tartare of ground beef mixed with butter flavored with cardamom and other spices—arrives fully cooked when it should be raw.

★ Meskerem

468 W 47th St near 10th Ave, Manhattan, 212-664-0520, subway: C, E to 50th St

At Meskerem you won't find mesob, those cute Ethiopian basket tables—the furniture here is plain and comfortable. Behind a black bar, bottles of tej are lined up, a honey wine that seems too sweet until its real utility is revealed—to staunch the burn of the food. Meals are served on stenciled metal trays overlaid with rubbery injera.

The vegetarian combo ($8.50) showcases the prominence of beans in the Ethiopian diet. You get six dishes, enough for two hungry diners. Two are particularly compelling: shiro features ground chickpeas in a moist toss of green onion and jalapeño pepper and looks and tastes like mom's potato salad until your mouth catches fire. Azifa, served cold, is an odd salad of brown lentils made earthier with ginger and horseradish that climb right up your nose. The national dish is doro watt ($9.50), a quarter chicken with a boiled egg in a thick red sauce. Made with Ethiopia's staple spice mixture berberé, this watt is hard to eat and easy to love. More subtly flavored is yedoro alecha, chicken with rosemary, onions, and a spice mixture that's like mild curry powder. [vegetarian friendly]

SOMALIAN

Yemen and Somalia Restaurant

231 W 116th St, near Adam Clayton Powell Blvd, Manhattan, 212-749-8241, subway: B, C to 116th St

Yemen & Somalia Restaurant represents a combo that's less strange than it might sound, since the two countries face each other across the Gulf of Aden, and have ancient trading ties. The proprietors are from Yemen, while the clientele is largely Somalian. The food includes offerings from both cuisines. This eight-table establishment has red tablecloths and a sign on the wall that spells out the rules of the house: "No smoking, No politics, No chewing kat." The latter is a leaf that's masticated for stamina by both nationalities. It's not illegal in this country—yet. It's futile to ask for a menu; each day, there's a single plat du jour ($8). On a recent visit, the meal began with a lettuce, tomato, and cucumber salad followed by a cup of curried lamb broth. The entree was a plate of rice with four bone-in hunks of lamb, nicely baked, and a tasty vegetable stew made with green beans, corn, potato, and okra, providing a viscous gravy absorbed by the rice. Served alongside was a homemade hot sauce of finely chopped green chiles, green onion, and yellow onion dressed with vinegar. On another visit we sampled a pleasantly spicy dish of finely chopped meat and carrots held together, sloppy-joe style, with tomato. [¢]

SOUTH AFRICAN

Madiba

195 DeKalb Ave near Adelphi St, Brooklyn, 718-855-9190, subway: D, M, N, Q, R to DeKalb Ave

Cobbled together of salvaged wood and Quonset-hut tin, it might be a grog shop in Soweto. There's a shelf crowded with hand-woven baskets, a couple of ostrich eggs, and a row of kerosene lanterns suspended near the ceiling—as if the electricity might flicker off at any moment.

First to hit the table is umgqushu stambu ($3), a tasty porridge of crushed hominy and kidney beans that, for many cash-strapped South Africans, constitutes an entire meal. The flavors of the so-called safari platter ($12) open a window into the world of the Voortrekkers, the contentious Dutch homesteaders who invented apartheid. Included are strips of biltong, dried beef cured to an intriguing semirancidity, and crumbly sticks of droewars, which taste like Slim Jims buried underground. A notably delicious dish originated in Portuguese Africa: peri-peri chicken livers, which come planted on a piece of toast that absorbs the spicy cooking oil.

The entree prices average $14, reminding you that you're in chi-chi Fort Greene instead of Johannesburg. Luckily, many of them are large enough to share. Sosaties are kebabs based on the Malay model, six massive meatballs redolent of onion, clove, and ginger. Bobotie is another Malay contribution, a great round pie filled with curried meat and boiled eggs. Reflecting the Huguenot heritage, oxtail poitjie dumps prodigious hunks of bony meat in a red-wine gravy loaded with vegetables and garlic, engagingly served in three-legged iron pot.

South African specialties

biltong
beef jerky

bobotie
Malay pie

bunny chow
vegetable curry in hollow bread

peri-peri
meat, fish, or poultry in hot sauce

sosaties
mutton meatballs

German
and Swiss

Most of the German restaurants in Manhattan date from the early 20th century, when there was a major Teutonic presence in Yorkville on the Upper East Side. Heidelberg (1648 2nd Ave, 212-628-2332) and Rolf's (281 3rd Ave, 212-477-4750) date from that era. Neither is particularly good.

Just as the German-American identity took a drubbing during two world wars, so did the fatty and starchy cuisine during the health-conscious '80s. But German cooking has bounced back, aided by beer lovers and the runaway popularity of Danube, David Bouley's haute-Austrian restaurant, and the advent of modern German places like Silver Swan and Hallo Berlin. But look to Queens for a number of establishments that still serve old-style German cooking, especially Niederstein's, favored by generations of German families attending funerals in the adjacent cemetery.

Swiss cooking has always lurked in the shadow of German, French, and Italian, but the multi-cuisine approach has now become an advantage, especially among parties of diners that can't agree on what to eat. The menu at Roettele A.G. should please everyone.

GERMAN

★ Hallo Berlin

**402 W 51st St near 10th Ave, Manhattan,
212-541-6248, subway: C, E to 50th St
626 10 Ave at 44th St, Manhattan,
212-977-1944, subway: A, C, E to 42nd St**

A paradise for sausage lovers, these German beer
gardens claim to be "the wurst restaurants in New
York." The menu runs the gamut from the lowly
weiner to the imperial Berliner curry—a supremely
delicious knockwurst dusted with raw curry powder.
Bring your vegetarian friends, since the sides are so
good, they can stand alone: crusty fried potatoes,
sweet-and-sour red cabbage, German pickles, and
homemade spätzl. There are several forms of pickled herring, but also a fresh herring filet doused with
a choice of six different sauces, of which mellow
mustard is the best. Skip the Königsberger klopse,
stark white meatballs that do a good imitation of cream of wheat. Wash it all down with the
sinister-sounding Köstritzer Black Lager. Lunch specials served till 5 p.m. [¢]

German specialties

Berliner curry
*knockwurst with
curry powder*

headcheese
pressed pork product

jaegerschnitzel
*breaded veal cutlet
with mushroom gravy*

sauerbraten
*beef roast in
a tart marinade*

spätzl
*free-form
homemade noodles*

Killmeyer's Old Bavarian Inn

**4254 Arthur Kill Rd near Storer Ave, Staten Island,
718-984-1202, subway: none**

This ancient tavern, nearly 150 years old, sports an intricately carved mahogany bar and
stuffed animal-head trophies in profusion. Lately it has been garnering enthusiastic plaudits
from critics and diners alike, partly, no doubt, due to its unexpected and obscure location in a
borough not known for its exciting food scene. A remarkable beer list that runs to over one
hundred varieties overshadows the food. The very Bavarian wursts—bratwurst, weisswurst,
knockwurst—are the things to get. Also don't miss the potato pancakes.

Niederstein's

**69-16 Metropolitan Ave, Queens,
718-326-0717, subway: M to Middle Village/Metropolitan Ave**

If this were Manhattan, it would be the mother of all theme restaurants—poised in the middle
of Lutheran Cemetery, with gravestones and funerary sculptures climbing the hill out back like
a well-framed shot from Night of the Living Dead. On Sunday, the thronged rooms are dotted
with funeral goers in an atmosphere of perpetual hush. A special Sunday menu offers dinners
in the $20 range: a delicious jump-starter of cucumbers bathed in dill and cream, appetizer or

soup served with rye and rolls, tossed salad, an entree and two sides, dessert, and coffee or tea. Germans have never been known as light eaters. Appetizers include chewy headcheese, ox-tongue salad, a heap of intensely smoked ham called rauchfleisch, and sweet herring in oniony cream sauce, but stick with the melon or fruit cup if you hope to go the distance. Soups change daily and run to ponderous goulash (heavy on the ghoul) and the dieter's choice, consommé with liver dumplings.

Other Teutonic fare includes the oink-intensive Bavarian platter featuring knockwurst, bratwurst, and pork loin on a generous bed of homemade kraut flecked with bacon. There's also a safety cushion of sculpted mashed potatoes in case a heavy forkful sends your hand plummeting to the plate. The sauerbraten is somewhat less satisfactory because the massive slabs of beef are short on vinegary tang. Note that on non-Sundays you have to order a la carte, with entrees hovering slightly in the $10 to $15 range—and still too much to eat.

Silver Swan

41 E 20th St near Broadway, Manhattan,
212-254-3611, subway: R, N to 23rd St

This restaurant looks very German inside, with comfortable booths, beer signs, and an imposing bar in the front room. To enjoy the bar menu, which has several unadorned German favorites at prices discounted from the dining room (where boar is king), you must sit in the front room. You can, for example, get a good-sized portion of two weisswurst, bratwurst, or knockwurst, with hot potato salad, and red cabbage or sauerkraut for around $10. Goulash and sauerbraten are also available. A full list of German beers, including seven wheat beers served in half-liter flasks, is another magnet to draw you to this laid-back spot.

Zum Stammtisch

69-46 Myrtle Ave at Cooper Ave,
Queens, 718-386-3014, subway: none

Sit under the moose head in the Bavarian-fantasy dining room and enjoy some of the best German food in town. Begin with ox tongue salad—the pickled meat sliced thin and served with lettuce and onions—then order the house specialty, jaegerschnitzel, a huge veal cutlet breaded, fried, and smothered in mushroom gravy. The restaurant is also justifiably proud of its homemade head cheese and goulash soup, a close cousin of chile con carne. For dessert, don't miss the hot raspberry sundae.

SWISS

Roetelle A.G.

126 E 7th St near Ave A, Manhattan, 212-674-4140, subway: F to 2nd Ave

The charming, ivy-draped garden out back would be reason enough to visit this unique East Village cafe, but the pan-European comfort food should provide a further incentive. Go Gallic with the steak au poivre, German with the sauerbraten, or Italian with a handful of pastas. Uniquely Swiss offerings are found mainly among the appetizers—ruby-red air-dried beef called viande de grison, and melted raclette cheese served with boiled potatoes, cocktail onions, and cornichons. Or, of course, there are four fondues—it's bound to come back into culinary fashion one of these days.

Swiss specialties

fondue
melted cheese dip

raclette
melt-and-scrape Swiss cheese

viande de grisons
air-dried beef

Ghanaian
and Nigerian

For the last decade Francophone restaurants, mainly from Senegal, Guinea, and the Ivory Coast, have held sway over the city's West African food scene. Now it's the turn of the Anglophone countries like Ghana and Nigeria. Both depend heavily on the indigenous and multifarious yam, the first plant cultivated in Africa.

One common pattern for meals is a bowl heaped with mash from which pieces are nipped off with the fingers of the right hand and dunked in a gravy, known as "soup." Mashes may also be made from cassava, potatoes, rice, and corn meal, while soups run to okra, peanut, palm nut, and, in Nigeria, egusi, a raunchy puree of melon seeds flecked with greens, somewhat resembling runny scrambled eggs. The delightful musky flavor comes from dried shrimp. Egusi is an acquired taste that produces an intense craving after two or three exposures.

GHANAIAN

African American Restaurant

1987 University Ave near Burnside Ave, Bronx, 718-731-8595, 4 to Burnside Ave

This successor to the Bronx's African Restaurant is an alliance between a Ghanaian and an American cook, who present the food of two continents side-by-side on the same steamtable. On the African side, you have a choice of two or three mashes every day, including kenkey and a fufu based on potatoes rather than yuca or plantain. There are also a couple of soups offered for the mashes, and a choice of stewed chicken, resilient and fatty oxtails, or a fried fish, usually porgy. On the other side are collards, macaroni and cheese, meat loaf, fried chicken, black-eyed peas, and Creole rice. The only thing I didn't like was the candy-coated barbecue chicken. Open 24 hours on the main drag in University Heights. [¢]

Ghanaian specialties

fufu
mash of yuca, plantain, or potatoes

kenkey
fermented cornmeal mash

omo-tuo
mashed rice

romo
lamb soup

soup
sauce for mash

waachi
black-eyed peas and rice

Ebe Ye Yie

2364 Jerome Ave near W 184th St, Bronx, 718-563-6064, subway: 4 to 183rd St

Run, don't walk to this Ghanaian eatery, situated among the rolling hills of University Heights. A neon sign in the window, modified from a previous occupant, says simply "A Restaurant." The homemade kenkey, made from fermented corn pone, is particulary tasty—dense and beige and served with a plastic knife so slices can be lopped off. Or go with a milder mash like omo-tuo, made from rice, or a potato-based fufu with the texture of rubber and silk. To accompany the mach choose soups like goat and beef, or simple fried fish garnished with an amazing dried-shrimp relish. For vegetarians, there's waachi, a combo of black eyed peas and rice that's the forerunner of the soul-food staple, hoppin' john. [¢]

In God We Trust

441 E 153rd St, Bronx, 718-401-3595, subway: 2, 5 to 3rd Ave-149th St

Among the many amazing features is a wall of Astroturf next to the tables, which makes for some comfy leaning after downing your fufu and soup. This Ghanaian cafe, just north of the commercial South Bronx area known as the Hub, is a neighborhood oddity—its steam tables loaded with fragrant peanut and palm-oil soups rather than the pork, beans, and rice of neighboring joints.

Begin by selecting a mash, a hefty starch cylinder that arrives wrapped in aluminum foil, each variety with a distinct texture, flavor, and aroma. Yam fufu is bland and soft as a pillow, springing back when you poke it. Omo tuo, pounded from rice, has a clean taste and a pellucid whiteness that's almost disturbing. Made from fermented corn meal, kenkey generates a flavor somewhere between caviar and old gym socks. Next pick a soup: peanut is my favorite here—tomato-tinged and minimally goobery. Palm nut comes a close second, tasting more of meat than palm oil. Into the soup is dropped your choice of whatever flesh presents itself on a given day—oxtail, goat, beef, chicken, or fried fish. Alternately, choose romo, a "light soup" already containing lamb in a strong broth. To further vary the terrain, ask to have okra or spinach dabbed on the surface of your combo. The meal will set you back about $6.50. [¢, kid friendly]

Obaa Koryoe

3151 Broadway near Tiemann Pl, Manhattan, 212-316-2950, subway: 1, 9 to 125th St

Another Ghanain merits special mention, a favorite of Harlemites and Columbia students alike. Obaa Koryoe, named after its female proprietor, has been a mainstay in Morningside Heights for 15 years. Though the food is mainly from Ghana, there are also Nigerian, Sierra Leonean, and pan-African dishes offered. The comfortable setting is foliage intensive, and a shop selling African curios on the premises serves to put you in the mood. Watch for waachi, a delicious casserole of rice and black-eyed peas that establishes the culinary link between African and African-American chow, and don't miss the groundnut soup, if it's available. This is the most above-ground West African restaurant in the city. [kid friendly]

NIGERIAN

★ African Village

724 Myrtle Ave at Walworth St, Brooklyn, 718-722-4770, subway: G to Myrtle Ave

African Village mounts the most sophisticated Nigerian menu in town, not pulling punches when it comes to strong flavors and strange textures. The long room is dotted with small tables surrounded by comfortable upholstered chairs, while on one wall the gravity-defying endowments of several carved female statues would make Hugh Hefner pop another Viagra. The room culminates in a bar that actually serves alcoholic beverages, a rarity among the town's mainly-Islamic West African eateries.

Nigerian specialties

aagbono
bush mango-seed sauce

amala
yam-flour mash

egusi
melon seed sauce

suya
Hausa beef skewers

yam porridge
sweet potato mash

For those accustomed to fufu that arrives in a foil-wrapped cylinder, African Village's pounded yam comes as a pleasant surprise. The recently pummeled white tuber forms a fluffy and amorphous mound, so light it might blow away. Other mashes include amala, cooked up from a dried cassava meal with an arresting gray-brown color and musky odor. The country's signature soup, egusi, is thickened with dehusked and crushed melon seeds that generate a color and texture like fine scrambled eggs. The astringent dried leaves of the shrub Vernonia anyadalina (called "ougou") sharpen the nutty flavor of this wonderful sauce. Demonstrating their genius as food chemists, Nigerian cooks make a soup of chopped greens and agbono, the seeds of the bush mango. These impart a viscosity more powerful than okra, so that the sauce pulls away from the bowl in oozy tendrils. Pièce de résistance for me was the goat pepper soup, which, in addition to regulation lumps of goat also contained chitlins and kidney.

Demu Cafe

773 Fulton St near S. Portland St, Brooklyn,
718-875-8484, subway: A, C to Lafayette Ave

Yam porridge, a dappled mixture of white and orange yams, is lightly mashed and flecked with plenty of crushed red pepper. Also sampled: amala, a mash made from yam flour— moist, dark brown, and shaped like a small beret. We asked for vegetable soup—a tomato and palm oil blend that was thick with a chopped, spinach-like green. We also ordered fish and goat, to be flung in the soup. Our fish consisted of the front half of a bluefish and back half of a mackerel, like some gene splicing experiment gone bad.

The dining room is spacious and comfortable. A serving window looks into the kitchen, where the Demu family is busy cooking. Each day the cafe has only a few of the dishes listed on the menu. Ask your Demu what's available. If you want to eat with your right hand the way most Africans do, the server will bring you a white plastic tub of water to wash with. This neighborhood hangout often hosts literary events in the evenings, and it's only steps away from BAM.

Greek

Even though much of the Greek population has departed Astoria—counterintuitively migrating east to places like Bayside, Queens, or further into Long Island—the vast majority of the city's Greek restaurants are still located there. The restaurateurs know that when New Yorkers want to eat Greek, they hop on the N. While most Astorian spots are not quite as inexpensive as you'd like them to be (full dinners often average $20 or more), they're still about half the price of ballyhooed "authentic" Greek spots in Manhattan like Molyvos and Estiatorio Milos.

Don't forget that most coffee shops are still being run by Greek immigrants and offer a handful of specialties, which means that your cheapest taste of Greek will often be found right on the corner.

GREEK

Christos Hasapo-Taverna

41-08 23rd Ave, Queens, 718-726-5195, subway: N to Astoria/Ditmars Blvd

If you're tired of the usual steakhouse, here's a welcome alternative. Located in an obscure corner of Astoria and comfortably furnished with antiques, this Greek taverna concentrates on beefsteaks, serving charbroiled T-bones, filets, shells, and chops, all displayed in their raw state by the front door. Starters are more recognizably Attic—old favorites like tzatziki, tarama, stuffed grape leaves, and grilled octopus, and harder-to-find items like steamed dandelion greens, home-cured sardines, and kokoretsi—bundled and skewered lamb innards heavily flavored with garlic and oregano. [$]

Joe Jr.

482 6th Ave at 12th St, Manhattan, 212-924-5220, subway: F to 14th St

This sometime celebrity hangout, the king of Greek coffee shops, offers a handful of Hellenic specialties each day. The moussaka is particularly fine, layered with eggplant, tender potatoes, and light bechamel, though you can skip the canned peas on the side of the plate. Also avoid the gyro platter, made with a rubber version of the good lamb you sometimes get. Best bet is an abundant Greek salad made with crisp ingredients and avalanched with sharp feta. [¢]

Laterna

47-20 Bell Blvd, Queens, 718-423-1245, subway: Long Island Rail Road to Bayside

Fleeing Astoria, a segment of the Greek community has relocated to Bayside's Northern Boulevard, where there's a Greek Orthodox Cathedral, pastry shop, grocery store, and Laterna, a huge restaurant that hosts tumultuous extended-family events. We sat on the balcony and enjoyed thick-sliced roast lamb inundated with tart sauce; an abundant and cheap Greek salad; lemon-roasted potatoes; and an excellent mezedes (or meze) plate of grilled sweetbreads, sausages, skordalia, and haloumi, a Cypriot cheese, as a four-year-old in a white tuxedo, a wedding party's youngest member, gyrated around the room imitating Elvis.

Nick's Place

550 7th Ave at 39th St, Manhattan,
212-221-3294, subway: N, R, 1, 2, 3, 7, 9 to Times Square

Not to be confused with Uncle Nick's, this nominally Greek luncheonette is hidden in the bowels of a building with no sign of any sort—you have to know it's there. You may also enter via the loading dock at 205 West 39th Street. Neighborhood garmentos go for the entree-sized salads, the best of which features slices of fresh turkey with beaucoup greens. Nick also does kebabs and burgers at a small grill at the end of the room (the feta burger is tops). On the whole, Greek standards like spinach pie are average; the best is moussaka. [¢]

S'Agapo

34-21 34th Ave, Queens, 718-626-0303, subway: G, R to Steinway St

In the shadow of the Kaufman Astoria Studios and a little off the beaten path, S'Agapo is my fave among the Astorian Greeks, a choice recently confirmed by a meal that featured a special of Macedonian-style roast pork—huge gobbets of oink well-marbled with fat and bathed in drippings alive with subtle flavor. Good too was a red snapper done "savori"—rubbed with fresh tomato and braised in a wine and citrus marinade. In spite of an excellent grilled octopus, the best starter is a zingy puree of roasted red peppers and garlic that goes great on the crusty bread.

Snack

105 Thompson Street near Prince St,
212-925-1040, Manhattan, subway: 1, 9 to Houston St

Doubling as a grocery, this nifty new cafe and carryout is festooned with symmetrical piles of Hellenic products facing a neat row of bright white tables decorated with the tiny Greek flags. The fare is all room temperature, all vegetarian, and you can probably guess the menu: cheese and spinach pie, eggplant dip, Greek salad, stuffed vine leaves, and an especially delicious beet salad incorporating roots and stems sprinkled with olive oil, red wine vinegar, and oregano, then topped with a dollop of skordalia. Just the thing for a Greek picnic in your apartment. [vegetarian friendly]

Uncle George's Greek Tavern

34-19 Broadway, Queens, 718-626-0593, subway: N to Broadway

Uncle George's looks like a Greek diner, which it is. Revolving in the window on a brace of spits are a pig and a lamb, while at another rotisserie inside the restaurant, a chorus line of 100 or so chickens practice their high kicks. The waiters are expert at ignoring you. Every once in a while, one of them goes running down the central aisle carrying an eight-foot sword rammed through a pig on the way to the rotisserie; you better pray he doesn't trip, or you're going to be on the skewer.

The large entrees range from $8 to $12 and include several lemony-salty, roasted potato halves. Roast pork consists of a full pound of meat, cut in inch-and-a-half cubes, some fatty and some lean, rubbed with sage, salt, and pepper before roasting, and sprinkled with dried oregano. (Dried oregano is sprinkled on top of nearly everything here.) A good starter is tzatziki—a plate of yogurt mixed with cucumber, chopped onion, and loads of raw garlic. You spread it on bread. Saturday is the only day you can savor rabbit and onion stew. The restaurant's best deal is the tiny aluminum carafe of retsina (the Greek wine flavored with resin from the casks in which it is stored) for $1.

Uncle Nick's Greek Cuisine

747 9th Ave near 50th St, Manhattan, 212-245-7992, subway: C, E to 50th St

Huge, grainy, black and white photographs line the walls: a peasant family sits at a table, jovial men in a taverna stare into the camera like deer caught in headlights. The photos of turn-of-the-century peasants set the stage for the thoroughly excellent and unpretentious grub you'll find at Uncle Nick's Greek Cuisine. Cuisine? Not by a long shot. This joint's a monument to just plain food. The palette of flavors is comically narrow: a squeeze of lemon here, a splash of wine vinegar there, a sprinkle of dried oregano, and maybe some garlic, all applied with a restrained hand. Why the restraint? This is food remembered from childhood. The art here is not in the seasoning, but in the grilling. In fact, as you enter the long dining room, the most prominent feature is the tandem charcoal grills behind a counter. On them you will see fish sizzling. The red snapper is the most celebrated ($15), outsized and prepared for the grill by simply rubbing it with salt; but even better is the humble porgy ($12), served two to a plate. Its sharper flavor, almost mackerelish, complements the dark flavor of the charcoal. Note that the proprietors have opened a fancier Greek wine bar next door.

★ Zenon

34-10 31st Ave, Queens, 718-956-0133, subway: N to Broadway

Zenon is from Cyprus, although the constituency is mainly Greek. Accordingly, don't miss Greek Night every Wednesday, when the place blows up. The menu features rotating specials, with heavy emphasis on seafood and lamb. Valiantly we ate our way through the menu: squid and shrimp salad, pickled beets, deep-fried zucchini, tzatziki, taramosalata, lamb chops, chicken, grilled octopus, fried calamari, and smelts so fresh they could have flung themselves out of the pan. All admirable, but the dishes you'll remember as you make your way home are skordalia, a garlic and potato puree served as a pita dip, and grilled haloumi, a Cypriot cheese that's been boiled in whey and mildly flavored with mint. Zenon is most highly recommended.

Zodiac

30-15 Newtown Ave near 31st St, Astoria, Queens,
718-726-3995, subway: N to 30th Ave

This neophyte forgoes all the standard big feeds of Greek cooking, like moussaka and grilled fish and meats. Instead, the menu concentrates on hot and cold meze, plus pizza and burgers. The grilled octopus, engulfed in lemony broth, was especially tasty, while a dish of baked shrimp and feta was marred by rubberiness. You can't go wrong with the Greek salad, abundant in volume and dressed with olive oil and sharp red-wine vinegar. The breezy dining rooms are bordered by sidewalk tables, and Zodiac is destined to become a favorite for enjoying a snack and a retsina.

Haitian

A walk down nearly any major thoroughfare in Flatbush will take you past a string of tiny Caribbean eateries, mainly Trinidadian, Jamaican, Guyanese, and Haitian. For a recent stroll I picked Nostrand Avenue, exiting the 2 train at Newkirk, one stop short of Brooklyn College. Topside I found a neighborhood of brick storefronts and three-story apartment buildings interspersed with modest Victorian homes. Standing on the corner is St. Jerome's, whose crenelated towers ringed with scowling griffins make it look more like a castle than a Roman Catholic church. Many of the local businesses are Haitian, including botaniques, bakeries, convenience stores, and a radio station so small that the DJ sits in a miniature booth a few feet from the sidewalk. Explore this area and the other not-too-distant Haitian district centered at Rutland Road and Rockaway Parkway in East Flatbush, and you'll find a good number of small, pleasant eateries where little English is spoken and the food is a tasty combination of African and French. Though little known to non-Haitians, it's one of the best cuisines of the Caribbean.

HAITIAN

Eve's Restaurant

1366 Flatbush Ave near Farragut Rd, Brooklyn, 718-859-4874, subway: 2 to Brooklyn College/ Flatbush Ave

It's a pleasant room, simple and spotless—eight tables with red and white tablecloths, ceramic seashells filled with paper napkins, and red artificial flowers. A woman in a white apron is seen cooking through a door at the rear of the room. Even though it was 12:30 P.M., lunch was not yet being served. So I had breakfast, a choice of cornmeal or plantains served with fish, beef liver, or cow's feet. I picked the cornmeal and was served a plate loaded with cornmeal and pink beans cooked in fish stock—a very African-style mash. Accompanying the cornmeal was a small bowl of stewed cow's feet, big squares of foot flesh with a rubbery texture (maybe not for everyone), in a delicious broth, seasoned with thyme, garlic, carrots, and onion. I poured the stew over the cornmeal and dug in. [¢]

Haitian specialties

acra
taro fritters

bouillon
chicken pot-au-feu

griot
marinated and fried pork

lambi
conch stew

legumes
meat-and-vegetable stew

Krik Krak

844 Amsterdam Ave near 101st St, Manhattan, 212-222-3100, subway: 1, 2, 3, 9 to 96th St

This tiny Haitian lunch counter, brainily named after a book by Edwige Danticat, soared to excellence the minute it opened a couple of years ago. The lambi, a savory conch stew widely reckoned to be the national dish, was as tender as I've ever tasted it, the gravy laced with strips of sweet red pepper. The griot was also exemplary—pork chunks marinated, boiled, and then fried to produce a concentrated porkiness. Deploy the blistering hot sauce, which masquerades as a tiny serving of cabbage slaw. Feeling flush? Get the fried snapper, strewn with onions and peppers and accompanied by a fine creole sauce. On the weekends there's often bouillon, a homestyle stew that's the Haitian answer to Mexican pozole.

Rose's Restaurant

1046 Rutland Rd near Rockaway Pkwy, Brooklyn, 718-774-1635, subway: 3 to Sutter Ave-Rutland Rd

This East Flatbush cafe, perpetually festooned with Christmas lights, is the ideal spot to get some down-home Haitian cooking, and the ineffable Frenchness of it all will be readily apparent. Tender medallions of conch are fricasseed with plenty of lima beans and other vegetables in a rich red sauce. The dish called légumes—French for vegetables—is mainly goat, with only a smattering of vegetables to justify the name. Another Haitian favorite is griot (here spelled "grillot")—pork chunks boiled in a marinade of lemon, garlic, and spices, then fried in oil, for a crunchy exterior and mellow, chewy interior. One of the best features of Rose's is the dish of vinegary hot sauce on the table, ramified with carrot and cabbage so it almost seems like a salad. Don't miss the Haitian bakery between the subway stop and the cafe, where they have an interesting collection of Haitian cookbooks in French and English. [¢]

Le Soleil

877 10th near 57th St, Manhattan,
212-581-6059, subway: A, B, C, D, 1, 9 to 57th St

Favored by Haitian cabdrivers, and one of the last remaining vestiges of the Upper West Side Haitian community known as Bois Verna, this restaurant boasts a dining room decorated with brightly colored paintings of palm trees and island huts. The clientele converses amiably and eats with evident gusto. There is a different menu for each day of the week comprising eight or so dishes (all $10 to $12). When I stopped by, three were available. I ordered the conch (lambi) and a fried red fish with sauce. The lambi was smothered in brown sauce tasting of garlic and onions. The fish—a red snapper strewn with onions and sweet red peppers in a spicy red sauce laced with vinegar—was large and done to perfection. All entrees were accompanied by plain rice cooked with beans or white rice with soupy red beans. You also get a whole boiled plantain. The servings are so large, one could easily be shared by two.

Yoyo Fritaille

1758 Nostrand Ave near Clarendon Ave, Brooklyn,
718-469-7460, subway: 2, 5 to Newkirk Ave

A Haitian friend recommended a place with the rollicking name of Yoyo Fritaille. Red neon signs in both windows sputtered "YOYO," and a yellow overhang offered Bega, Acra, Marinade, Lambi, Tassot, Griot, Banane, Patate. Most fall into the category of "fritaille," or fried things. Once inside, I found steam pouring from the food receptacles. The counterman removed every lid to show what was underneath. The first held big chunks of griot (pronounced "gree-oh"), one of Haiti's greatest dishes, which looked so delicious I immediately ordered some ($6). It's made from chunks of pork marinated in garlic, shallots, spices, and bitter orange, then boiled until the liquid evaporates. Next, the pieces are fried, which further anneals the ingredients to the surface, resulting in a chewy exterior and moist interior with the flavors intensely concentrated. Other fried items included slices of white sweet potato, plantain, sausages that tasted suspiciously Polish, and, most interesting of all, acra—amorphously delicate fritters of shredded taro root reminiscent of ones made in West Africa. My favorite nonfried item was "legumes"—a stew of vegetables and beef, with the disintegrating vegetables forming a thick sauce. [¢]

Indian, Pakistani, Bangladeshi, Sri Lankan, and Tibetan

These overlapping cuisines continue to have an expanding presence in the city; in fact, as neighborhood Chinese restaurants disappear, they are often replaced by neighborhood Indian or Pakistani—a new phenomenon here, but one that's been in place in Britain for decades. The biggest story, though, is the runaway multiplication of Pakistani places. No longer pretending to be Indian, they now boast their ethnicity, offering distinctive specialties like "steam roast" meats, marvelous spice-laden biryanis, and variety meats and minces done on the tawa, a flat griddle. While Bangladeshi food—or, at least, food made by Bangladeshi cooks—has always been available along the East Village's 6th Street, Sri Lankan cooking remains a rare anomaly on the West Side of Manhattan, with only two restaurants. More numerous are the Tibetan places, almost constituting a mini-fad, but the food often seems a pallid mixture of Indian and Chinese, and I only have one to recommend.

With the exception of a few Pakistani places, all the eateries in this section are a good bet for vegetarians since even the meatier places have a menu that's at least one-third vegetable matter. Accordingly, only the strictly vegetarian places have been marked "vegetarian friendly." To wrap yourself in the most intense Indian atmosphere, go to Curry Hill on Lower Lexington Avenue between 26th and 31st Streets, or Jackson Heights on 74th Street and 37th Avenue, where, in addition to many restaurants, you'll find Indian newsstands, sari shops, spice stores, and other delights. For a great Pakistani neighborhood, see Swad, below. The best way to get to know an Indian or Pakistani restaurant is the lunchtime buffet, which invites a physique-destroying pig-out, and gives you a good idea of the potential of the kitchen. A restaurant that scrimps on its buffet ingredients warns you that its more expensive dishes are probably not too great either.

INDIAN

Bay Leaf

**49 W 56th St near 6th Ave, Manhattan,
212-957-1818, subway: N, R to 57th St**

Expense aside, the food is a magical mystery tour of the subcontinent, focusing mainly on Northern India. From Lucknow comes murgh zaffrani, chicken in a saffron cream sauce further thickened with cashews and almonds, the subtle nuttiness a perfect foil for the saffron. Another good choice is from Madras: kodi mellagu, chicken in a fragrant sludge of black pepper and curry leaves. The leaves lend a remote sweetness, and the dish is so heavy with pepper that you can smell it 20 feet away. From the vegetarian section of the menu comes bagare baigan, a spectacular dish of tiny purple eggplants from the city of Hyderabad. The sauce is made with coconut milk and lemon juice, and the aubergines are cooked firm. The appetizers are largely forgettable—you're much better off ordering another entree to be shared. An exception is khaman dhokla ($6.00) from Gujarat, delectable spongy cakes made with lentil and chick-pea flours, yellowed with turmeric, sprinkled with black mustard seeds and shredded coconut. [$]

Indian specialties

alu chat
tamarind-dressed potatoes and crisps

iddly
South Indian vegetarian dumplings

kachori
smooshed-pea fritters

uthappam
rice-and-lentil pancakes

masala dosa
rice-and-lentil crepe with potato filling

mukmara
lemon chicken

palak paneer
Mughal spinach and cheese

Bombay Kitchen

**113-25 Queens Blvd, Queens,
718-263-2065, subway: E, F to 75th Ave**

In addition to the standard menu from north and south, this Forest Hills kosher Indian features dishes from the three Jewish groups of India, inspired by Copeland Marks's "Sephardic Cooking." Most derive from the Calcutta Jews, who emigrated from Baghdad in the 18th century. There's mukmura, chicken in a lemony sauce of almonds and raisins, and pantras, blintzes stuffed with curried vegetables. Unfortunately, while the food is fascinating, it isn't wonderful—the offerings seem more like recipes than finished dishes. [kid friendly]

Chinar

**204 W 50th St near Broadway, Manhattan,
212-245-6453, subway: 1, 9 to 50th St**

Not the greatest Indian restaurant in the world, this batik-decorated shoebox is nevertheless a wonderful dining resource in the Times Square area—a budget purveyor of all your favorites:

palak paneer, alu paratha, tandoori chicken and fish, even a sprinkling of South Indian choices like masala dosa. Particularly recommended on the 118-item menu are mixed-vegetable Navratan curry and alu chat, a snack of potatoes in a tangy tamarind dressing. Watch the chalkboard outside for super-cheap daily specials that often include a free beverage. [¢]

Chola

232 E 58th St near 3rd Ave, Manhattan,
212-688-0464, subway: 4, 5, 6 to 59th St

Never in New York has the neglected food of South India received so much attention. Look in the Dakshin Specials section to find "more kozhambu" ($12.95), a stew of baby okra and spongy dumplings in a thick buttermilk sauce redolent of mustard, onions, and curry leaves. These leaves (pronounced "kari") are central to southern cooking, imparting a pungent fragrance somewhere between lemongrass and bay leaf. Find them also in avial malabar ($12.95), a favorite of Cochin, a former Dutch colony on the Malabar coast. A cumin-laced mélange of carrots, zucchini, and eggplant thickened with coconut and yogurt, it's pleasingly mellow and tart at the same time. Other estimable oddities include three dishes from the Jewish community of Calcutta. Their Middle Eastern origins are reflected in the lemon, slivered almonds, and yellow raisins of chicken makmura ($14.95). Phall ($16.95), by contrast, is a fusion of English and Indian cooking—tender hunks of lamb in a thick tomato sauce from which powerful flavors of garlic, cilantro, and cinnamon emerge. It's the only dish on the menu that set my mouth on fire. [$]

★ Chowpatty

809 Newark Ave, Jersey City, NJ,
201-222-1818, subway: PATH to Journal Sq

Jersey City's Little Gujarat, four blocks north of the PATH station, is three solid blocks of Indian businesses with names like Patel's Video, Patel's Cash and Carry, and Patel Snacks. In their midst is Chowpatty, a restaurant that features three vegetarian cuisines of the subcontinent: Mughal, South Indian, and Gujarati, the latter unlike either North or South Indian. The selection of vegetables, for example, includes choices totally unknown to Westerners—like tindora, a small, cucumber-shaped gourd that grows on an ivy-like vine, and tori, which looks like a dildo with spiny ridges, and has a slightly bitter flavor. These are often prepared by a dry-cooking method that involves very slow frying in oil with spices, with no water added. One dish cooked this way is tindora bataka, strips of gourd and sweet potato flavored with cumin and asafetida, which has a pleasing leathery texture. Another choice is undhiu, a wild mélange of ten vegetables that demonstrates the full range of Gujarati flavors. The vegetable combos, 15 in all, are served with tiny pooris, pappadums, tomato chutney, pickled peppers, and little bowls of ghee with lumps of jaggery, unrefined brown sugar. Indians are inveterate snackers, and a good deal of the Chowpatty menu is devoted to snacks (called farsan) such as kachori and samosa. More elaborate snacks called chat are made by throwing a couple of farsan onto a plate and dumping yogurt, chutney, tamarind sauce, fried mung beans, chopped onions, and crisp-fried noodles on top. [vegetarian friendly]

Curry in a Hurry

119 Lexington Ave at 28th St, Manhattan,
212-683-0900, subway: 6 to 28th St

Those who remember the cramped quarters of the original place on 29th Street—the first Indian fast-food on Curry Hill—will be impressed by these spacious corner digs. The food still rates a solid "B"—whether it's Mughal vegetarian stuff like alu gobi and saag paneer, tandoori specialties like chicken tikka and lamb kufta, or South Indian masala dosa and iddly, the latter two served with a wonderful chunky sambar that almost outclasses the main dish. The best part is the second-floor dining room with its big picture windows, making the room almost romantic when uncrowded. Dig the unique chutney bar—fresh green chiles; raw onions; rice pudding; chutneys of cilantro, coconut, and tamarind; salad fixin's; lemon wedges; and, best of all, an astringent pickle of green olives, chile pepper, and lime.

Darbar East

239 First Ave near 14th St, Manhattan,
212-677-0005, subway: L to 1st Ave

Not to be confused with the expensive place in Midtown called Darbar, this small and cheap place in the hospital district nevertheless excels at fresh and carefully prepared Indian food, with a few Nepalese dishes thrown in for good measure. Particularly tasty are chicken makhani, with torn pieces of tandoori chicken immersed in a mellow yogurt sauce, and lamb pasand, thickly gravied with sweet-spice accents. Unless you're in a hurry, skip the steamtable offerings in favor of the wider-ranging carryout menu, which can also be ordered for eat-in. [¢]

★ Dosa Hutt

45-63 Bowne St near Beech Ave, Flushing, Queens,
718-961-6228, subway: 7 to Flushing/Main St

Three blocks east of Main Street, Bowne Street seems a quiet thoroughfare of frame houses and trim apartment buildings. But a surprise is in store—a few blocks south of Franklin Street the houses part to reveal the gray eminence of a Hindu temple with three ornate towers dominated by the elephant-headed Ganesh. Their observances completed, cheerful knots of Indians go next door to Dosa Hutt, a strictly vegetarian three-table shoebox where four employees gyrate behind the counter frying, steaming, and bumping into each other like Keystone Cops. The 20-item menu features variations on the mainstay breakfast and lunch dishes of South India: dosa, uthappam, vada, and iddly.

Dosa are the heart of the menu, offered in eight types. The standard masala dosa ($2.50) is not particularly large, but the wrapper is crisp and well-browned, and the filling more complex than most, featuring dal and cashews tossed with a potato mixture accented with cumin, onions, and curry leaves. The best is the "special butter masala dosa" ($3), so drenched in ghee that you can smell its nutty fragrance anywhere in the neighborhood. Nearly every dish is served with a cup of homemade coconut chutney. The sambar—a thin dal soup for dipping and drinking—is admirably functional. The only other main-course is uthappam, a fermented lentil-flour pancake dotted with vegetables and priced from $2 to $3.50. Slices of green chile are fried into the pancake, but if the merely incendiary is not good enough for you, go for the "hot pepper and peas uthappam." I dare you to eat more than half of it. [¢, vegetarian friendly]

Jackson Diner

37-47 74th St near Roosevelt Ave, Queens,
718-672-1232, subway: E, F, G, R, 7 to Roosevelt Ave/Jackson Heights

OK, this Little India mainstay is never again going to be what it once was. The charming earlier location, which really was a diner, slung perfect, if modest, Indian food to hordes of demanding Indian and Pakistani shoppers. Now it's a yuppie joint with all the charm of an airline terminal, and the food has slipped several notches, too. A goat curry sampled lacked flash, while a lamb saag that used to be a friend's favorite dish was way too salty. Several subsequent visits to see if the kitchen had settled into a groove found that it hadn't. Your best bet is to go for the still-glorious luncheon buffet from 11 to 4 on weekdays.

Madras Cafe

79 Second Ave near 5th St, Manhattan,
212-254-8002, subway: F to 2nd Ave

This strictly vegetarian cafe is a breath of fresh air in the East Village's Curry Corridor, the first in this Bangladeshi zone to specialize in Southern Indian cooking. We especially liked the lentil soup laced with lemon and cilantro, spongy iddly dumplings, and lemon rice studded with cashews and toasted dal. Dosai are available in seven variations, but even better are the uthappam, spongy fermented rice-and-lentil pancakes. The menu is rounded out with breads and curries of eggplant, green beans, cauliflower, and homemade cheese. [vegetarian friendly]

New Madras Palace

101 Lexington Ave near 26th St, Manhattan,
212-889-3477, subway: 6 to 28th St

Seven years ago Madras Palace went out of business, after being the first on the block to offer kosher-certified vegetarian south Indian fare. Now it's back, sadly transformed from an informal carryout to a sit-down restaurant. But the dosa are as good as ever, well-browned and sprawled across the plate, offered in a record-breaking 15 variations. The ambitious menu rounds out with dozens of north and south Indian dishes, of which some of the more interesting are coconut uthappam, masala cashews, and "iddly in rasam bowl"—creamy steamed dumplings served in a broth reminiscent of Chinese sweet-and-sour soup. [kosher, vegetarian friendly]

Thali

28 Greenwich Ave near 10th St, Manhattan,
212-367-7411, subway: A, C, D, E, F to W 4th St

This narrow establishment, decorated in eye-searing tones of red, orange, and yellow, offers a single tray of food (a "thali") at lunch and dinner. The tray contains a series of small dishes such as, at a recent lunch, dal, yellow rice, savory potatoes and cauliflower, a paratha, tangy carrot salad, and a milk-based sweet, all for $6. Dinner, at $10, is double the food. Sometimes the dishes are prepared in Gujarati fashion: slowly dry-cooked with a little oil, no water, and mild spices. I can't wait to go back. Finally, vegetarian food served the way most Indians eat it. [vegetarian friendly]

Tiffin

18 Murray St near Church St, Manhattan,
212-791-3511, subway: 1, 2, 3, 9 to Chambers St

Named after a multi-dish midday meal, and also the stackable metal containers used to deliver it to office workers in India, this new restaurant (cousin to Thali) makes fresh forays into the largely uncharted territory of vegetarian Indian food. The three part prix fixe ($20) meal could begin with chawal sevaiya, a rice-noodle salad dotted with peanuts, or tomato rasam, a cereal-thickened roast tomato stew. Favorite main courses included sindhi sai bhaji, a flavorful variation on saag paneer, and jaipuri khazan, a blend of vegetables in a fruity curry. Though some of the dishes are too sweet or timidly spiced, Tiffin is a great resource for downtown vegetarians. [vegetarian friendly]

Vatan

409 3rd Ave near 29th St, Manhattan,
212-689-5666, subway: 6 to 28th St

Who says theme-restaurant food has to be bad? Made to look like an Indian Village circa 1900, this comfy serves the cuisine of the westernmost state of Gujarat in a multicourse, fixed-price meal ($19.95). No ordering from a menu! It's also all-you-can-eat, so don't be shy about asking for seconds. Thrill to tiny samosac and kachori served with an array of sweet chutneys and acerbic pickles, dals to be mopped with miniature pooris (brought hot), and kedgeree, a rice, onion, and lentil casserole, served with a white gravy laced with fenugreek. It's strictly vegetarian, and you won't miss the meat. [kid friendly, vegetarian friendly]

PAKISTANI

Bangal Curry

**111 Church St near Murray St,
Manhattan, 212-267-8342,
subway: 1, 2, 3, 9 to Chambers St**

Open 24 hours, 7 days in a neighborhood just north
of the twin towers where most eateries close on the
weekends, this tiny Indian features noticeably fresh
vegetarian and meat-bearing entrees at bargain-
basement prices. We dined lavishly on chicken
makhani, cauliflower curry, and, best of all, potatoes
cut like french fries and sauteed with gira (cumin
seed) and hot pepper pods—a home-style treat
rarely seen in restaurants. These dishes over rice
with papadam, mixed pickle, and soda came to just
over $5. Dig the mural of tea-leaf pickers on a hill-
side. [¢, vegetarian friendly]

Pakistani specialties

biryani
spice-dotted fried rice

chicken jalfrazi
*with onions and
green peppers*

karahi gosht
*thick Hyderabadi
goat stew*

mutton champ
grilled lamb chops

paya
braised cow feet

steam roast chicken
*steamed tandoori
variation*

Bukhara

**1095 Coney Island Ave, Brooklyn,
718-859-8033, subway: D to Ave H**

Jog past the big-screen TV, where mooning lovers cavort and sing in English-subtitled Hindi,
to the outsized L-shaped steam table. Pick earthy goat stew, loaded with potatoes in a choco-
late-brown gravy, or, even more intense, a fricassee of kidneys and long green chiles. Don't
neglect the snacks on the glass shelf, like samosa, pakora, and the A-1 potato fritters—fried
rounds of mashed spuds flecked with red chiles. This restaurant, a cabby favorite, is
Pakistani—not Uzbek, as the name would suggest. Super-delicious. [¢, halal]

5 Stars Punjabi Indian Cuisine

13-15 43rd Ave, Queens, 718-784-7444, subway: E, F to 23rd St/Ely Ave

This Long Island City Punjabi is located in a futuristic diner that looks like it was designed by
Mies van der Rohe—all aboard for your flight into outer space! The menu offers some twists
and turns on the usual Indian fare, as with a paratha stuffed with ground cauliflower and fennel seeds that is typical of the tawa cookery of the Punjab. Also estimable are the carefully
prepared biryanis—which are light, lemony, and cashew-studded—and anything made with
goat. Expect to rub elbows with plenty of Sikh cabbies, for whom this is a favorite hang. [¢]

Halal Indo-Pak Restaurant

1750 1st Ave near 91st St, Manhattan,
212-987-8150, subway: 4, 5, 6 to 86th St

Don't be misled by this no-nonsense thimble of a place—the food is prepared with great care and affection. Check out karahi gosht, a thick stew of goat attributed to the city of Hyderabad, or anything made with lamb. Skip the tandoori items, which may be a little old and tired, and concentrate on what's on the steam table. Vegetarians will find an array of selections in a Mughal vein, like the tasty palak paneer. Open 24 hours, this restaurant is a resource in a food-challenged neighborhood. [¢, halal]

Khyber Kebab

207 10th Ave near 23rd St, Manhattan,
212-727-0144, subway: C, E to 23rd St

Don't believe the sign that says Chelsea Big Wok; persevere into the dilapidated premises that serves some of the best Pakistani food in Manhattan. You need go no further than the fish cakes that sit on the counter, deep-fried hockey pucks of kingfish laced with onions, scallions, and a touch of fennel seed. Request the homemade cilantro chutney for dipping. Also estimable is a meatless curry of pumpkin and cabbage with the bright taste of cardamom and cumin. No kebabs in sight, though. Open till 4 a.m. [¢]

Pakistan Tea House

176 Church St near Reade St, Manhattan,
212-240-9800, subway: A, C, 1, 2, 3, 9 to Chambers St

Don't miss the tandoori fish at this gently-named eatery, mobbed at lunch with a diverse crowd of businesspeople, artists, and cabdrivers. Also, don't confuse this location with several imitators that have sprung up in the immediate neighborhood with similar names. Accept no substitutes! The broad range of breads, many cooked in the tandoor just inches from your face, would be reason enough to visit, but also try the chicken jalfrazi, made with fresh onions and green peppers that miraculously retain their character in the thick stew. Even when it has to be prepared to order, the food here is really fast. Open 24 hours. [¢]

Pearl Palace

60 Pearl St near Broad St, Manhattan,
212-482-0771, subway: N, R to Whitehall

Not quite as good as Pakistan Tea House, this way-downtown 24-hour eatery may be perfect if you're making your yearly pilgrimage to the Statue of Liberty, or visiting a rich uncle on Wall Street. The all-you-can-eat lunch buffet is the ideal way to experience the Pakistan-oriented menu. Especially recommended: okra masala, onion kulcha (a stuffed bread), and the splendid ginger chicken, aromatic with sweet spices. [¢]

⭐ EAST VILLAGE TRUCKSTOPS

For a cheap meal on the run, it's hard to beat the East Village's Pakistani truckstops. Bread, rice, and two steamtable dishes run less than $5 in most cases. They're hard to spot—many masquerade as the grocery stores they once were. Made to address the 24-hour dining needs of Pakistani and Bangladeshi cab drivers, anyone is welcome. The most famous is the walk-down Punjabi (114 East 1st St, 533-9048), where a couple of narrow wooden counters invite you to stand up and nosh. The fare is strictly vegetarian, and the starch component is provided by whole-wheat rotis. My favorite dish is saag, a puree of spinach dotted with onions and laced with hot chiles, and there's always a tumeric-laden dal-and-yogurt curry. Just down the block is the not-quite-so-good Pak Star Deli (78 E 1st St, 260-5884), where the sunny disposition of the Bengali counterguy almost makes up for inferior chow. His hot tea, however, is wonderful: prepared by immersing a tea bag in hot water with plenty of milk and sugar, then dipping a jet from an espresso maker and blowing bubbles till the whole beverage is a creamy froth. Pak Punjab (40 E 3rd St, 614-0107) is the underachieving cousin of Swad in Brooklyn, and the food isn't quite as good—although this joint offers a lot more selection than the other places. Especially good are the bulging potato samosas and the chicken-ball and boiled-egg stew. Perhaps the most abject of these dens is Lahore Deli (132 Crosby St, no phone), where the food is every bit as good as the other three despite its entirely decrepit appearance. Order not from the refrigerator case, but from the plastic tubs on top, used for dishes that have just been created. My potato and eggplant curry rocked emphatically on a recent visit.

Swad

1107 Coney Island Ave near Avenue H, Brooklyn, 718-421-2727, subway: D to Ave H

A panoramic window peers into the tandoori chamber, offering a cinematic view of an elderly chef, her head swaddled in white linen, methodically handclapping dough into round nans. Fragrant with toasted sesame and finished with a lick from the tallow pot, they're the best nans you've ever tasted. Meaning "taste" in Punjabi, Swad is the latest steamtable joint on a stretch of Coney Island Avenue that's become the center of Brooklyn's Pakistani community.

Rice here is treated not as an accompaniment, but as a meal in itself. Beige colored and dotted with pieces of tender chicken, biriyani ($4) swarms with whole spices like nutmeg and cardamom, a legacy of ancient trade routes. Another Pakistani passion is paya ($5)—cow feet braised into an oily and gummy stew loaded with bits of skin, cartilage, and integument, like an unfinished batch of mucilage. Every day new dishes ($4-$6) appear on the steam table. One late Sunday evening we enjoyed a curry of lamb and bitter melon, the quinine bite sweetened with masses of caramelized onions. Another time there was a gingery and thickly gravied goat curry, while a few days later a soupy dish of long green squash dotted with jalapenos left a lasting impression. [¢, halal]

Tabaq 74

73-21 37th Rd, Jackson Heights, Queens,
718-898-2837, subway: E, F, G, R to Jackson Heights/Roosevelt Ave;
7 to 74th St-Broadway

If it weren't for the dearth of vegetables, this place might be designated successor to Jackson Diner. The meat-heavy Pakistani menu is mainly wonderful, especially "mutton champ"—five strongly aromatic chops rubbed with spices and charcoal-grilled (amazingly, $7). Also dig the tawa-cooked keema, a dish of minced meat inflected with garlic, onions, and cilantro, and, for a change of pace, the yogurt-dunked ginger chicken. Of the meager number of vegetable offerings, the dry-cooked okra triumphs. For dessert, skip the instant coffee in favor of an especially creamy and firm rice pudding. [¢, halal]

BANGLEDESHI

Darul Kabab

39-26 61st St, Queens, 718-396-6361,
subway: 7 to Woodside-61st St

Lurking in the shadow of the sprawling elevated LIRR station in the heart of Woodside and decorated like a Holiday Inn lobby, Darul Kabab has an awning cryptically inscribed "An Authentic Indian Cuisine" and offering Indian, Pakistani, and Bangledeshi food. Lush pictures of Bangladesh might move you to exclaim—"Wow, it must be paradise there." Oddly, what sounds like Chinese music plays over the P.A. The food, too, has a few flourishes that might be regarded as Chinese. Biriyani is a favorite in Bangladesh, and, while the mutton version (kacchi biryani, weekends only—$6.95) was heavy with big chunks of meat nuanced with the usual range of sweet spices like cinnamon, clove, and ground coriander, the shrimp version was more like shrimp fried rice. Goat curry was especially thick and meaty, with only a few bits of potato. Surprisingly, the best dish was an amazing concoction selected from the steam table featuring big swatches of green loofah matched with pieces of hot green chile in a lemony yellow gravy.

Bangledeshi
specialties

fish masala
spice rubbed and sauteed

kacchi biryani
mutton fried rice

loofah
ridged green squash

roshgulla
sweetened
homemade cheese

shawi
rice-noodle dessert

SRI LANKAN

Taprobane

**234 W 56th Street near 7th Ave, Manhattan,
212-333-4203, subway: N, R to 57th St**

Try the strange-sounding black curry—chunks of tender
lamb in a midnight brown sauce powerfully flavored with
toasted fennel, coriander seed, coconut, and fenugreek.
The spice combinations for most of the dishes, like pork
red curry and beef smore (no graham crackers or
chocolate involved), are novel enough that you'll know
you're not eating Indian food. One of the best items at
this Sri Lankan restaurant (one of only two in town, the
other: Lakruwana, 358 West 44th Street, 957-4480), is
the hopper—a bowl-shaped lentil pancake cradling a
poached egg, served with a zippy onion relish.

*Sri Lankan
specialties*

black curry
*lamb in toasted
coconut sauce*

hopper
bowl-shaped pancake

lampries
*banquet of many
small dishes*

sambol
onion relish

smore
*fish cooked in spicy
coconut paste*

string hopper
rice-noodle pancake

TIBETAN

Tibet Shambala

**488 Amsterdam Ave near 84th St, Manhattan,
212-721-1270, subway: 1, 9 to 86th St**

Each day, Tibetans drink as many as 40 cups of bocha, a hot beverage made from brewed tea
churned with butter. Tinted an iridescent yellow-gray, it's mock chicken soup. You may be presented with a free cup as you study the menu. Momo are dumplings similar in appearance to Chinese
pot stickers, but with distinctively Tibetan fillings. One variety, shogo-fried momo ($7.25), is stuffed
with creamy potatoes flavored with turmeric, green onions, and cilantro. You get eight fried in clari-
fied butter (like Indian ghee) and served with a pristine, lightly dressed slaw of carrots and red and
white cabbage, and an irresistible brown chili sauce—richly textured and heavy on the cilantro.
Luksha shamdey ($8.95) is a soupy curry of lamb and potatoes. The serving is generous, but the
most remarkable feature is how unspicy it is. Tibetan
cooking tends to be less spicy than its Indian and Chinese
counterparts, perhaps because of the geographic isolation
imposed by the high mountains that circle the country.
Nevertheless, the muttony goodness of the stew is memorable. Vegetarianism has a positive religious value for
Tibetans, and this is reflected in the high proportion of
vegetarian dishes on the menu. One of the best is thaba
nezom ($7.25), a handsome platter loaded with three cold
salads: potatoes and green peas, black-eyed peas, and
tofu and cauliflower. By the way, it's served with a homemade flatbread, called bhale, brought warm to the table.

*Tibetan
specialties*

bhale
round flatbread

bocha
butter tea

luksha shamdy
curried lamb soup

momo
noodle dumplings

International

This slew of places is particularly useful for groups who can't decide among themselves what kind of food they want to eat—each eatery has enough diverse selection to satisfy everyone, and the food is across-the-board good. Nevertheless, none represents the apex of any particular ethnic cuisine, although you'll find plenty of cross-cultural surprises in these fusion crucibles.

INTERNATIONAL

Ansuya's Caribbean Cafe

411A Amsterdam Ave near 80th St, Manhattan,
212-580-6050, subway: 1, 9 to 79th St

Tiny but comfy, this new cafe and carryout offers a pan-Caribbean menu featuring jerks, rotis with curried fillings, Cuban chicken with mojo sauce, Trinidadian snacks like phulouri (split-pea fritters), and, odd man out, Argentine skirt steak with a weird chimichurri sauce. But consult the chalkboard for the most spectacular dishes, such as Guyanese shrimp-and- pumpkin stew, and, best of all, a rich oxtail from St. Kitts loaded with meat and carrots, redolent of allspice, and served over mountains of rice and peas. Pour on the citrusy hot sauce!

Black Betty

366 Metropolitan Ave near Havemeyer St, Brooklyn,
718-599-0243, subway: M, N, R to Union St

Taking a page from the Oznot's Dish book, this jazz bar has added an adjacent dining room and mounted a menu loaded with North African and Middle Eastern influences. The biggest thrill was the Moroccan paella, the standard Iberian product with couscous substituted for rice. It came saturated with an excellent shellfish-and-chicken broth that would have made cardboard taste good. The rest of the menu is a mixed bag: the Israeli avocado salad needed more dressing, eggplant done three ways was delicious, while the turnovers called boreks had a crust like cast iron.

Boca Chica

13 1st Ave near Houston St, Manhattan,
212-473-0108, subway: F to 2nd Ave

The food at this lively pan-Latino is all over the map: Brazil, Mexico, Chile, Puerto Rico, Cuba, even Spain. Some of the dishes lack authenticity, but who cares when they taste so good? Brazilian is best—check out the Bahian moqueca de peixe, which features shrimp and red snapper in a sauce made with coconut milk, bell pepper, garlic, and onion. Another winner is conch ceviche with diced cucumber, tomato, and cilantro—a perfect summer salad.

Cafe Asean

117 W 10th St near Greenwich Ave, Manhattan,
212-633-0348, subway: A, B, C, D, E, F, Q to W 4th St

The short menu at this thumb-sized Pacific Rim cafe offers the greatest hits of Vietnamese, Thai, and Malaysian cooking. Top honors among starters go to chicken satay, beef and vermicelli salad topped with crushed peanuts and ringed with basil, and crab and asparagus soup.

Nor did the entrees disappoint: our faves were tofu and perfectly cooked vegetables in a lemongrass stir-fry, and an awesome curried squid. Refreshingly for this type of restaurant, the decor is strictly Martha Stewart, and the staff couldn't be nicer.

Elora's

**272 Prospect Park W near Windsor Pl, Brooklyn,
212-718-6190, subway: F to 15th St/Prospect Park**

A pair of cooks—one Mexican and one Dominican—make this Windsor Terrace eatery unique. Add the proclivity of both for Iberian chow, and you have a vast range of culinary territory. From a menu of biblical proportions choose paella, Cuban sandwich, tripe soup, pork burrito with mole verde, oxtail stew, or a simple plate of pernil or tacos. One of my faves is the home-style Mexican dish called chilaquiles: crisp strips of leftover tortillas mobbed with cheese, chiles, and tomatillo sauce. Delicious! French doors open onto the pleasant street, on the northern verge of Greenwood Cemetery. [¢]

Emerald Planet

**2 Great Jones St near Broadway, Manhattan,
212-353-WRAP, subway: 6 to Bleecker St**

Just when you were getting terminally bored of burritos, along comes the wrap—the burrito reborn with an international catalog of ingredients ensconced in wildly colorful tortillas. In pleasant digs, this place purveys downtown's best, with silly geographic identifications such as Kathmandu: grilled coconut shrimp in green curry with mango salsa, green beans, bamboo shoots, and rice. (Hey, where do they get shrimp in Nepal?) The other half of the menu is devoted to smoothies that feature fruit combinations with optional additions like spirulina, bee pollen, and lecithin. The decor is high tech, and you'll feel welcome to sit around, either inside or outside, as long as you like. [outdoor dining]

Havana Pies

**245 East 14th Street near 2nd Ave, Manhattan,
212-254-1884, subway: 4, 5, 6, L, N, R to Union Sq
219 East 23rd Street near 3rd Ave, Manhattan, 2
12-684-3330, subway: 6 to 23rd St**

Empanadas, invented in the Galician region of Spain and perfected in South America, are turnovers filled with meat or cheese. Here the humble pie is redefined by international stuffings. The crawfish étouffée is fantastic, jammin' with pink tails in a lively sauce, as is the curried vegetables, creamy with coconut milk that provides a slightly sweet edge. But the greatest praise should be reserved for Cuban pernil asado—thick slices of garlicky pork roast. Pies may be ordered deep-fried or baked (the latter surprisingly good), and you'll have trouble choosing among the 20 varieties offered. Three make a meal for around $5. [¢]

Komodo

186 Avenue A near 12th St, Manhattan,
212-529-2658, subway: L to 1st Ave

Those who knew Avenue A when this was a crack block will be surprised at Komodo, a
new neighborhood joint that melds the cooking of Mexico and Southeast Asia. Also
surprisingly, most of the dishes work. The chicken corn chowder—laced with coconut milk
and properly spicy—blew us away, as did the sirloin topped with fried kumamoto oysters—
a nifty idea—and shivered fried leeks. And while the snapper filet cooked in a banana leaf
was a bit mushy and bland, the mesclun salad dressed with pecan vinaigrette more than
made up for it.

Mesopotomia

98 Ave B near 3rd St, Manhattan,
212-358-1166, subway: F to 2nd Ave

With wall treatments that look like leaks from an upstairs flat, this bistro feels more like the
East Village than ancient Iraq, though the menu hails from India, Italy, the Middle East, North
Africa, and even Belgium. You can't go wrong with appetizers like the Turkish-leaning grilled
eggplant ladled with spicy yogurt, or the salad of shrimp, tomatoes, and parsley tossed with
olive oil. I wasn't so hot on the entrees, but, in fact, my favorite starter could make a whole
meal: salade Mesopotamian, with feta, green peppers, tomatoes, merguez sausages, and
baby lettuces.

Mezze

10 E 44th St near 5th Ave, Manhattan,
212-697-6644, subway: 4, 5, 6, 7 to Grand Central

This lunch-only pan-Mediterranean—created by celebrity chef Matthew Kenney—can't
decide whether it wants to be a fancy salad bar or a real restaurant. Feathery babaganoush
and hummus, ordered from the menu, were without peer; the curried shrimp risotto was spectacularly briny and cheesy. Also recommended are Moroccan spicy carrots, charcoal-grilled
asparagus accented with preserved lemon, and, especially, a salad that paired potatoes and
yams flavored with cilantro and astringent curry leaves (no relation to curry powder). Perch on
the balcony to be waited on, and compare the bald spots of the men grazing at the salad bar
far below.

Radio Perfecto

190 Ave B near 12th St, Manhattan,
212-477-3366, subway: L to 1st Ave

Niftily furnished with dozens of Bakelite radios from the '30s and '40s, and lighting sconces made from electric drills, this alphabet bistro offers a range of relatively inexpensive possibilities from solid comfort food like chicken pot pies, fried calamari, and pastas, to attempts at haute cuisine like a mousse of chicken livers and port wine garnished with onion marmalade —it's weird at first, but gradually grows on you. Pork roast with black beans and yellow rice— a tip of the hat to the neighborhood—-was less than perfecto, but the Belgian fries were some of the best in town.

★ Republic

37 Union Sq W near 17th St, Manhattan,
212-627-7168, subway: 4, 5, 6, L, N, R to Union Sq

This self-consciously hip noodlery touts peasant food from Vietnam, China, Thailand, Japan, and Malaysia, much like Kelley and Ping down in Soho (127 Greene St., 212-228-1212).

¡O¡ SUPER DUPER

Celebrity chef Johannes Sanzin has created in Souperman (77 Pearl Street, 212-269-5777) a haute soup joint in a colonial strip-mall downtown. There are 12 or so selections each day, and a few are good enough to justify the absurd prices common to all the overpriced soup places. Among Sanzin's creations, I liked the organic winter vegetable, subtly flavored with mint, while I thought the Thai free range chicken was too oily and low on flavor, despite scads of chicken and mushrooms. All the soups joints, including the ubiquitous and not-that-good Daily Soup chain owe their inspiration to Soup Kitchen International (259A W 55th, 212-757-7730), a quirky joint that you know all about if you've studied the "Soup Nazi" episode of Seinfeld. Despite criticism leveled at the TV show, the rules of engagement are accurately represented. The soup is from the dense and complicated school. The seafood bisque is the pièce de résistance—pieces of lobster, shrimp, real crab, and scallops in a thick pink puree. Other varieties include lentil, matzoh ball, sweet red pepper, chicken vegetable, and creamless mushroom. Flavor secrets run to garlic in huge chunks, parsley, and mustard seeds. Be prepared to line up and wait, and be sure to have your money ready.

The setting features supersize blowups of the human figure in noodle ensembles and suave, polished-wood picnic tables that encourage you to eat and get lost quickly. It's not uncomfortable, but you feel like you're in some posh re-education camp. As for the food, it goes from ho-hum to inspired, often presenting conventional dishes improved with a single unexpected flavor or element. The Vietnamese standard of barbecued pork ($9) marinated in soy/garlic is fine, until the undersauced rice vermicelli in the bottom of the bowl bores you in the latter half of your feed. Anything vaguely Malaysian, like spicy duck in curry broth with taro chips, is fab, or actually, anything preceded by the word "spicy." Best appetizers are grilled Japanese eggplant ($5.50) and, surprisingly, the perfect fried wontons mired in sweet sauce wearing a crown of mâche. [outdoor dining, kid friendly]

Rice

227 Mott St near Spring St, Manhattan,
212-226-5775, subway: 6 to Spring St

What a concept! This cafe and carryout specializes in rice-based dishes, with a choice of basmati, Japanese short grain, sticky, brown, and, somewhat inconsistently, barley and couscous. Available in large and small sizes, the majority of the dishes are in an Asian vein, like Vietnamese grilled chicken, Thai beef salad, and Indian curry with yogurt and banana. There's also a selection of plain sauces priced at a dollar apiece which can be paired with any grain, including eggplant caviar, almond yogurt, and mango chutney.

Italian

This section demonstrates the vast range of Italian cooking styles currently available in the city, many at bargain prices. These range from Neapolitan—New York's earliest Italian group—to more recent introductions like Milanese, Emilia-Romagnan, Tuscan, Roman, and Sicilian (see box). Not all involve smothering red sauces, but if you really love tomatoes, as I do, you'll visit one of the more ancient Neapolitan places in Manhattan or Brooklyn, like Andy's Colonial, Bamonte's, Beatrice Inn, Cino's, or Totonno's—you'll feel like you've been dropped onto a movie set, and the greatness of the food will show you how far Chef Boyardee had to go to ruin it. Pizza spots, in general, are not included—that's another book entirely.

ITALIAN

★ Andy's Colonial

2257 1st Ave at 116th St, Manhattan, 212-410-9175, 6 to 116th St

Mexican eateries are eclipsing Puerto Rican in this East Harlem nabe—but if you look closely, you can still see a few vestiges of the old Italian community that once existed here, and I don't mean Rao's. Andy's is a throwback—just a bar, really—that serves excellent Neapolitan food. You'll have to order judiciously, but this is easily done with dishes like eggplant rollatini, stuffed with feathery ricotta that must be made fresh somewhere in the near vicinity—it tastes like it's only a couple of hours old. The menu is scrawled on a chalkboard, and there are more choices than you'd expect from the tiny kitchen. One evening, fettuccine was sauced with tomatoes and flecks of prosciutto, which lent a pleasantly salty tang. Retrograde dishes like garlicky clams oregonata are also done with a special flare. The ancient chef will come out to see if you liked your meal, and, as you exit, you'll have to elbow your way past a throng of good old boys in the smoky bar. Though mobbed in the evenings, you can often find a table in this restaurant in the afternoons.

Italian specialties

crostini
toast with topping

eggplant rollatini
wrapped around ricotta and baked

ribollita
Tuscan bread soup

stracciatella
Roman eggdrop soup

vastedda
Sicilian spleen sandwich

Bamonte's Restaurant

32 Withers St near Lorimer St, Brooklyn, 718-384-8831, subway: L to Lorimer St

Founded in 1900, this restaurant was new when Italian immigrants from the town of Nola first carried the giglio through the streets of Williamsburg. When Robert Moses's BQE sundered the neighborhood five decades later, Bamonte's persisted beneath the superhighway as patrons retreated to the suburbs. Walk into its shadowy bar, where waiters in tuxes stand in pools of eerie pink light, through a wooden arch that leads to the dining room, and find walls covered with photos of Dodgers—like dem Bums were still in Brooklyn.

Originating in the Campania region, the food is unabashedly southern Italian: seafood-heavy and tomato-sauced, and yes, they probably have a tanker truck of the red stuff parked out back. Start your meal with shellfish—perhaps an ancient concoction like clams casino ($6.95), each clam surmounted by a half-rasher of bacon, with a layer of chopped tomatoes in between to referee the strong flavors; or mussels marinara ($7.95), a mountain of glistening black shells drenched in garlicky marinara, an elemental interplay of clear and sharp flavors. In addition to seafood, the entrees favor veal, poultry, and pork. But in a joint like this with such a strong working-class heritage, you need make no apologies for choosing pasta as a main course. The homemade ravioli ($9.95) is absolutely superb: giant cheese-stuffed pillows with a velvety wrapper bathed in sauce that remains light despite its ground-meat component. Or check out the lasagna regionale ($11.75), stuffed with chicken and spinach, and nicely browned on top.

Beatrice Inn

285 W 12th St near W 4th St, Manhattan,
212-929-6165, subway: 1, 2, 3, 9 to 14th St

This ancient whitewashed restaurant recalls the day when everyone sought out their own Village Italian hideaway, and tried to keep it a secret. The food is straight out of the Fifties, from the iced shrimp cocktail, to the baked clams, both commendable, to a less-than-exciting fried calamari with a tomato sauce that will put you to sleep. For a second course, go with the homey pastas like a spaghetti with meat sauce and a doctrinaire lasagna oozing ground meat and cheese, and veer away from the heavier and more expensive meat courses.

Cafe al Mercato

2344 Arthur Ave near E 187th St, Bronx,
718-364-7681, subway: B, D to Fordham Rd

The Arthur Avenue Retail Market, at 2344 Arthur Avenue in the Belmont section of the Bronx, is one of the last operating covered markets in the city, built by Fiorello LaGuardia in 1940 to get the pushcarts off the street. Stalls sell meat, cheese, fruits and vegetables, gardening supplies, dry pasta and pulses, coffee, and olives. Most products are unmistakably Italian; if you have any doubts, look up and see row upon row of small Italian flags under the lofty ceiling. Against the rear wall of the market is Cafe al Mercato, with a seating area separated from the rest of the market by a low, faux-brick wall. Displayed in glass cases at this Sicilian spot are rice balls, crusty loaves of bread, roasted peppers, stuffed shells, and several rectangular pizzas, available by the slice, a recent collection including one with broccoli rabe against a backdrop of particularly good cheese. An olive slice had abundant green and black olives, chopped parsley, and a welcome dose of fresh garlic, while a tomato slice featured fresh tomatoes on a bed of cheese, with a sprinkle of dried oregano (and no tomato sauce). If you're sliced-out, try the frittata, a crustless pie of eggs and vegetables cooked in the pizza oven. [¢, vegetarian friendly]

Chianti

8530 3rd Ave near 85th St, Brooklyn,
718-921-6300, subway: R to 86th St

Recommended by a beat cop as we desperately searched for a Norwegian restaurant that no longer existed, this Bay Ridge Italian's gimmick is "family style"—platters of pasta so big that you feel like a small child as they're delivered. The farfalle primavera was particularly good, hosed with cream and dotted with peas, carrots, and mushrooms. The appetizers also delighted, especially the zuppa di mussels, bathed in white wine, tomato, and garlic and more than enough for four people; but the chicken and veal platters were a profound anticlimax and skimpy to boot. Stick with the pastas!

Cino's

243 DeKalb Ave near Vanderbilt Ave, Brooklyn,
718-622-9249, subway: D, M, N, Q, R to DeKalb Ave

Poised between Fort Greene Park and Pratt University, this ancient Italian specializes in the unreconstructed fare of Southern Italy, and all depends on their knockout red sauce, chunky with tomatoes and garlic and engagingly sweet. Chameleon-like, it changes character with everything it goes on, from the wonderful eggplant rollatine, stuffed with ricotta and prosciutto, to the linguini with shrimp sauce, generously dotted with crustaceans. Start with the Roman-style stracciatella (called "spinach eggdrop" on the menu), which will remind you of the Chinese soup, or the mixed salad, rife with tangy pickled vegetables. [kid friendly]

Da Andrea

557 Hudson St near Perry St, Manhattan,
212-367-1979, subway: 1, 9 to Christopher St

The warm octopus appetizer really stands out at this modern Village Italian, tossed with cubes of potato in a light pesto dressing, as does the vinegary salad of cucumber, tomato, and onion mantled with toasted bread crumbs. Dating couples have already discovered this dark and intimate retreat, pleasantly low on decor. Entrees of lamb shank sided with mushroom-dotted potatoes and zuppe di pesce with five types of seafood are also fab, but bargain hunters will be satisfied with the pastas as a second course, all priced less than $10.

Driggs Pizzeria

558 Driggs Ave near N 7th St, Brooklyn,
718-782-4826, subway: L to Bedford Ave

The front is a pizzeria with all the usual stuff; in back is a dining room with plastic-covered tables and pictures of sports figures—LaMotta, DiMaggio, and, perhaps anomalously, Don King. The eats (entrees $6 to $14) selected from a chalkboard over the kitchen are much better than you'd expect: ricotta-stuffed eggplant parmesan and penne a la vodka, which comes in a light tomato sauce fortified with cream, blessedly light on the booze. But it would be a mistake to neglect the grub in the front part of the joint, especially the pizza tricolore and the wonderful, retrograde meatball parmesan hero ($3.25).

Giovanni's

2343 Arthur Ave near E 187th St, Bronx,
718-933-4141, subway: B, D to Fordham Rd

Little Italy in the Bronx rarely gets a new restaurant these days. This one specializes in brick-oven pizzas with an unusually thick crust, chunky tomato sauce, and great latitude in topping options. The same pies are cheaper if you get them made in the regular oven, but who would be so crazy? I sat in the funky front room, but there is also a more formal (and more expensive) restaurant in back. After pizza, step across the street to Madonia Brothers Bakery (2348 Arthur Ave, 718-295-5573) and grab a cannoli—the rich ricotta filling is squirted into the shell when you order, so the pastry stays crunchy.

Grano

21 Greenwich Ave at 10th St, Manhattan,
212-645-2121, subway: A, B, C, D, E, F, Q to W 4th St

At this offspring of the popular Borgo Antico, the rabbit is exemplary—swathed in a thick, dark sauce and heaped with polenta, sided by barely steamed baby carrots. A similar bunny ragu is also poured over papardelle, but king of the pastas is a spaghetti-like tagliolini, blackened with squid ink and dotted with intensely flavorful baby clams. The entrees are so rich with olive oil, you might want to start with one of the more modest appetizers, like the grilled summer vegetables or mozzarella and tomatoes.

★ 'ino

21 Bedford St near 6th Ave, Manhattan,
212-989-5769, subway: 1, 9 to Houston St

With equipment limited to a toaster oven and a double-size Cuban press, and deploying only a handful of pungent ingredients, this Milanese-style paninoteca specializes in oddball sandwiches. Bruschetta are tiny toasts heaped with combos like roasted garlic with arugula oil; panini include variations on the toasted cheese sandwiches pressed to grooviness; while tramezzini are effetely made with crustless white bread—the best smearing lemon mayo on arugula, tomato, and cubes of pancetta to create an Italian BLT. There are plenty of good wines by the glass, but if it's breakfast time, you'd better stick with the excellent cappuccino. Go in the morning or afternoon to avoid the crowds at this ultrahip spot. [vegetarian friendly]

L & B Spumoni Gardens

2725 86th St near W 11th St, Brooklyn,
718-372-8400, subway: N to 86th St

OK, so this picturesque Bensonhurst old-timer (founded 1939) doesn't have the best Italian food in town, but the servings are voluminous and the price is right. My faves include eggplant Sicilian, a giant domed casserole of eggplant and ziti topped with browned mozzarella, and a garlicky vodka linguine dotted with peas and mushrooms. The perfect fried squid appetizer is enough to feed four, even though the "spicy" tomato sauce turns out to be bland. Though it seems out of character, the salad of oranges, walnuts, and baby lettuces is the second-best appetizer. Don't miss the spumoni ice cream, even if it's the dead of winter. [¢, kid friendly]

Luca Lounge

220 Ave B near 12th St, Manhattan,
212-674-9400, subway: L to 1st Ave

Pushing the northern verge of Avenue B's restaurant row almost to Stuy Town, this glorified pizza joint has one of the nicest backyard gardens in the East Village. Beyond the handful of excellent, thin-crust pizzas, the pickings are slim: a couple of salads, a slender cheese-and-fruit plate, tomato bruschetta—with no pastas or main courses. So stick with the wine and pizzas, the best of which is carciofi, topped with plenty of artichokes on a four-slice crust imbued with a smoky taste from the wood-fired oven. [vegetarian friendly, outdoor dining]

Lupa

170 Thompson St near Houston St, Manhattan,
212-982-5089, subway: A, B, C, D, E, F, Q to West 4th St

In a city gone crazy for the rustic pleasures of Tuscan food, and still carrying a torch for Neapolitan, Lupa adjusts the geographic focus to Rome, delivering bold flavors like fennel, lemon peel, mint, anchovy, raisin, and, of course, garlic. Among the Roman offerings are an unforgettable potatoless gnocchi ($11), kneaded with ricotta into puffy knuckles that punch through a stout sauce of ground fennel sausage; and a fettuccine Alfredo profound in its buttery and cheesy simplicity. Patrician, too, is an oxtail alla vaccinara ("butcher's style") sloughing handsome quantities of meat and fat into a sweet-and-sour gravy, finalized with a spray of toasted pignoli. And when you order pollo alla diavolo ($13), don't expect it to come Florentine style, smeared with a paste of onions, garlic, and parsley. Instead, Lupa paves its crisp-skinned version with crushed black peppercorns, a killer variation on southern fried chicken. Testa di polipo ($8) melds baby octopus heads into a submarine head cheese, stuck together with natural octopus crazy-glue. The black-and-white slices make a beautiful picture on the plate, but for most of us, they taste a little too much like, well, head cheese. Caution: hard to get a table at this glam spot; reserve in the back room way in advance, or go midafternoon.

Malatesta Trattoria

649 Washington St at Christopher St, Manhattan,
212-741-1207, subway: 1, 9 to Christopher St

The menu offers simple northern Italian fare with a focus on Emilia-Romagna. With its cities strung like beads along the Emilian Way just north of Tuscany, this region is home to parmesan cheese, prosciutto di Parma, and balsamic vinegar, all lavishly deployed at Malatesta. One evening a delectable special of risotto con funghi ($13) was creamy with grana, a lighter, sweeter cousin of parmesan, and underscored with white wine and mushrooms. Subsequent specials have been equally beguiling, including a salad of lightly poached calamari ($7.00) tossed with celery, tomato, parsley, capers, and olive oil, vivified with a few squeezes of lemon.

As befits a restaurant with its origins in the Italian breadbasket, baked goods excel. Most remarkable is piadina ($5), a regional flatbread that's like a flour tortilla, only stiffer. It comes warm from the oven and folded over a choice of four fillings, of which the best is, unexpectedly, plain steamed spinach. Predictably, the foremost pasta is tagliatelle al ragù ($10), airy ribbons in a hopelessly rich sauce of ground meat, butter, and disintegrating vegetables, a combination associated with Bologna.

Pepe Verde

559 Hudson St near Perry St, Manattan,
212-255-2221, subway: 1, 9 to Christopher St

It's rare to find a cafe where a new language is being invented, but that's the case at Pepe Verde, where the Italian managers and Mexican cooks have developed a patois halfway between Spanish and Italian. This synergy also extends to food, especially the amazing chicken, bacon, and guacamole hero, a personal favorite. It represents one of the most righteous uses for boring chicken breast. The pastas here are also excellent, made on the spot and bursting with garlic and fresh herbs. Enjoy soccer and motorcycle racing on the tube as you wait, twin obsessions of the proprietors. [vegetarian friendly]

La Pizza Fresca

31 E 20th St near Broadway, Manhattan,
212-598-0141, subway: N, R to 23rd St

Lofty-ceilinged and skylighted, this handsome cafe highlights pizzas flash-cooked at high temperatures in a wood-burning brick oven, featuring toppings of scintillating freshness. Unfortunately, the prices will make you gasp—the humble cheese-and-tomato Margherita sets you back about $10 for a pie that provides four tiny slices. Pastas, salads, and desserts are also offered, but highest honors go to a pie: quattro stagione, topped with prosciutto, mushrooms, mozzarella, and artichoke hearts that never saw the inside of a can; it might just be worth the price. Turning its back on over a century of American pizza making, this place also boasts of its certification from a benevolent association of Neapolitan pizza bakers. [vegetarian friendly]

Ribollita

260 Park Avenue South near 21st St, Manhattan,
212-982-0975, subway: 6 to 23rd St

This informal Florentine is the successor to Il Crostino, a neighborhood fave with much lower prices. Many of the best dishes remain intact: a splendid lasagna-of-the-day, bruschetta made with superior olive oil and tomatoes, maccheroni Bolognese, humble meat balls in tomato sauce, and the Tuscan bread stew from which the restaurant derives its name. Notable newcomers include crespelle, thin crepes wrapped around cheese and spinach and sauced with béchamel and tomato puree.

Totonno Pizzeria Napolitano

1524 Neptune Ave near W 16th St, Brooklyn,
718-372-8606, subway: B, D, F, N to Coney Island/Stillwell Ave

Another old-timer prey to rumors of sliding downhill is Coney Island's Totonno Pizzeria Napolitano, located a couple of blocks inland from the beach in a neighborhood of auto body shops and rickety wooden houses. I'm happy to report that on a recent visit the pizza was still wonderful in all its sloppy glory, with a thin, charred crust, high-quality mozarella in slices, and especially rich pepperoni. The pie is awash with a sauce that some may regard as too damp, but so what? Eat it with a fork. Zagat calls the staff rude, but to me, they're the soul of humble hospitality. Note: Pies only, open Wednesday through Saturday, dough runs out early in the evening, about 8 p.m.

Valdiano

659 Manhattan Ave near Nassau Ave, Brooklyn,
718-383-1707, subway: G to Nassau Ave

Way off the tourist track, Vallo di Diano occupies the semiarid lower stretch of Italy's Campania. On a hillock in the center sits Teggiano, a town whose history harkens back to the Greeks. Now debuting in nearby Greenpoint is Valdiano, a restaurant founded by Teggiano immigrants. A recumbent San Cono—the town's 11th-century patron saint—waves from atop the china cupboard.

Campania is particularly proud of its fresh cheese, which finds its most perfect use in mozzarella in carrozza ("in a carriage"—$4.50), which slabs the white stuff between two pieces of bread, dips the assemblage in egg batter, then fries it into a crisp and oozy toasted cheese sandwich. This peasant classic is sided with a gravy boat of excellent chunky marinara for dipping. Involtini di melenzana ($5) is another dairy masterpiece, rolled fried eggplant around a filling of fresh ricotta, topped it with tomato sauce and mozzarella, and roasted it to bubbly brownness. Even more remarkable is the salad of broccoli di rapa ($4), a strong-flavored relative of turnip greens glossed with a bitterness-softening dressing of olive oil and garlic. Literally breathtaking is an idiosyncratic penne all'Arrabbiata, noodle cylinders drenched in a thick sauce that's tweaked with scorching green chiles.

Veronica Ristorante Italiano

240 W 38th St near 7th Ave, Manhattan,
212-764-4770, subway: 1, 2, 3, 7, 9, N, R to Times Sq

Get there early if you want a seat at this venerable, lunch-only cafeteria in the Garment Center. The long counter presents a daunting array of choices, including nearly every Italian dish you've ever heard of. The linguine under the shrimp scampi is miraculously firm, with five jumbo shrimp well-coated with olive oil, garlic, and bread crumbs. Though many of the selections are swamped with red sauce, everything isn't red and dead—they do wonders with cream, veal stock, and pesto; and if none of these appeal, there are plenty of salads and sandwiches, as well.

¡O¡ THE REAL FOCCACCIA

"Focacceria" sounds like a trendy Tuscan bakery, but in parts of Brooklyn it denotes an old-fashioned Sicilian eatery specializing in snacks that can be eaten standing up, including short dishes of vegetables and seafood, and, especially, sandwiches made with seeded rolls called focaccia. Flooded with Sicilian immigrants in the 1950's, Bensonhurst boasts the biggest concentration. Focacceria (7118 18th Ave, 718-232-9073) exudes a glow that seems to come from the profusion of fresh vegetables ($3-$5) heaped up inside: strips of breaded zucchini, stuffed artichokes, broccoli rabe sauteed in garlic, well-oiled fava beans, and a tart pickle called giardiniera featuring crunchy cauliflower and big green olives. The seafood selection is nearly as attractive, but the signature at Gino's (7118 18th Ave, 718-232-9073) is vastedda ($3), a marvelous sandwich that piles boiled cow spleen on a split focaccia, avalanches it in snowy ricotta, then adds coarsely grated parmesan. Spleen? Pretend it's liver. Caravello's (2313 86th St, 718-946-5700) crouches in the shadow of the elevated B; the outside looks like a pizzeria, but penetrate deeper into the Formica interior and find a steamtable offering a few dishes of real distinction. Powerful flavors of onion and garlic infuse a wan pork and potato stew ($5), while the tomato-drenched lasagna is appealingly whomped with garlic. Joe's of Avenue U (287 Avenue U, 718-449-9285) is like a '60s diner, with booths large enough to accommodate extended families, who drift in Saturday afternoons to graze among old friends. The pasta con sarde ($6.50, Fridays and Saturdays only) is spectacular: bucatini heaped with sardines roughly mashed with fennel, pignoli, and currants. Spoon in the toasted breadcrumbs to form a thick sauce. At 96, Ferdinando's (151 Union St, 718-855-1545) is the oldest and most picturesque of the Brooklyn focaccerias, retaining its pot-bellied stove and ancient vastedda-making set-up. But more popular among its patrons than vastedda is "panelle special," a sandwich that substitutes chick pea fritters for spleen. These fritters are ravioli-like and faintly smoky, the perfect complement to the sharp grated cheese.

West Brighton Italian Grocery

1215 Castleton Ave near Taylor St, Staten Island, 718-448-1168, subway: none

This ancient salumeria, whose business card carries the cryptic inscription "Milk Farm," fabricates excellent hot and cold heroes on crusty bread, including one heaped with mortadella, capicola, provolone, lettuce, and tomato, then inundated with wine vinegar and tasty olive oil.

Watch carefully for the daily pasta specials, priced around $5. On a recent afternoon it was a perfect lasagna oozing equal proportions of mozzarella and ricotta, with a subtle Bolognese sauce, the finely ground meat taking a back seat to a tart, coarse tomato puree. The mild tasting pasta fagioli soup wasn't bad, either. [¢]

Zito's East

211 1st Ave near 12th St, Manhattan,
212-473-3400, subway: L to 1st Ave

Spawned by a beloved bakery on Bleecker, this cafe cum pizzeria has the requisite brick oven, from which sail pizzas that are a notch above most in this genre: the crust a little thicker, not charred quite as much, and furnished with a more generous quantity of toppings (my faves: artichokes and extra garlic). The menu also offers a broad array of other Italian dishes, with the innumerable pasta/sauce combinations an especially good deal—most are priced a little over $5. The dining room is more spacious than you'd expect from the narrow storefront. [¢]

Jamaican, Vincentian, Grenadian, and Bajan

O f all the Caribbean islands, Jamaica has the most interesting and varied cuisine. It makes abundant use of fresh seafood, chicken, and pork and uses a broad range of flavors from an exciting variety of sources. Chinese indentured workers introduced soy sauce. African slaves provided green onions, cilantro, many of the cooking techniques, and the love of hot peppers. The Spanish, both directly and via Spanish-speaking Caribbean islands, introduced the use of salt cod and cooking techniques involving yellow onions, green peppers, and vinegar. Curries came directly from India and via England, Trinidad, and Guyana. Jamaicans also have unusual botanicals to cook with: ackee, breadfruit, and allspice, an indigenous nut that Jamaican cooking (especially the technique known as jerking) makes spectacular use of.

The other Anglophone islands in this section boast their own memorable dishes but, while they share Jamaica's major culinary themes, they lack its range.

JAMAICAN

Jams

**518 9th Ave near 39th St, Manhattan,
212-967-0780, subway: A, C, E to 42nd St**

Sporting a jaunty white fedora, Lady Saw the
Undisputed DJ Queen presides over this tiny
Jamaican cafe, where the specialties include
ackee—a weird fruit that cooks up like scrambled
eggs—tossed with salt cod and onions, and
callaloo—the stewed green tops of the taro plant.
More mundanely, they turn out a decent chicken,
either jerked or Southern fried, and an even better
brown stew fish, with your choice of snapper or kingfish sauced with onions, garlic, tomatoes, and okra.
Also grab the homemade ginger, sorrel, and sea-
moss drinks. [¢]

*Jamaican
specialties*

cow cod
bovine penis soup

escoveche porgy
fried and pickled fish

jerk
*meat or chicken
barbecued with
spice paste*

patties
*beef or vegetable
turnovers*

rice and peas
*coconut-drenched
red beans and rice*

Maroons

**244 W 16th St near 8th Ave, Manhattan,
212-206-6640, subway: A, C, E to 14th St**

Nothing is better than a plate of green tomatoes, crumbed and carefully fried. They join a list
of other distinguished appetizers at this Jamaican and soul food cafe, cunningly fitted into a
single tenement apartment. Barbecue ribs are dense and sweet, cooked to the point where the
meat and sauce fuse. The cod fritters are equally accomplished, dotted with scallions and
miraculously devoid of denseness. Though the jerk chicken suffered from an overdose of
cooking school technique, it was delicious nonetheless, but the catfish filet was overwhelmed
by butter. For sides, pick the callaloo over the mac and cheese. [$]

Negril

**362 W 23rd St near 9th Ave, Manhattan,
212-807-6411, subway: A, C, E to 23rd St**

This is a good place for an island splurge, if you don't mind paying over $10 for entrees at din-
nertime, and want something with a little more ambiance than, say, Daphne's. The skillfully
spiced fare runs to curry goat (dig it), jerk pork (dig it), and jerk chicken salad (skip it). The
bilevel dining room is a particular delight, with the wall-sized aquarium occasionally diverting
the couples at the bar from mooning into each other's eyes. Lunches are much cheaper, with
plenty of specials around $10, including good rotis. There's a slightly less desirable version of
this place in Hell's Kitchen called Island Spice (402 W 44th St, 212-765-1737).

Dee's West Indian Bakery

97-17 57th Ave near Lefrak City, Queens,
718-699-1398, subway: G, R to Woodhaven Blvd

Situated on the ragged northern frontier of Lefrak City, this minuscule Jamaican cafe has two hot selections per day, plus the usual array of patties, cakes, and tonics like Tan-Pon-It Long and Zion. Oxtails stewed with butter beans are particularly savory; alongside you get stewed cabbage and rice and beans cooked in coconut milk. Other typical choices include brown-stew chicken, curried goat and, only at breakfast, saltfish and ackee. For something sweet, try tamarind balls or rainbow cake. [¢]

Royal Bake Shop

215A E 170th St near Grand Concourse, Bronx,
718-681-9160, subway: 4, B, D to 170th St

What a contrast between the beef patties they sell at pizza parlors and the ones served here! The annatto-tinged pastry is fresh and light. The filling is very spicy, with the meat ground so fine it's almost pureed. Patties are $1 each; two would make a fine, filling lunch. Eat them as the Jamaicans do, in a coco bread (70¢). As specialized as a hot dog bun, this yeast bread has been folded prior to baking to make a shape like a baseball glove. The combination of coco bread and patty is sublime—the spicy filling of the patty shining through two carbo layers, one puffy, one oily. Royal Bake Shop doesn't sell much else, but these are good enough to warrant a special visit. [¢]

Strictly Roots

2058 Adam Clayton Powell, Jr. Blvd near 123rd St, Manhattan,
212-864-8699, subway: A, B, C, D to 125th St

This vegetarian eatery (their slogan: "We serve nothing that crawls, walks, swims, or flies"), with its comfortable tables and velvet painting of Haile Selassie in a suit, has created a cuisine that rivals any other in depth and interest. Sure, there are predictable Jamaican standards like vegetable-stuffed patties, banana bread, and sorrel punch, but take a gander at the steam table: a delicious succotash of green beans and limas, crisply fried tofu balls, an herby potato mash sweetened with orange yam, and a lasagna that substitutes TVP (textured vegetable protein) to create a dead-ringer for its Italian prototype. [¢, vegetarian friendly]

Sylvia's Restaurant

674 Nostrand Ave near Bergen St, Brooklyn,
no phone, subway: A, C to Nostrand Ave

The restaurant's name and the mural—a straw-hatted boy fishing while, over his shoulder, a family picnics in a lush meadow—might make you think this is a soul-food joint. Think again; this eatery, which features a savory liver-and-dumpling breakfast, is Jamaican. Heartier meals are based on fried fish, curry beef, and brown stew chicken, and come with a salad, slices of fried plantain, a hunk of cassava, and white rice soaked with a generous quantity of brown lentils. Don't let them stint on the habanero hot sauce, and expect the regulars lined up along the counter to be impressed. [¢]

★ Toyamadel

**1709 Amsterdam Ave near 145th St, Manhattan,
212-491-4492, subway: 1 to 145th St**

An absurdly filling breakfast is served all day at this handsome Jamaican eatery. I picked cod and callaloo—taro leaves stewed with shards of savory salt cod sided with boiled plantain and starchy dumplings. The kitchen, seen through the counter window, is a paragon of gleaming modernity, while roots tonics, patties with coco bread, and other baked goods are dispensed through a separate window. Curry chicken with rice and peas was also irresistible. All combos are conveniently available in small, medium, and large sizes, and Toyamadel is steps away from Riverbank State Park. Picnic time! [¢]

Universal Kitchen

**737 Lydig Ave near Holland Ave, Bronx,
718-239-0636, subway: 2, 5 to Pelham Pkwy**

This carryout excels at curries. My $4 lunch included curried goat, with the surprise inclusion of finger-shaped dumplings, heaped over a generous mound of coconut-laced beans and rice. Though not homemade, the patties of chicken or ground beef are also fab, laced with the subtle perfume of scotch bonnet peppers and perfect when crammed in a mitt-shaped coco bread. The proprietors couldn't be more accommodating, and you can see the food being prepared through a heart-shaped window, beside which a swinging door into the kitchen is inscribed "Cleanliness is Godliness." [¢]

Brawta

**347 Atlantic Ave at Hoyt St, Brooklyn,
718-855-5515, subway: A, C, G to Hoyt-Schermerhorn**

The stretch of Atlantic Avenue near the Long Island Railroad terminus has been a hotbed of Caribbean restaurants, but never has one opened so far west. The spiffy interior has black and red tiles of the bumpy industrial sort, and vases of orange and pink gladiolus. In a niche in one wall is a shrine to Bob Marley, and the interior is so pleasant that I sat when I had intended to carry out. The jerk chicken dinner ($7.50) consisted of five small pieces that had been marinated and roasted—very tasty even though it hadn't been charcoal barbecued. There was a generous quantity of rice and peas on the side, and the hot and heavenly jerk sauce had been poured over everything. There was also a salad of shredded romaine, carrots, and red cabbage dressed with French dressing. The escoveche porgy, advertised on the chalkboard menu as hot and spicy, was the only dish carrying that warning. It wasn't. The head-on fish was smothered in pickled carrots and onions, and was plenty good anyway. [kid friendly]

⦿| JERKIN' IT

There are so many jerk joints in parts of Brooklyn and the Bronx that they merit an entire book. Though the recipe originated in Jamaica, every Caribbean island has its own spice mixture and jerking techniques. In the islands, jerking is usually done in a busy open-air market or by the side of the road, using a split sixty-gallon drum. Recipes vary, but in Jamaica the jerk coating usually contains green onions, ground allspice, garlic, fiery Scotch bonnet peppers, soy sauce, and chicken or pig blood. Here, the blood is often omitted and the jerk is often baked instead of barbecued. Following are my three favorite versions in the city.

Danny and Pepper (771 Flatbush Ave, Brooklyn, 718-284-9187) shares a store with a Korean fish market, and the fishmongers and jerk sellers size up every customer and seem visibly disappointed if you move to the opposite side of the store. Outside is a 60-gallon drum, the emblem of great jerk. Inside, a serve-yourself refrigerator holds tonics with names like Agony Drink and Front-end Lifter, as well as D&G ginger beer. The chicken is moist and pink inside, with the pinkness resulting from marination rather than undercooking. The skin is nicely charred and crusted with jerk seasonings, which in this case run more to green onions, oregano, and thyme. Refuse the offer of free bread; instead, ask for festival, a sweet torpedo-shaped fritter.

At Norman's Jerk Chicken Restaurant (167-20 Hillside Ave, Queens, 718-297-2803), the chicken has a lot more soy sauce in the jerk covering than is usual, and I figure it's the influence of the Guyanese and Trinidadian restaurants in the neighborhood. Norman's occupies a corner store and looks like an old lunch counter, with a couple of booths and a row of stools. A sign over the counter offers breakfasts of mackerel and banana, ackee and codfish, and porridge and liver. Another place to get great jerk is Jerk Center (1296 E Gun Hill Rd, Bronx, 718-798-4966), located in a former gas station in the Bronx, where the plexiglas window displays bottles of Aunt Linda's Colonic Bitters. You can smell the charcoal jerk smoke blocks away. The fragrant chicken or pork jerk (the latter's preferred) lies on top of Jamaican rice and peas—pink beans and white rice stewed with sweet coconut milk— with a homemade hot pepper vinegar poured over everything. Other main courses include oxtails, brown smothered chicken, curry chicken, curry goat, fried or steamed fish, and ackee. Soups include pepper pot, cow cod, fish tea, and mannish water, a stew of goat parts, green banana, potatoes, and other vegetables.

Daphne Caribbean Express

233 E 14th St near 2nd Ave, Manhattan,
212-228-8971, subway: L to 3rd Ave

What was once a mediocre Jamaican restaurant called Daphne's Hibiscus moved down the street and adopted the fast-food format. The curried goat roti ($6), a rolled flatbread sandwich, was meat-heavier than it needed to be, and came from the soupy school of roti construction—be prepared to wield knife and fork. Best surprise was a dish called mackerel and bananas, which contained savory chunks of skin-on mackerel and two kinds of plantain—sweet fried and starchy boiled. And as if that weren't enough, the entree also contains floury dumplings. Yum! Main dishes are available in small portions—big enough for any normal person—for $5.95; large portions are $7.95. [¢]

VINCENTIAN

Louise's

54 Rockaway Ave, Brooklyn,
718-574-7514, subway: A, C, J, L to Broadway-East New York

Heralded by a wall-size mural of palms flanking a cool lagoon and an outsize papier-mache hamburger, this cavernous East New Yorker specializes in the food of the Caribbean island of St. Vincent. Antillean specialties run to savory oxtails, deep fried fish filets, and an awesome curried chicken with just the right amount of heat (lots). The island women who run the joint couldn't be nicer; and when they ask how you liked your meal, you'd better say "very much, thank you." The menu is rounded out with burgers and further mainland fare. [¢, kid friendly]

BAJAN

★ Culpepper's

1082 Nostrand Ave near Lincoln Rd, Brooklyn,
718-940-4122, subway: 2 to Sterling St

Sporting an electric-blue awning, Culpepper's is a Bajan cafe a few blocks south of Eastern Parkway in the Brooklyn's Prospect-Lefferts Gardens. The neighborhood is home to Haitians, Jamaicans, Dominicans, Trinidadians, and Barbadians, who call themselves Bajans. The eatery is mainly carry-out

Bajan specialties

coo-coo
cornmeal porridge

flying fish
favorite catch

cutters
Bajan sandwiches

during the day, but in the evening the doors swing open to reveal a spotless white dining room that's quickly becoming an island clubhouse. While the British colonial heritage of Barbados is preserved in its architecture, baked goods, and the lilting speech of the islanders, much of the food is African at heart. Coo-coo ($8) is a steamed porridge of cornmeal kneaded with butter and flecks of okra, sliding easily down the gullet. It's served with a choice of fish doused with a plenitude of wonderfully thin and aromatic sauce— red-tinged and slightly oily. With chunks of fresh tomato and scads of onions, it's strikingly different from the "brown stew" gravy of other Caribbean joints. Though kingfish is a popular choice, go for steamed flying fish instead, the island's favorite catch and a real Bajan passion. Dewinged, deboned, extensively marinated, and cut crosswise into thin pieces with the hatched skin attached, flying fish has firm white flesh and a mild, almost meaty flavor that goes well with the delicate sauce. [kid friendly]

GRENADIAN

TCB'S Jerkin Chicken

769 Nostrand Ave near Sterling Pl, Brooklyn, 718-363-8100, subway: 3 to Nostrand Ave

TCB's Jerkin Chicken, a narrow Crown Heights carryout with a multinational menu, lists lambi, rotis, jerks, cowfoot souse, and other island specialties that may be unfamiliar to those born on larger land masses. I was curious about oil down ($7), which prompted the counterguys to divulge they were from Grenada, not Jamaica—I'd stumbled on their national dish. This Fridays-only tour de force is a farrago of green plantain, cocoyam, corned oxtail, and dense flour dumplings shaped like swollen fingers, simmered for hours in coconut milk. A few pieces of curry chicken are thrown in at the last minute. With only a trickle of concentrated sauce, this ridiculously rich dish needs to be chased with an island drink: white foamy Irish moss ($3), made from seaweed; mauby, concocted of bitter carob bark; or sorrel, a blindingly red hibiscus-flower tea mimicking Kool-Aid.

With a name like Jerkin Chicken, you'd expect the signature product to rock, and it does (half a bird, $5.50). Though the spice coating seems thin, the succulent fowl bursts with jerk flavor, attracting throngs of patrons at peak hours. Even better is jerk pork ($6 per half pound), a real oddity in this chicken-happy neighborhood: hunks of fatty meat—some surrounding bones you didn't know a pig had—oozing midnight sauce with a distinctively Grenadian flavor. Antilleans do know how to live large. [¢]

Grenadian specialties

oil down
multistarch oxtail stew

Irish moss
sweet seaweed beverage

callaloo
taro leaf soup

curried lambi
conch

Japanese

Not so long ago, sushi was a rich person's pursuit in Japan, since raw-fish meals often cost the equivalent of $400 or more. Americans can pat themselves on the back for aiding in the democratization of sushi, and in the invention of new sushi styles, like the California roll and the Boston roll, which have put our imprint on the culinary form. These developments, of course, have mixed consequences, one of which is that you can get bad sushi on nearly every street in the city nowadays—desiccated, fishy-smelling, maybe even unhealthy. The list below includes places that are still good, and in one case, a world class sushi bar—Kuruma Sushi—that's so expensive you can easily blow a hundred dollars in fifteen minutes.

New York continues to accumulate Japanese specialty restaurants offering tonkatsu, okonomiyaki, soba, fugu, and other arcane delights.

JAPANESE

Akida

**42-32 Bell Blvd, Queens,
718-224-8196, subway: none**

Of the Japanese restaurants on Bayside's burgeoning sushi strip, this one looked the best. We knocked
back yellowtail, mackerel, and broiled eel nigiri-zushi
in short order, then switched to the more exotic
assemblages from the Chef's Special Roll section of
the menu. Best was the spider roll, spiny with fried
soft-shell crab and cooled with cucumber. Also
memorable was the tiger roll of eel and shrimp
moistened with ginger dressing. Tomoe Sushi it's
not, but at half the price, it ain't bad. Enjoy a 25%
discount between 5 p.m. and 8 p.m.

Chikubu

**12 E 44th St near 5th Ave, Manhattan,
212-818-0715, subway: B, D, F, Q to 42nd St**

Probably the only spot in town that serves fugu caught in the wild (other places use farm-
raised fish, nearly devoid of poison) is Midtown's Chikubu. The fugu chef's certificate of quali-
fication is displayed in the cloakroom. The fugu sashimi is sublime, pinwheeled on the plate in
thin translucent slices crazed with fine filaments and topped with a little wad of dyed radish.
The condiment of choice? Tabasco sauce—in Japan an exotic ingredient. The other sushi and
sashimi also rock, and wash it all down with a tipple of sake flavored with toasted fugu fin.
Also watch for seasonal specialties like "sweet young honey bee with soy sauce." [$]

Genki Sushi

**9 East 46th St near 5th Ave, Manhattan,
212-983-5018, subway: 4, 5, 6, 7 to Grand Central**

Why is the face on the logo frowning? This sushi bar serves some of midtown's best in a
sunny, street-level room that's the atmospheric antithesis of the usual nigiri-zushi purveyors.
The plates rotate around an amoeba-shaped prep area on a cunning metal conveyor belt,
color-coded according to price ($2.50-7.50), as Brazilian music floods the premises. Most
mind boggling was the eel, broiled to order and flopping extravagantly over the rice lozenges,
but nearly its equal was the belly tuna (toro) imported from Chile, intensely pink and creamy.

Japanese specialties

fugu
multipart blowfish meal

katsudon
*egg and fried pork
over rice*

oden
broth with odd additions

okonomiyaki
eggy pancake

soba
buckwheat noodles

toro
*fatty belly tuna sushi
or sashimi*

udon
gluey wheat noodles

Haru

433 Amsterdam Ave near 82nd St, Manhattan,
212-579-5655, subway: 1, 9 to 79th St

Finally, the Upper West Side has broken the sushi barrier, and it's no longer necessary to go south to get a decent piece of fish. Haru's menu concentrates on incredibly fresh sushi and sashimi, often sprinkled with electric-red flying fish roe and served Korean style in filets so huge that they droop over the ends of the rice wad and trail along the plate. This oceanic luxuriance has packed the place, and even all the sidewalk tables are often filled, although who'd want to sit in the 90-degree heat in clouds of auto effluvia to eat their sushi?

★ Hasaki

210 E 9th St near 3rd Ave, Manhattan, 212-473-3327, subway: 6 to Astor Pl

Kudos to the architect who designed this timber-intensive subterranean space, preceded by a sunken patio and pair of anterooms decorated with dramatic stone treatments and a stand of live bamboo. In spite of credible versions of sukiyaki, teriyaki, and soba, the raw fish still rules at Hasaki, where four crackerjack chefs simultaneously wield knives. The regular combos are fantastic, but pay closer attention to the specials like negi toro, a huge wad of belly tuna (the much-revered fatty kind) ground up like steak tartare, tweaked by chopped scallions, topped with three kinds of damp seaweed and one kind of dry, and looking like a fatal undersea accident. The regular menu also offers sushi surprises, like kinuta eel, a maki roll sans rice with a super-thin curl of cucumber standing in for the usual seaweed wrapper. Kinuta hamachi is even more stunning: raw yellowtail, scallion, and cooked shrimp inside the same cucumber membrane. This would be good enough on its own, but it comes with a delicious dipping sauce of blonde miso paste mixed with lemon, fancily served in a lemon rind.

Aftertimes, skip the desserts and go for the Japanese coffee. If you thought the French and Italians were anal about their coffee-making, witness the Japanese: the apparatus looks like a kid's chemistry set, with a Florence flask on the bottom and beaker on top. I won't explain the scientific principle, but as the coffee shoots upward, all eyes will be on your table. [$]

Jeoladdo

116 E 4th St near 1st Ave, Manhattan, 212-260-7696, subway: F to 2nd Ave

Here's the gimmick: a Japanese restaurant with Korean touches combined with a screening room for independent films. The menu emphasizes sushi, which is painstakingly fresh and, for now at least, cheap by local standards. Typical maki rolls are priced two-for-one in the $5 range, but look to the "House Roll" section to find more colorful creations, often made with real crab. My favorite part of the menu, though, offers Korean pancakes called jeon, made with egg and gooey rice starch studded with oysters, shrimp, or squash.

★ Katsuhama

11 E 47th St near 5th Ave, Manhattan,
212-758-5909, subway: E, F to 5th Ave

Push your way past the pre-fab sushi counter and find one of the most interesting Japanese restaurants in town, a real tonkatsu-ya—an eatery that specializes in lean, thin-sliced pork cutlets (known as "hire") expertly fried and served with a sauce like brown ketchup. A mortar filled with roasted sesame seeds is also provided—grind the seeds up very fine and mix them into the sauce. Better yet, order katsudon: a dish of pork-topped rice glazed with sweet egg sauce. Other less interesting fried items like shrimp and chicken breast are also available.

Sapporo East

245 E 10th St at 1st Ave, Manhattan,
212-260-1330, subway: L to 1st Ave

Granddad of the East Village's cheap Japanese, this joint offers the best combination of value and good food. The once-innovative menu is now rear guard. Their katsudon and seaweed salad are still among the best in town, and the sushi is fresh and edible, if not distinguished. For higher-brow sushi, go to sister restaurant Shima. For hipster spotting, depend on Sapporo East.

🍽 SLURP, SLURP

Whether you crave soba or udon, Manhattan provides a plethora of great Japanese noodle houses. All can be counted on for a satisfying bargain meal. Here are a few of my favorites: Menchanko-Tei (39 W 55th St, 212-247-1585; 131 E 45th St, 212-986-6805; 257 World Trade Center Concourse, 212-432-4210) is king of the authentic Japanese noodle joints, reflected in the favor shown this chain by Japanese diners. Don't look for teriyaki, sushi, or tempura; the menu is centered on soups crammed with noodles or rice and served in big metal bowls. Try the eponymous menchanko, weighed down with udon, chicken, Chinese cabbage, fish balls, Japanese sweet potato, tofu, and miraculous gooey islands of rice cake. The condiment provided tastes oddly like Indian lime pickle. Another specialty is oden, a Japanese comfort food that lets you mix and match from among a list of nine strange-sounding elements like fish cake bar fly, beef tender, mixed fried tofu ball, and Devil's tongue jelly, all deposited in a thin sweet broth.

Long the choice of students and slumming Nipponese businessmen, long-running Sapporo (152 W 49th St, 212-869-8972) is one of Times Square's last good, cheap ethnic eateries. With nary a piece of sushi in sight, the menu is strictly no-nonsense Japanese comfort food. Don't

miss the gyoza, dumplings whose wrappers are stuffed with savory meat and greens, steamed, and then pan-fried to a crisp brown on one side. This noodle joint is especially cozy in winter but, if you come by during the summer, you can get the pièce de résistance: hiyashi chuka, a bowl of cold noodles in a slightly sweet broth, topped with ham, chicken, egg, fish cake, green onion, shredded ginger, cucumber, and corn—a wild and flavorful combo! Tokyo La Men (90 University Pl, 212-229-1489), a cutely named noodle shop, occupies a narrow room with tons of plastic flowers hanging from the ceiling. Thrill to hokey names like Viking La Men and Stamina La Men, then order ten sin, brought in a huge white bowl that holds a quart of brown broth laced with mushrooms and beef. A broad omelet strewn with shredded red ginger and ribbons of spinach floats on top. Excavation reveals thin noodles, kernels of sweet corn, and tiny pieces of mushroom.

Who would guess that the elegant Soby-ya (229 E 9th St, 212-533-6966) is a humble Japanese noodle shop? It's the East Village's first, offering hot and cold assemblages featuring udon and soba. All the soup combinations sampled were excellent, including curried chicken with soba, and udon with a mushroomy vegetable mélange. You can easily eat for under $10, but who could resist the appetizers like homemade shumai, tempura by the piece and, lost in the extensive sake menu, a bar snack of raw baby squid marinated in a fragrant dark liquid.

Finally, if you thrilled to the movie Tampopo, you can relive the experience at a couple of places that make their own soba from scratch (at fiendishly elevated prices). Restaurant Nippon (155 E 52nd St, 212-758-0226) owns a farm in Canada where they grow their own buckwheat to make a soba that's 20% wheat/80% buckwheat, making it a little more rubbery than average. Dig the warm-weather lunch special, starting with a couple of pieces of inari-zushi, followed by a green salad, and climaxing in a heap of cool mori-soba—buckwheat noodles displayed on a bamboo screen. Honmura An (170 Mercer St, 212-334-5253), even more expensive, makes their soba from buckwheat flown in from Japan, and rolls it out in a little shack right inside the dining room using a series of successively smaller dowels. The soba are pale and coarse-grained, breaking off at just the right moment, like none other on this side of the planet. Eat them in hot broth with a pair of tempura prawns that are so big, one would be enough. Or try any of the dozen other hot and cold permutations. Honmura An is considered one of the city's most sublime dining experiences.

★ Kuruma Sushi

7 E 47th St near 5th Ave, Manhattan,
212-317-2802, subway: E, F to 5th Ave

I've seen sushi heaven and its name is Kuruma Sushi. Begin your voyage with toro sashimi, and the kindly sushi chef, who obviously knows his stuff, will inquire politely, "How fatty do you want it?" Your reply, of course, is "As fatty as you can make it." What floats over the partition and eases onto your plate are two wobbly diamonds of perfect fish flesh, bright pink and crazed with little veins of fat like Kobe beef, and so unutterably tasty that you could walk out the door right then and still feel satisfied. But you won't. The further swatches of sashimi, and later, fingers of sushi arrive in synchronous profusion, and you'll be certain to taste things you've never had before, and will probably never have again. Eating sushi there is like riding a very expensive taxi—plan on spending about $25 per person for every five minutes on the meter. [$]

Mie

196 Second Ave near 12th St, Manhattan,
212-674-7060, subway: L to 1st Ave

The proprietors must have been prescient when they opened this Japanese old-timer in 1965; over the next three decades it was joined by dozens of comparable East Village restaurants. This was one of the first places in town to serve sushi, and the output remains above average, with an intriguing list that sometimes includes butterfish, cockle, and smelt egg. Even more important—the comfortable subterranean rooms have empty seats when inferior joints in this sushi-wise neighborhood are mobbed. Favorite dish: a vinegary octopus salad found on the special menu card. [kid friendly]

Mottsu

285 Mott St near Houston St, Manhattan,
212-343-8017, subway: B, D, F, Q to Broadway-Lafayette

This punningly named Japanese restaurant ("mutsu" means bluefish) excels at sushi, as you can tell by the long arc of the sushi bar that dominates the minimalist space. The generous California roll might be the best in town, luxuriantly smothered in flying-fish roe. Other interesting short dishes included nuggets of tempura-fried filet mignon, miso soup dotted with cockles, and king crab legs propped among seaweed, daikon, and cucumbers in a light vinaigrette. The short list of entrees contains unexpected selections (chicken stuffed with mozzarella), but you can easily make a meal of non-entrees.

Otafuku

236 E 9th St near 2nd Ave, Manhattan, 212-353-8503, subway: 6 to Astor Pl

This rustic stall delivers what other East Village Japanese eateries have long disdained: okonomiyaki—eggy pancakes that originated in Osaka and which constitute a major form of fast food throughout the country. The name means "cook what you like," and what you like in this case is shrimp, unsmoked bacon, or squid embedded in a vegetable matrix of cabbage, green onions, corn, pickled ginger, and egg. The nicely browned product is glopped with barbecue sauce, powdered seaweed, smoky bonito shavings, and, unless you stop them in time, mayonnaise. Also offered: fried octopus balls called takoyaki. [¢]

Shima

188 Second Ave at 12th St, Manhattan,
212-260-6303, subway: L to 1st Ave

A special oyster appetizer knocked me out—three delicate kumamoto oysters doused with light and citrusy ponzu sauce and strewn with pickled daikon. This Japanese restaurant is the upscale successor to a favorite NYU spot that recently closed, and cousin to First Avenue stalwart Sapporo East. For chilly nights try oden, a steaming broth of tofu, fish cake, boiled egg, radish, and a translucent loaf of devil's tongue starch. Stir in the hot mustard! For greatest contrast pick zaru soba, buckwheat noodles served on a bed of ice cubes and crowned with crisp shredded nori.

Taka

61 Grove St near 7th Ave South, Manhattan,
212-242-3699, subway: 1, 9 to Christopher St

The restaurant is named for its female proprietor who, in addition to being the sushi chef, also makes all the nifty crockery used by the restaurant. (When was the last time you saw a female sushi chef?) She has never handed me a bad piece of tuna, which is more than I can say for many other itamae.

Tomoe Sushi

172 Thompson St near Houston St, Manhattan,
212-777-9346, subway: N, R to Prince St

Another downtown fave, Tomoe Sushi is mobbed every evening. The reason? The sushi list is longer than other downtown spots, the clientele hip, and the fish obsessively fresh. The difficult choice often runs to more than 50 varieties, and includes Stimson clam, cockle, abalone, sea eel, fatty tuna, and amaebi—not the notorious plague of the third world tourist, but tiny shrimp with a firm texture that pop in the mouth and leave a sugary aftertaste.

Yakiniku West

218 E 9th St near 3rd Ave, Manhattan,
212-979-9238, subway: 6 to Astor Pl

Even though Yakiniku West bills itself as a "Japanese rural steak house," the specialty of the house is not native to Japan, but an adaptation of do-it-yourself barbecue techniques learned from the Korean immigrants who opened bulgogi shops in Tokyo. In the middle of each table is a domed grate encircled by a series of holes that draw the smoke away with ruthless efficiency—a distinct improvement over bulky overhead hoods in Korean joints that leave your clothes reeking of smoked fat. The menu, five square feet and copiously illustrated with color photos, allows you to plan your dinner like a general plotting a campaign. The best deals are several set meals that include soup, salad, rice, kimchee, two sauces for smearing and three for dipping, meat and veggies, tea, and ice cream. Cheapest is short ribs of beef ($14.25), cut from the bone in long strips and well-marbled with fat. All the meats are available a la carte, but the connoisseur's attention will stray to the variety meats, priced $3.50 to $6.50 for a modest portion: pig foot, tripe, intestine, liver, and, best of all, tongue, which has a novel spongy texture and seems goof-proof—it tastes good burned or raw.

Yoshi

201 East Houston St near Essex St, Manhattan, 212-539-0225, subway: F to 2nd Ave

Improbably located in the shadow of Katz's, this new Japanese restaurant offers spaciousness and cheapness as reasons for seeking it out. The $11 bento, always available, is one hell of a feed: thick planks of tuna, salmon, and yellowtail sashimi; shrimp and vegetable tempura; rice; fried chicken wings; huge serving of salmon teriyaki; and assorted steamed vegetables. Other portions are also on a grand scale, such as the "tofu steak" appetizer of four deep-fried pillows smothered in multi-mushroom sauce; it could well serve as an entree.

 JAPANESE SHOPPING MALL

To jaded New York palates, Japanese food is old hat. We've enjoyed innumerable orders of tempura, teriyaki, and sushi, and Japanese restaurants have become as familiar to us as Greek coffee shops were to our dining forebears. But if you want to taste some Nipponese food you probably haven't encountered before, hop over to Yaohan Plaza (595 River Rd, Edgewater, New Jersey, 201-941-9113), the all-Japanese mall. A shuttle bus leaves from Gate 51 at the Port Authority Bus Terminal, South Building, and costs $2 each way. Yaohan is right on the Hudson, on a ribbon of land below the wooded cliffs of Fairview. One building is long and low, with stores that sell Japanese products such as superhero action figures, golf clubs, karaoke CDs, and Hello Kitty stuff. There's also a larger, hangar-size structure, containing a supermarket and a food court, which has 11 establishments arranged on three sides of an airy seating area. Grab a table by the window and enjoy a spectacular view of Manhattan, with Riverside Church and Grant's Tomb as focal points.

Jewish

This section features Jewish-American eateries—some kosher, some not. Expect the food to be in an Eastern European vein. Due to the Jewish dietary laws, these eateries naturally sort themselves into two camps. Delis are more profuse in this day and age but, as recently as 10 years ago, the grand dairy restaurants, like the defunct Hammer's (where the movie *The Front* was filmed) and Dubrow's in the Garment Center, figured prominently in the city's dining landscape. Go to Diamond Dairy or Ratners (138 Delancey St, Manhattan, 212-677-5588) for a little of the old atmosphere. For Jewish Sephardic styles, consult the Middle Eastern, Central Asian, and Indian sections of this book.

JEWISH

B & H Dairy Restaurant

**127 2nd Ave near St Marks Pl, Manhattan,
212-505-8065, subway: 6 to Astor Pl**

B & H has been hanging around since when this
stretch of Second Avenue was known as the Yiddish
Broadway, adhering to the same dietary rules as
Diamond Dairy, below—which means fish is OK, but
there's no meat on the premises. This place stays in
business because the food is cheap and good, and
the dairy regimen is popular with neighborhood vegetarians and those who would just like to eat light
for a change. To that end, the soups are what is
most often ordered: mushroom barley, matzoh ball,
red borscht, cabbage, and (my fave) vegetable,
which features green beans, carrots, potatoes, and
cabbage in a light and flavorful broth. The best part
is always the buttered homemade challah (here called "holly bread") that comes on the side. I
always get a double order. Omelets, matzoh brei, noodle pudding, and fish round out the
menu. [¢]

Jewish specialties

borscht
hot or cold beet soup

challah
braided egg bread

cholent
bean stew

matzoh brei
eggs scrambled with broken matzoh

Nova
translucent smoked salmon

stuffed derma
onion sausage

Barney Greengrass

**541 Amsterdam Ave at 86th St, Manhattan,
212-724-4707, subway: 1, 9 to 86th St**

The name sounds like a cartoon character, but Barney Greengrass ("The Sturgeon King")
couldn't be more serious about fish. This Upper West Side landmark dispenses chub, lox,
Nova, kippers, sable, whitefish, pickled herring, sardines, and sturgeon, whose faintly smoky
and boneless white flesh is likely to be preferred by youngsters. Examine the showcase and
proceed into the dining room; curiously, it's wallpapered with scenes of New Orleans. Here you
can order thin slices of any fish, served with lettuce, olives, tomatoes, onions, pickles, and a
toasted bagel. Of several fish-and-eggs combos, my favorite is scrambled eggs with
caramelized onions and Nova.

Diamond Dairy Restaurant

**4 W 47th St near 5th Ave, Manhattan,
212-719-2694, subway: B, D, F, Q to 47-50th Sts/Rockefeller Ctr**

Dramatically poised on a balcony above the National Jewelers Exchange, this old-fashioned
Ashkenazi Jewish dairy restaurant features the usual dairy dishes, including blintzes, puddings, and rivers of sour cream. Baked fish is a particular specialty, but even better is cholent,

a garlicky bean stew. All hail the orange kugel floating on top! Enjoy watching the jewelry transactions down below as you dine, and go as soon as possible, before this New York institution goes the way of Dubrow's and Hammer's.

Galil

1252 Lexington Ave near 85th St, Manhattan,
212-439-6203, subway: 4, 5, 6 to 86th St

This glatt kosher restaurant, newly refurbished, has an intriguing Moroccan bent. The lamb tajine is particularly good, featuring a huge shank sweetened with prunes and raisins served on a bed of couscous in a painted ceramic tajine (the serving is enough for two), while Moroccan fish balls, a quintessential Sephardic dish, are bathed in a cumin-inflected tomato sauce and sided with good fries. The fish of choice is mushat, or St. Peter's fish—firm fleshed and nicely charred from the grill. Also dig the vegetable-stuffed pastries known as Moroccan cigars, and the excellent mint tea. [kosher]

Jay and Lloyd's

2718 Avenue U near E 27th St, Brooklyn,
718-891-5298, subway: D to Avenue U

Critics go crazy for Adelman's, a kosher deli on Kings Highway in Brooklyn. But I find their corned beef too fine-grained, their matzoh ball soup too Campbell's-tasting, and their pastrami only adequate. And the twerpy decor is for the birds. Much better on all counts, and only a few blocks seaward, is Jay & Lloyd's. The pastrami's great, thickly rimmed with spices, moist, and generously wadded in the sandwich. It's cut not too thin and not too thick, and delivered with no pretensions whatever. They also offer a kosher version of the Catskill sandwich fave RPG, usually made with anisey Chinese roast pork on garlic bread topped with duck sauce. Here, veal is substituted for pork. [kosher]

★ Katz's

205 E Houston St at Ludlow St, Manhattan,
212-254-2246, subway: F to 2nd Ave

Visit this century-old deli before they decide to raze it and build a high-rise condo. Tip the carvers $1 before you order and get a sandwich big enough for two—my usual choice is a combo of pastrami and corned beef on a club roll. If you know what's good for you, order it lean. The preferred beverage is Dr. Brown's Cel-ray, a celery tonic that's a Lower East Side favorite, but skip the limp and mealy fries.

Pastrami Queen

1269 Lexington Ave near 85th St, Manhattan,
212-828-0007, subway: 4, 5, 6 to 86th St

More thickly rubbed with spices and more aggressively salted and smoked, Pastrami Queen's product is deeply flavored and almost purple in color, and it's sliced thicker than at other delis. Also, the sandwich is human-sized, which means small by industry standards. The Queen was once situated in Forest Hills and called Pastrami King, until the removal of a courthouse to another neighborhood caused them to rethink location. The pastrami is actually better now. The bilevel room has too much buffed wood, and the matzoh ball soup is pallid—an afterthought at a joint where all the energy goes into the excellent pastrami. [kosher]

Second Avenue Deli

156 2nd Ave at 10th St, Manhattan,
212-677-0606, subway: 6 to Astor Pl

While the corned beef is superior at Katz's, pastrami is the thing to get at the Second Avenue Deli—leaner than usual, firm, smoky, and deep ruby in color. For those seeking a less rough-and-tumble venue, this kosher haven takes its theme from the Jewish theater district that used to flourish along this thoroughfare—that's Joey Adams sitting at the big table in the Molly Picon Room (or it was until he died just before the pub date of this book). The deli is also a good place to experience the arcana of Ashkenazi cooking, from stuffed derma, to kasha varnishkas, to creamy noodle pudding, achieved without cream, of course. [kosher]

Korean

Long gone are the days when every Korean restaurant in town had an identical menu, usually with no English translations. Ten years ago the patrons of these places were overwhelmingly Korean, and there was a particular thrill venturing into them. Though the welcome was never less than warm, it was disappointing to be served only the blandest and most unchallenging pan chan that could be dredged up. You'd look tearfully down into your bowl of white cabbage kimchee while the diners at the next table were enjoying spicy raw meat, pickled skate, and fiery kimchees.

Nowadays, these restaurants expect non-Koreans, and no longer make themselves look like private clubs. In addition, specialized Korean restaurants have appeared. Walk along 32nd and 35th Streets in Manhattan and marvel at all the new types, and the beckoning intent of their facades. In addition to new noodles joints, pastry shops, and dumpling houses, there's a place obsessed with soft bean curd (Cho Dang Gal, 55 W 35th St, 212-695-8222) and another that specializes in cooking with ginseng (Ahp Ku Jung, 10 W 32nd St, 212-594-4963). Even though Manhattan is in the vanguard of innovation, similar things have been happening in Flushing and Elmhurst. Typical prices at most Korean restaurants range from $8 to $22 per dish. You can often avoid these relatively expensive prices by taking advantage of lunch specials, usually in the $5 to $10 range, sometimes with two or three courses.

KOREAN

Broadway Noodle

**82-53 Broadway near Elmhurst Ave,
Queens, subway: G, R to Elmhurst Ave**

This modest noodle shop features Chinese dishes
with surprising twists that begin with the arrival of
serious cabbage kimchee and sweet yellow daikon
pickle—betraying the Korean bent of what's to
follow. We especially enjoyed "rice with vegetable
and pork with starch noodles," which, in case you
had any doubt, is a carbohydrate barrage of rice
tangled with mung-bean threads, and "noodles with
hot chop suey soup" which was served in a bowl like
a basketball cut in half, featuring squid and shrimp
with Italian spaghetti in an incendiary red broth. [¢]

Do Hwa

**55 Carmine St at Bedford St, Manhattan,
212-414-1224, subway: 1, 9 to Houston St**

This offspring of the East Village's Dok Suni, partly owned by Quentin Tarantino, pulls fewer
culinary punches in its presentation of Korean fare in a hipster setting. Go for the wonderful deji
kalbi, spareribs annealed with a thick sweet sauce, or any of the several pajun, savory pancakes loaded with chiles, scallions, and your choice of seafood or vegetables. While a pricey
pair of sea bass fillets left us cold, the beebimbop—a rice, beef, and vegetable assortment
topped with a runny egg and delivered in a sizzling crock—was one of the best in town (mix
vigorously before eating). Depending on where you live, it just might beat going to 32nd Street.

Haejo

**46-25 Kissena Blvd, near Cherry St, Queens,
718-461-4782, subway: 7 to Flushing/Main St**

Kissena Boulevard is the strip-mall capital of Korean Flushing, lined with clusters of barbers
and beauty shops, greengrocers and video stores, bars and restaurants—among them Haejo,
billed as "Korean-Chinese" on the green awning. Curiously, a grainy black-and-white TV hov-
ers up near the ceiling, featuring a burly man yanking thick doughy ropes and smashing them
against a counter with lethal force.

Though it offers nearly a hundred diverse dishes that spin Chinese food for Korean tastes, the
raison d'être for Haejo is homemade wheat noodles of the sort that were carried across the
Yellow Sea by Chinese refugees from Shandong Province in the '50s, and still made mainly by

---

Korean specialties

beebimbop
*many-ingredient
rice farrago*

bulgogi
beef barbecue

kimchee
spicy cabbage pickle

mandoo
meat-stuffed dumplings

naengmyum
North Korean noodles

pajun
giant gooey pancake

pan chan
small appetizing dishes

soju
sweet-potato liquour

Chinese expatriates. Several feet long and of squarish circumference, the noodles are never cut with a knife, but break off naturally when the guy's done whacking. They may seem ordinary at first, but your admiration increases with every bite. The single variety is hidden in the second "Soup" section, designated "noodles with brown sauce" ($5.50), "noodles with special brown sauce" ($6), "noodles with special brown Peking sauce" ($6.50). More Korean-tasting is "noodles with hot seafood soup" ($7.95), a broth of liquid fire. Note the address carefully—there is a seafood joint with same name nearby.

Ishihama

319 5th Ave near 32nd St, Manhattan,
212-696-9386, subway: B, D, F, N, Q, R to 34th St

This restaurant concentrates on sushi with a Korean perspective (even providing a dish of kimchee alongside each serving), but other Japanese standards like teriyaki and tempura are also available. The sushi is well-formed and fresh, and recommended items include hwe-dup bop—a salad of rice, raw fish, and greenery in a sweet chile sauce—and natto hand roll—an if-you-dare combo of scallions and mucoidal fermented soy beans. Best of all, a free side dish of raw sea squirt in hot sauce that landed on our table one evening. Wash it down with O.B. beer (the favorite of gynecologists everywhere) or a bottle of soju, a sweet potato liquor (now usually made from grain) that's like a weak vodka.

Mandoo

2 W 32nd St near 5th Ave, 212-279-3075, subway: 6 to 33rd St

This nifty Koreatown newcomer specializes in dumplings, made right in the window. The modernistic dining room is all angles and blond woods, and selections include baby mandoo, nearly a score of tiny dumplings with a pork-and-scallion filling; kimchee mandoo, stuffed with the sweltering cabbage condiment; and the euphonious haemool mool mandoo, filled with a combination of shrimp and sea cucumber and colored fluorescent orange due to the addition of carrot to the dough. Noodles, rice dishes, and desserts round out the menu, and the perfect conclusion to a meal is sujeonkwa, a cold sweet broth flavored with cinnamon, like Mexican horchata. [¢, kid friendly]

New York Kom Tang Soot Bull House

32 W. 32nd St near Broadway, Manhattan,
212-947-8482, subway: B, D, F, N, Q, R to 34th St

The newly refurbished and expanded favorite is outfitted with special tables with a metal-lined depression and an awesome hood overhead. Stoked with live charcoal, the actual grills are brought to the table as soon as you order. There are 19 items in the barbecue section of the menu, the most extensive selection on the block, including such arcana as tongue, kidney, tripe, and—for rock fans—beef heart. The portions aren't enormous by American carnivore standards, and the grill is so close to the diners that it cooks your face as surely as it cooks the meat. Maybe you should have ignored the hostess and stayed downstairs, where all non-barbecue parts of the menu are available, among them casseroles, fried fish, rice and noodle dishes, sushi, and soups, one of which is kom tang, the earthy beef-and-noodle soup for which the restaurant is named. My favorite choices, however, are the hotpots and porridges. The latter are hearty rice gruels, bland by Korean standards, such as abalone porridge, which has tiny chunks of carrot and green onion, with the abalone providing more flavor than substance. The porridge comes with a raw egg yolk in the middle topped with a haystack of dry seaweed, both of which should be vigorously mixed in before eating.

Olympic Garden

79-06 Broadway, Queens, 718-335-4646,
subway: E, F, G, R to Jackson Heights/Roosevelt Ave; 7 to 74th St-Boadway

Occupying a commanding position opposite Elmhurst Hospital, Olympic Garden is a stone and glass box with a Vegas flair. But despite the name, it's not a Greek diner anymore; for a decade this diner has served Korean food. The spread of pan chan, the small dishes that arrive free of charge at the start of the meal, rivals any I've seen. On one visit we received a table-bowing nine plates, including sweet pickled daikon shreds, delicious asparagus tips smeared with bean paste, tart sticks of wobbly fish cake, a fiery salad of broad-leaf parsley, and, best of all, a kimchee of Chinese cabbage dotted with raw oysters.

With meat-bearing entrees in the $15 range, Olympic Garden is priced on par with other Korean restaurants in the city, but the servings are significantly larger. Bulgogi was enough to share among four, although instead of arriving neatly pinwheeled on a platter, it came in a big wad. The beef is too lean, anyway, so order the jaeook gooey, ribbons of pork tenderloin that really are gooey with a dark marinade. But don't get trapped in the barbecue section, 'cause you'll miss hae mool pajun ($12.95), one of the outsize pancakes for which Koreans are famous. And who could avoid ordering something called angler sea toad casserole? Not me. It's one of those red stews brought to the table boiling, rife with bean curd, cayenne, and green onions. Indeed, the pieces of spiny fish were so ugly we wondered what the face looked like.

Shin Jung

136-33 37th Ave, Queens,
718-460-5026, subway: 7 to Flushing/Main St

If you're a fan of chandeliers, here's your place—the double dining room has dozens. The food is straightforward Korean, entirely lacking Japanese flourishes, and deploying superior raw materials. The meat in the unmarinated beef rib—our favorite barbecue—was spectacularly well-marbled, ceremoniously snipped from the bone by our waitress as we watched. Also recommended are the mung bean pancakes, three to an order and crammed with vegetables and beef, and the whole grilled mackerel. The beverage of choice is soju, quaffed from tiny glasses between bites.

Terminal House

306 W 40th St near 8th Ave, Manhattan,
212-695-4080, subway: A, C, E to 42nd St

The sinister name makes it a great place for a personal Last Supper, as does its location on Manhattan's seediest block—40th Street just west of Eighth Avenue, where strange characters hang out gibbering under the Port Authority's south rampart. Don't be deterred! Terminal House is one of the best cheap Korean restaurants in the city.

The bill of fare has no English whatsoever. Once again, don't be daunted: the choices are spelled out in Roman characters and include several familiar standards like beebimbop, a rice dish decorated with assorted vegetables and ribbons of pork and egg, and kimchee jige, one of those Korean casseroles crammed with ingredients and brought to the table boiling. Subsequent visits identified further standouts: soon du bu, a flocculence of soft bean curd veined with red and freighted with oysters and unusual mollusks, pointy feet protruding. Unable to make an identification, we waved one at the waitress and she obligingly drew a picture of a sea-snail shell. For chile freaks, there's yook ge jang, long tendrils of beef mobbed with egg, luridly floating in the red fumet like a severed head—totally X-Files, but also irresistibly delicious. [¢]

Malaysian, Indonesian, and Philippine

Though the Buddhist Chinese constitute 35 percent of the population in many parts of Malaysia, the Islamic majority has had all too much success convincing them to get lost—which probably explains the marked increase of Malaysian restaurants in town. The food of this group is a grab bag of Chinese, Indian, Portuguese, aboriginal Malay, Thai, and other Southeast Asian influences, all of which come together in the cooking of the Straits Chinese, a subgroup resident in the Malay Peninsula for over two centuries.

A few years back, Malaysian eateries began to appear on the frontiers of Chinatown, distinguished by prices considerably lower than those of the Cantonese and Vietnamese places that preceded them. For a mind-boggling $2.95, you could get a large plate of rice and choice of three entrees from among the jumble of dishes displayed in the window. Now more ambitious Malaysian restaurants have begun to appear in Chinatown, with many becoming multibranch empires and locations in Soho, the Upper West Side, the Village, and elsewhere.

Though New York boasts myriad Malaysian restaurants, Indonesians you can count on the fingers of one hand. Fifteen years ago Atlantic Avenue's adorable Bali Rice Shop introduced the satay to Brooklyn, then promptly croaked. That loss was finally redressed in 1993 when Java Rijsttafel surfaced in Park Slope, although, as the name implies, this pint-sized cafe specializes in the scarf of Java rather than Bali. Neither had much effect on the city's Indonesian restaurant deficiency, since these islands are only two in an archipelago of 8,000, many with unique cuisines.

As for Filipino restaurants—there are fewer than there were fifteen years ago, when nurses and doctors were recruited en masse from the Philippines to staff area hospitals, especially Beth Israel. This migration gave rise to the concentration of eateries and groceries you can still find today around the corner of 1st Avenue and 14th Street. Sadly, the touro-touro joints that once graced 9th Avenue behind the Port Authority are now vanished, but you can still see Philippine institutions in Woodside, Queens, along Roosevelt Avenue.

MALAYSIAN

Malaysian Rasa Sayang

**75-19 Broadway, Queens,
718-424-9054, subway: E, F, G, R to
Jackson Heights/Roosevelt Ave; 7 to 74th
St-Broadway**

Only steps away from the Jackson Heights stop, this
Elmhurst Malaysian eatery excels at popiah, refresh-
ing summer rolls stuffed with tempeh, crisp fried
onions, and greenery, then topped with a pair of
sauces; and rendang, cubes of beef shank slow-
cooked in a coconut gravy laden with sweet spices
and garlic. Our loudest cheers, though, were
reserved for a special of tilefish braised in a ginger
broth—a dish elicited by asking the waitress what
kind of fish was on hand, and then letting the chef
prepare it in the most appropriate way.

*Malaysian
specialties*

ABC
*ice dessert with
wiggly jellies*

achat
*sweet pickled
vegetable salad*

beef rendang
dark coconut-milk stew

pasembur
*sprout, jicama, and
shrimp-fritter salad*

popiah
vegetable burritos

roti canai
*chicken curry with
floppy pancake*

Nyonya

**194 Grand St near Mott St, Manhattan,
212-334-3669, subway: 6, J, M, N, R, Z to Canal St
5323 8th Ave near 54th St, Brooklyn,
718-633-0808, subway: N to 8th Ave**

Ignore the pricey suggestions of the waitstaff and go for some of New York's best home-style
Malaysian cooking at bargain prices. Start with the wonderful pasembur, a sharable salad of
sprouts, jicama, cucumber, and tofu surmounted by herb-flecked fritters smothered in chile
sauce, then proceed to "squids wrapped in silver foil"—rings of steamed cephalopod made
triply tart with lemon, lemongrass, and lime leaves. Other faves include achat, a plate of sweet
pickled vegetables dulled with sesame seeds, and yam rice, a $1 side of rice, yam, pork, and
assorted vegetables that could almost be a main course.

Proton Saga

**11 Allen St near Canal St, Manhattan,
212-625-1163, subway: F to East Broadway**

This attractive eatery—pridefully named after the first car to be manufactured in Malaysia and
not some grade B science fiction movie—presents an Islamic perspective on Southeast Asian
food. The achat is sublime, a tart and sweet salad of shredded vegetables topped with sesame
seeds and crunchy peanuts. The no-pork menu focuses on seafood, of which sting ray is
something of a house specialty. Have it Malaysian style, smothered in chile sauce, the tender

flesh pulling easily away from the radiating spines. Also don't miss peanut cake, an Indian-style paratha filled with crushed goobers.

Satay Hut

**135-25A 40th Road near Main St, Queens,
718-321-0842, subway: 7 to Flushing/Main St**

Provocatively located just down the street from a public housing project called the Bland Houses, the food at Flushing's Satay Hut is anything but insipid. The roti canai, a gossamer pancake bunched and presented with a small bowl of chicken curry, is assertively hot, and so is the even better coconut variation sometimes available. Out-hotting these is beef rendang rice —fiery gobs of meat with the spicing twisted in a decidedly Indian direction. Paradoxically, the "chili chicken (Indian style)" didn't taste very Indian at all, although these breaded and mildly spiced morsels beat the pants off Chicken McNuggets. [¢]

★ Sentosa

**3 Allen St near Division St, Manhattan,
212-925-8018, subway: F to East Broadway**

Killer selections at Sentosa, a new restaurant offering a Singaporean perspective on Malaysian cooking, include lobak ($6.95), an omnibus dish with something for everyone, including fried bean curd served with a pair of sauces, meat-stuffed tofu skin, shrimp pancakes, pickled vegetables, and a scary black egg that transmits light like obsidian. At intervals a chef appears at a marble-topped table to roll dough for rotis. He flings them in the air and spins them like pizzas to achieve the thinness so prized in roti canai ($1.95), a small bowl of chicken curry accompanied by the bread wadded like a silk handkerchief for dipping. The same rotis are available stuffed with egg and finely chopped vegetables (roti telur) or crushed peanuts ("peanut pancakes," on the dessert menu).

The recent appearance of fresh Southeast Asian herbs in Chinatown markets has been a boon to Sentosa. The pandan, or screw pine, has long tapered green leaves that were formerly available only in dried or frozen form. Fresh, they sing with a flavor somewhere between vanilla and gym shorts. Encounter them in pandam ayam ($7.95), a heap of fried chicken wings wrapped with shredded-leaf bows like birthday packages. Paired with clove, this subtle herb also infuses coconut rice (75 cents). Fresh Indian kari (the ancestor of the English word "curry") leaves are exploited in kari ikan kepala ($14.95), a tour-de-force of gluey fish heads in a coconut-milk broth rife with okra, onions, and sweet peppers. The cheeks are the best part. [kid friendly]

★ Taste Good

82-18 45th Ave, Queens, 718-429-9234, subway: G, R to Elmhurst Ave

Taste Good boasts an ambitious menu of Chinese-Malaysian fare behind a sign humbly offering Chinese noodles. Nasi lemak ($4) is a perfect illustration of the cuisine's complex piquancy, a revered luncheon dish that sets coconut rice amid small dishes selected for their contrasting tastes and textures, in this case a heap of roasted peanuts, a chicken-and-potato curry in soothing coconut gravy, a dice of cucumbers, and a dense sambal of pickled anchovies in a tart, tamarind-driven dressing. Appetizer is a misnomer at Taste Good, where it designates a series of entree-sized selections more properly referred to by their Sino-Malaysian name chia thit tho, meaning "to be eaten for pleasure."

With low prices and huge portions, Taste Good provides little opportunity to blow much money (a table of six big eaters recently gorged themselves for under $50). Even the more expensive House Specials compensate with gargantuan portions. Dried curry asam prawn ($15.95), for example, dumps nine behemoths into a sweet chile sauce. If you're not Malaysian, the waitress will offer to remove the heads and shells; don't let her, since the orange fat (and most of the flavor) is deposited in the head, and the crunch of the exoskeleton nicely offsets these too-fleshy beauties. Dried curry fish meat ($9.95), is another estimable variation on the very wet "dried curry" formulation, this one featuring slices of tilapia in a tureen of thick sauce enlivened, Thai-style, with variegated bell peppers. [¢]

INDONESIAN

Bali Nusa Indah

651 9th Ave near 45th St, Manhattan, 212-974-1875, subway: A, C, E to 42nd St

In spite of its name, and the gamelan music trilling over the P.A., Bali Nusa Indah is entirely Javanese in its outlook. The sole Balinese dish is Bali nusa fish ($13.50), a fried snapper strewn with red bell peppers, tomatoes, and onions—a bit of a bore compared with the rest of the menu, which tends to be righteously spicy. Not overwhelmed by peanuts, the sauce that drenches the satays in sate ayam ($9) is vividly fishy and fiery. Also stunning are otak-otak ($3), fingers of fish mousse steamed in banana leaf; a superior gado-gado amplified with vinegary pickled vegetables, but curiously lacking boiled eggs; and nasi goreng ikan asan, a fried rice featuring morsels of salted fish.

Indonesian specialties

ayam opor
chicken in coconut sauce

embek-embek
Sumatran soup with dumplings

gado-gado
boiled salad with peanut sauce

ketjap
sweet-sour marinade

otak-otak
fish mousse in banana leaf

sate ayam
chicken brochettes with peanut sauce

Indonesia is the botanical home of clove, nutmeg, mace, black pepper, and cassia—spices over which Arab and European traders contended for centuries. Luxuriant combinations of these intensify the meat and poultry offerings at Bali Nusa Indah. Ayam opor ($9) is my favorite: chicken chunks, crisp skin adhering, dunked in a sienna-tinted sauce redolent of coconut and sweet spices.

Indonesian Mission to the United Nations

**325 E 38th St near 1st Ave, Manhattan,
212-972-8333, subway: 4, 5, 6, 7 to Grand Central**

If you pass the surveillance camera's muster, you may proceed through a maze of construction debris to the tiny subterranean lunchroom. A set meal ($6) is provided each weekday from 1 till the food runs out about 1:30. On a recent afternoon it began with a soup subtly flavored with fish sauce and black pepper freighted with nearly weightless shrimp crackers. The main course was a sculpted mound of rice mediating a gingery dish of chicken and broccoli and an angry sambal of shrimp, potatoes, and red chiles, both delicious. But most amazing was the dessert—a two-shades-of-pink Jello gateau smeared with sweetened condensed milk and fruit cocktail. Diplomacy dictates that you dive in and eat the whole thing. [¢]

Java Indonesian Rijsttafel

**455 7th Ave near 14th St, Brooklyn,
718-832-4583, subway: F to 7th Ave**

Native to Java is a sweet-and-sour marinade of palm molasses, soy sauce, and vinegar or tamarind called ketjap, the forerunner of the red stuff that comes in disposable packets. Java Rijsttafel's ayam panggang ($9.50) wraps this inky cloak, fragrant with garlic and ginger, around a chicken breast, then paints it with lemongrass oil for a patent-leather shine. A couple of other Javanese specialties are bakwan ($3), splendid corn fritters dotted with shrimp, and pastel ($2.95), turnovers stuffed with fine rice noodles whose pastry reflects four centuries of Dutch colonialism. Unfortunately, much of the food at this Park Slope hideout tends to be bland; the peanut dressing on gado-gado—a salad of boiled eggs, tempeh, and vegetables—whispers when it should shout. The waitress confided that chiles and anchovy paste had been removed at the request of the regulars. Complain.

★ Warteg Fortuna

**51-24 Roosevelt Ave, Queens,
718-898-2554, subway: 7 to 52nd St**

Don't be fooled by the giant red awning that still flogs Colombian rotisserie chicken, Warteg Fortuna is the city's only working-class Indonesian cafe. Two parallel counters provide cramped seating for six diners. The kitchen is twice the size of the dining room, and it's an open kitchen, too, so you can't help wishing you were eating there instead of the dining room. No satays here, but a prix fixe menu ($3.75) that provides a complete meal. You may choose from a list of entrees that includes fish, chicken, beef, and lamb, accompanied by a plenitude of rice, and heaps of matchsticked green beans mixed with onions, and fried potatoes cubes with a vinegary glaze. Apart from these, the only other offerings include a very unusual soup called embek-embek ($5): elongated taro dumplings stuffed with egg yellow and cross section in a thin, hot, and sweet brown broth also heaped with cuke cubes and rice noodles. It had a spicy kick to it, so that the cook warned us with knit brows before handing the bowl over. There was also an alarmingly green angel food cake, a milky pink beverage that might have been Pepto Bismol, and a fried potato concoction that the Indonesians dining around us struggled to find an English word for. [¢]

PHILIPPINE

Elvie's

214 1st Ave near 12th St, Manhattan, 212-473-7785, subway: L to 1st Ave

This Philippine eatery belongs to a class known as "touro-touro," which means "point-point" in Tagalog. Everything for sale is displayed at the counter, and you make your selection by pointing. There are always at least ten main dishes and a host of snacks, like glutinous rice cakes and brochettes of chicken, pork, and anise-flavored sausage. Main dishes include oxtail with exotic vegetables in a creamy peanut sauce and a wonderful sweet-and-sour pork, made with hunks of crusty, Spanish-style roast pork in a sauce piquant with black peppercorns and bay leaf. The small dining room is decorated with colorful photos of the home country. [¢, kid friendly]

Philippine specialties

tosino
sweet pickled pork

ginataang sitaw
pumpkin stew

laing
pork and taro-leaf stew

balut
gestated egg

Manila Garden

325 E 14th Street near 2nd Ave, Manhattan, 212-777-6314, subway: L to 1st Ave

With skin like a lime, flesh like a tangerine, and fluorescent green pips, calamansi may be the world's smallest citrus fruit. The largest specimens measure an inch in diameter, yet such is their amazing tartness that four are enough to make calamansi ade ($2.75). It's the perfect beginning to a meal at Manila Garden, a largely overlooked East Village (well, almost) Philippine restaurant. Every Tuesday night an all-you-can-eat buffet features eight main dishes, rice, appetizers, soup, and dessert for under $15. On a recent foray, we sampled tosino, strips of pork cured in sugar, saltpeter, and cherry wine, then stewed in the pickle. Further down the row of gleaming receptacles we found paksiw na lechon, a perfectly roasted suckling pig carved so that a crisp swatch of skin adhered to each piece, with an odd dipping sauce of liver puree. Far less simple was ginataang sitaw, a stew of green yard beans and pumpkin thickened with coconut milk. Though tidbits of shrimp and pork meandered in the orange quagmire, the richness of the dish was entirely vegetable. Philippine food is unique in Southeast Asia, partly resulting from four centuries of Spanish rule. That influence is seen in bistek, a tangy entree of thinly sliced steak marinated in lemon and soy sauce, then fried with onions. Other Spanish-influenced selections include flan, chicharrón, and gambas—an adaptation of the familiar Iberian standard of shrimp fried in olive oil and garlic. Best of all, however, was laing ($9.50), an olive-drab slurry of fresh taro leaves cooked with coconut milk, fermented shrimp paste, pork tidbits, and hot chiles. Suggesting the humid taste of the jungle, it recalled the culinary contribution of the aboriginal Malay tribes—the food of the Philippines before the Spaniards invaded.

BALUT

Every region has food oddities idolized by residents and treated contemptuously by everyone else. Examples are Japanese fermented adzuki beans served at breakfast, which adhere to each other with gooey tendrils and taste like puke; Kansas City's fried brain sandwich; Vietnamese toasted crickets; and roast insect larvae enjoyed in Nigeria. My most recent encounter with a dish of this calibre is balut, boiled eggs sold in every Philippine grocery in town. At the New Manila Food Mart (351 E 14th St, 212-420-8182), the duck version ($1.50) sits in a lidded wicker basket with a gingham liner that Rebecca of Sunnybrook farm might have carried down the garden path. The more pedestrian chicken version (75 cents) is colored violet and sits in the refrigerator case. Peel the egg and take a bite, and you're in for a big surprise. The white is tinged yellow, and has an almost cheesy quality, with a slight tang of fermentation. The flesh is crazed with red blood vessels. Dig deeper and find a tiny, curled-up fetus.

Balut is the Tagalog term for a fertilized egg permitted to gestate for 15 days before being boiled. According to the counterman, the eggs should be reheated before serving. Duck eggs are most prized because of their size. A poll of Filipino friends revealed a diversity of opinion as to how the eggs should be eaten. One said they were good only immediately after boiling, still slightly runny. She also said that you throw the fetus away. Another claimed that, according to her mother, the slightly crunchy baby chick was the best part.

Mexican

Sunset Park, East Williamsburg, Sunnyside, Jackson Heights, and Corona have achieved prominence as Mexican neighborhoods over the last decade. But these have recently been aced out by East Harlem, where many of the traditional Puerto Rican businesses were taken over, first by Dominicans, and now by Mexicans. Neighborhood anchor is Casa El Rodeo, a store specializing in cowboy boots, hats, and saddles, as if East 125th Street were ranch country. The best Mexican in the region is right across the street—La Hacienda—although you'll find a half-dozen lesser eateries within a few blocks. Usually, I go for the tacos from the vendor just down the block, where you can select pig parts from a simmering display on a round guttered and sputtering contraption, just like they do in Mexico.

Nowadays, you're never far from a Mexican meal, and don't forget those churros they sell down in the subway, or the unbelieveable line of taco trucks on Roosevelt Avenue. There's one for every block from 72nd St all the way to Flushing Meadows Park.

MEXICAN

Downtown Bakery

**47 1st Ave near 3rd St, Manhattan,
212-473-6643, subway: F to 2nd Ave**

Over a clock featuring a color vignette of the Last
Supper with the clock hands poking out of Jesus'
midsection, the Day-Glo menu board lists Mexican
specialties in one column and gringo sandwiches in
the other. The Mexican selections at this former
Italian bakery are all antojitos ("little things you
crave"), including tamales, tacos, chimichangas,
enchiladas, and quesadillas. The counter lady
steered me away from the green sauce and toward
the mole poblano to go over my chicken enchiladas.
Two of these were doused with the pleasantly spicy
and sweetish mole, sprinkled with queso fresco, and
given a finishing zap in the microwave so that the
enchiladas were warmed but not mushed. A small,
undressed salad is added to the container post-zap.
At $3.50, this could be one of the best Mexican food
deals in town. Other promising selections: avocado
salad ($3.25) and pozole ($5.75), served with pork
tacos and only available on weekends. [¢]

Mexican specialties

chile relleno
*fresh chile stuffed
with cheese*

churros
Mexican donuts

horchata
*rice-and-cinnamon
beverage*

mixiotes
*chile-rubbed chicken
steamed in beer*

mole pipian
pumpkin-seed sauce

mole poblano
*complex sauce of
chiles and chocolate*

pozole
weekend hominy stew

★ Los Dos Rancheros Mexicanos

**507 9th Ave at 38th St, Manhattan,
212-868-7780, subway: A, C, E to 42nd St**

The food here is as close to Pueblan home cooking as you're likely to find in Manhattan.
Entrees come with soupy red beans instead of refried. Not only are the excellent cheese enchiladas not baked, they're not even stuffed—first bathed in fresh tomatillo sauce, then simply
folded over and dotted with queso seco and crema. I've dragged lots of friends to this place,
and everything we've tasted has been good. The chiles rellenos come bulging with cheese and
bathed in orange sauce; the mole poblano is more tart and dark-colored than usual; but best
is the mole pipian, a lumpy puree of pumpkin seeds tasting of pork, colored an unearthly
shade of green. It's probably out of a can, but it's still splendid. They have the usual weekend
specials of pozole and barbacoa, the former so thick with corn and pork there's little room for
broth, a tostada accompanying it piled high with beans, cheese, lettuce, and tomato. Keep
your eye on the grill in the front window for specials like grilled cactus paddles. [¢]

La Espiga II

32-44 31st St, Queens, 718-777-1993, subway: N to Broadway

Printed on the menu of this nifty Mexican bakery is the slogan: "No solo vendemos pan," which they translate as "We ain't just bread." Astoria's La Espiga II also sells Mexican groceries and an extensive menu of snacks: tacos, tamales, and tortas, Mexican-style sandwiches made with a crusty roll called a bolillo. These sandwiches are available in ten varieties, including queso de puerco (head cheese), chorizo, carnitas (fried pork bits), and queso amarillo (American cheese), all dressed with mayonnaise, pickled jalapeños, and pieces of avocado, then pressed under a weight on the griddle until warmed through. The spicy tamales are made with chicken and laced with moist veins of mole verde, a green sauce made with tomatillos, cilantro, and fresh green chiles. The weekend special, barbacoa ($6.50 a pound), is goat steamed in a banana leaf with chiles and salt. It's stringy and delicious, and half that quantity is enough for two. [¢]

La Hacienda

219 East 116th St near 3rd Ave, Manhattan,
212-987-1617, subway: 6 to 116th St

While most East Harlem Mexican eateries unambitiously offer tortas, tacos, and enchiladas, this joint decorated like a ranch house has a menu that runs to nearly 100 items, including comic English translations such as "spicy meat of the mole" and the appetizing-sounding "fat of chunk." There's a rotating gyro of pork al pastor, and a help-yourself condiment bar that includes pickled jalapeños and carrots, dried red chiles, and four sauces—two red, one green, and a thin guacamole for dribbling on tacos. Named after the sandal made from a rubber tire, huaraches are footprint flatcakes of masa with a rubbery texture something like a Colombian arepa. The stripped-down version ($2.50) of this Pueblan specialty is spread with green tomatillo sauce and then heaped with shredded lettuce, onions, crumbly cheese, and crema, a runny Mexican sour cream. For an extra dollar, savory strips of beef are thrown on top.

Gabriela's

685 Amsterdam Ave at 93rd St, Manhattan,
212-961-0574, subway: 1, 2, 3, 9 to 96th St

The food at this upscale Mexican diner is plain and honest, and the vast menu encompasses regional dishes. Still, about 80 percent of the menu is the typical cuisine of Mexico that you could find almost anywhere. Quesadillas are served three to an order, and consist simply of tortillas folded once over plain queso fresco. What makes them amazing is the tortillas, made right on the premises with a masa more finely textured than most.

The specialty of the house, chile-rubbed rotisserie chicken ($6.95 for half), is perfectly done. Three regional sauces can be ordered to go with the bird. My advice: shock the waitress and order all three—mancha manteles from Sinaloa, pureed bananas and chiles with a surreal orange color; Oaxacan mole negro, a smooth dark sauce with an underlying taste of raisins and a delayed incendiary kick; and a mole pipian attributed to the state of Jalisco. Dig the cured beef tongue Veracruz simmered with peppers, potatoes, olives, carrots, and tomatoes ($12.50).

Los Mariachis

805 Coney Island Ave near Dorchester Rd, Brooklyn,
718-826-3388, subway: D, Q to Cortelyou Rd

Premiering several years ago on a bleak stretch of Coney Island Avenue dominated by auto repair shops, Los Mariachis has blimped from a single storefront to an entertainment complex featuring a wedding hall and Tijuana-style curio shop. The signature dish, chicken mole poblano ($10.95), is a good introduction to the earthy, sauce-driven cuisine of Puebla. This mole is said to have been invented by a 17th-century nun, who, when faced with simultaneous visits from a governor and an archbishop, began throwing ingredients wildly into a pot. Dotted with sesame seeds and midnight brown, Los Mariachis' rendition is less chocolatey than most, featuring fruity highlights and several types of dried chiles. For chile enthusiasts, an even better choice is mixiotes ($9.50), a transcendent dish of skinless chicken pieces rubbed with pulverized ancho chiles, wrapped in parchment, and long-steamed in beer. Guisado de calabasas features chunks of pork and slices of zucchini slowly stewed in pureed calabash squash. Made with pumpkin seeds, the olive-drab pipian con pollo ($13.95) may be less than eye-appealing, but the delightful nutty taste and tomatillo tartness send the bland chicken into orbit. Friday evenings there's a strolling mariachi band. [kid friendly]

El Maguey y La Tuna

533 Grand St near Union Ave, Brooklyn,
718-965-3333, subway: L, G to Lorimer St/Metropolitan Ave

At the front of the restaurant is a grill where seven varieties of tacos—fresh corn tortillas wrapped around large quantities of coarsely chopped beefsteak, lamb, tongue, chorizo, or pork—are expertly turned out at $1.75 apiece. Taquitos al guacamole are even better, two

---

 WHAT IS YOUR TACO?

al pastor
marinated rotisserie pork

barbacoa
braised goat or lamb

cabeza
anything from the head, including brains, cheeks, ears, etc.

carne asada
grilled beef

carnitas
deep fried pork tidbits

cecina
salt-cured and air-dried beef

chorizo
skinless sausage

lengua
tongue

pollo
chicken

corn tortillas folded tightly around shredded chicken, deep-fried, and topped with guacamole, chopped iceberg lettuce, and plenty of grated queso blanco. Camarones ajillo are large shrimp sauteed Iberian style with margarine and tons of garlic. At $4.25, how do they do it? Entrees are generally $5 to $7, with none priced over $8. The arroz con pollo Mejicana—two chicken drumsticks and a thigh hidden by a mountain of orange rice with corn kernels and carrot chunks—is enormous but a bit bland. Mole ranchero is better: the same chicken parts covered in savory gravy spiked with hot chiles and chocolate, a stripped-down version of mole poblano. Chiles rellenos are some of the best in town. Warning—call first, restaurant has been open intermittently during the last year.

★ Matamoros Puebla Taqueria

193 Bedford Ave near N 7th St, Brooklyn, 718-782-5044, subway: L to Bedford Ave

Thread your way past corn husks, dried chiles, stacks of tortillas, and bales of fresh oregano at this Mexican grocery to find a darling miniature lunch counter serving antojitos, south-of-the-border snack fare. Taco choices comprise not only steak, chicken, and sausage, but also down-home treats like beef feet, tongue, and pork head—morsels of soft meat in an unguent gravy flecked with herbs. Other treats include overstuffed sandwiches dressed with jalapeños, and sopes, masa boats swamped with chicken, onions, and crema. Not as comfortable as nearby Vera Cruz, but the food's much better, and cheaper, too. [¢]

Mexico Lindo

459 2nd Ave near 35th St, Manhattan, 212-679-3665, subway: 6 to 23rd St

Lined with autographed photos of Latino celebrities whose names your parents would recognize, this old standby serves versions of Mexican food from the days before the cuisine was gourmetized and reduced to regions. Not a bad thing, considering the care they put into these ancient Tex-Mex renditions. Stick with the combos, which permute the raw materials of taco, enchilada, chile relleno, and tamale into the maximum number of pairings, but begin with the excellent garlic soup—good chicken broth, Chinese-style egg drops, and searing quantities of garlic. All it needs is a shake of salt.

Mi Cocina

57 Jane St at Hudson St, Manhattan, 212-627-8273, subway: A, C, E to 14th St

The skirt steak in the style of the ancient city of Querétaro is sublime—charcoal grilled, cilantro strewn, and profusely sided with a tamale, refried beans, guacamole, a limey relish of garlic and chile strips, and, of course, a warm tortilla stack. Just try to finish it. For vegetarians, there's a fine cazuela of zucchini, corn, onions, poblanos, tomatoes, and crema that's positively pre-Colombian. This haute Mexican boasts an earth-toned room accented with colorful tiles, and the drink of choice is Negra Modelo, the darkest Mexican beer. [$]

Mister Taco

2255 White Plains Rd near Pelham Pkwy, Bronx,
718-882-3821, subway: 2, 5 to Pelham Pkwy

Don't let the gringo name chase you away. A blessing to food-challenged Bronxdale, this new taqueria has some of the juiciest, overflowingest tacos in the city. Make sure you get the double-tortilla soft ones (instead of the hardshell variety) and the waitress will respect you. The cow tongue in the lengua taco is stewed to perfection, liberally dusted with crumbly cheese and cilantro; the barbaco—braised and pulled goat—taco is even better, with an additional dab of crema. The red chile sauce is hot as hell, while tomatillo sauce is soothingly cool. Colorful hand-painted murals enliven the room, and who could resist the panoramic view of White Plains Road? [¢]

El Rincon Mixteco

703 5th Ave near 24th St, Brooklyn, 718-369-0919, subway: N, R to 23rd St

At the far end of the dining room a gleaming kitchen can be seen through a small window. To the left a door leads to a sunny back yard, where I could see a gaggle of men constructing a small structure out of scrap wood. This small cafe near Greenwood Cemetery made me feel like I was in Mexico. Tacos ($2) are made with two tortillas and come neatly wrapped in white paper. The selection includes carnitas, cecina, lengua, pollo, al pastor, and barbacoa. The tortillas are thinly spread with guacamole, then a generous amount of meat is piled on with cilantro and raw onions. I also ordered the pozole ($3.50), which came in a deep bowl and contained large pieces of pork and chicken, flecked with oregano and epazote. With a squeeze of lime, it was about the best pozole I'd ever tasted. An excellent accompaniment is horchata ($1), a limpid beverage made from rice and cinnamon that comes in a tall soda-fountain glass, much more refreshing than it sounds. [¢]

Los Paisas

898 Amsterdam Ave near 103rd St, Manhattan,
212-961-1263, subway: 1, 9 to 103rd St

This cluttered grocery/cafe in an area sometimes known as the Valley serves a burgeoning Mexican community. Dig the flimsy looking wooden loft that doubles the area of the cafe to accommodate four tables total. A steamtable next to the cash register has the usual sauces: pipian, poblano, verde, rojo. The chicken, goat, or whatever, is brought up from the kitchen in the rear and sauced on the spot. A chorizo torta that I tried was an amazing bargain at $3.50, the roll packed with sausage scrambled with eggs, onion, tomato, lettuce, and a surprising quantity of sliced avocado rather than premade guacamole. Los Paisas is also a good place to stock up on your Mexican groceries: spices, Brooklyn-made tortillas, candy, soda, and beer. [¢]

¡O¡ WHAT? OXACAN!

A pal from Los Angeles disdains Pueblan food, calling it some of Mexico's worst. Where the action is, according to him, is Oaxacan. Naturally, L.A. has a slew of eateries where you can get the region's legendary seven moles—and I've got to admit, they're pretty damn good, with lots of crazy flavors you'll never find in New York. Until recently, we had no choice but to cry into our mole poblano, but now there's another way, and I don't mean driving to Los Angeles. New Brunswick, NJ now harbors Restaurant Oaxaqueño #2 (260 Drift St, 732-545-6869), and even if there is some question as to whether the current proprietors are really from Oaxaca, there are some serviceable Oaxacan specialties on the three confusing menus. Chuletas en huajillo ($6.25) turned out to be a trio of gnarled and tasty pork chops that won't lie flat In a brilliant red sauce bursting with finely ground chiles, with an undertaste of lard and a pleasing saltiness. The sinister black mole one-ups mole poblano—smoother, darker, subtler, with a bitter edge that comes from multiple overroasted chiles. Get it on lamb barbacoa or chicken. We also ordered carnitas in yellow mole, but instead of pork tidbits we got big floppy pieces of skin in a bright orange liquid. Dotted with pieces of cactus, the sauce was incredibly subtle, with an undertaste of cumin. As a side we ordered the nopales, but instead of the canned variety, we got three big fresh cactus paddles, spines burned off and both sides nicely charred, served with a few green onions with bulbs attached. When we carefully examined the menus at home, we discovered a dish that we had neglected—guisado de cabez de chivo en amarillo ($6.50), goat head soup. Damn! Not to mention tacos de chapulin—crunchy grasshopper tacos. The next time we went, they were gone, but we selected tlayuda ($3.50), an outsize homemade corn tortilla baked to brittleness and topped with black beans, jagged pieces of cecina, greenery, and a roasted jalapeño— Oaxacan pizza.

Tacocina

714 9th Ave near 49th St, Manhattan, 212-541-6969, subway: C, E to 50th St

Tacocina has a slick, fast-food presentation, and too many portraits of Frida Kahlo. The college-age staff are mainly from Mexico City, and somewhat bewildered. The tongue taco ($2.50), though not as fully stuffed, was first rate, with the glistening julienne of meat appropriately gelatinous and chewy. Other no-nonsense tacos from a list of 15 include hongos con elote (mushrooms and sweet corn), chuleta (pork chop), and an untranslated "suadero." The best thing on the menu is the tortilla soup ($2.75), which comes with an extra couple of bags of tortilla chips for immersion in the red, red broth, laden with a perfect balance of garlic, chile, and cilantro.

Tacos Nuevo Mexico

491 5th Ave near 11th St, Brooklyn,
718-832-0050, subway: F to 4th Ave-9th St

Behind a window choked with glowing beer signs is a room engulfed in green neon, where Santa stands at attention next to a potted cactus. No place in town serves such extravagantly stuffed tacos, two corn tortillas wrapped around your choice of spicy pork tidbits, mellow green-sauced tongue, veal brains, chewy broiled cheese, salt-cured beef, or elemental ground meat. Steaming cups of Mexican chocolate laced with cinnamon and almonds wash it down, or select from an extensive list of Mexican beers and sodas (grapefruit's the best). Excellent huevos rancheros swimming in soupy refried beans are available all day. [¢]

El Vaquero

2210 3rd Ave near 121st St, Manhattan, 212-426-0518, subway: 6 to 116th St

"The Cowboy" subtly announces its presence with a cactus-and-ten-gallon-hat logo on the awning. Located on a strip of hulking discount stores, the spare interior features a pulsating jukebox, a few tables covered with colorful textiles, and a bar that traverses the back of the room. A scatter of men with droopy mustaches swill Corona and Modela midafternoon. The menu has an assortment of $6 platos, but the joint exists for its antojitos. From a choice of three types of tacos ($1.50), out of an advertised list of seven, I pick chivo. It features two fresh corn tortillas folded over shredded goat, onions, and cilantro, and while it's not over-stuffed, the meat is tender, moist, and pleasantly gamy. A single sauce is offered, a fiery homemade puree of tomatoes and chiles. I was surprised to find that they had Negro Modelo, my fave Mexican beer, so I quaffed. [¢]

Middle Eastern

The Ottoman legacy can be seen in the common dining heritage of these countries, most obviously in the small dishes known as meze, often served at lunch or as appetizers: hummus, falafel, tabbouleh, and babaganoush (the spelling of these varies wildly). These can be found in almost all of the Middle Eastern restaurants below and are consistently tasty and good for you, too. But if you've become familiar enough to be on the verge of boredom, search out those dishes that differentiate the cuisines of the Middle East rather than unite them, like the kibbeh pie found in Lebanese places, or the salta of the Yemenis.

In this region of political and religious tumult, I had to make some tough calls. Do the Jewish Yemenites, for example, have more in common with the Muslim Yemenis with whom they lived for millenia, or with the Israelis who have been their hosts for a mere half century? Whether to clump the Lebanese and Syrians together, or award them separate categories? Following are my rather unsatisfactory groupings.

LEBANESE and SYRIAN

Al Dewan

29-36 30th Ave, Queens,
718-545-1700, subway: N to 30th Ave

The walls of Al Dewan are tiled with acres of rich brown marble. The floors, tables, and arches are the same smoky metamorphic rock. Add somber baskets of hanging plants and elegant light fixtures, and you feel like you're sitting in a mausoleum waiting for a funeral.

Many of the 48 maza on the menu, priced mostly from $3 to $5, are already familiar. The babaganoush is particularly good, the eggplant flame-grilled so it has a smoky flavor. Some are less familiar, like labni (or labneh): superthick sheep's-milk yogurt that's drained to thicken it. Get the version called labni maa toum, laced with enough crushed garlic to keep vampires away. Avoid the predictable salata Libnani and go for the fattoush, with cucumber, lettuce, tomato, onion, and deep-fried pita fragments in a dressing of vinegar and dried sumac. The best entree is dajaj meshwi, a deboned half-chicken marinated in yogurt, garlic, and lemon, then charcoal-grilled and served with a pungent garlic aïoli. Another fab entree is stuffed zucchini ($9.75): four large courgettes painstakingly hollowed and crammed with a mellow filling of finely ground lamb and rice.

Lebanese and Syrian specialties

kibbeh
meat or pumpkin fritters

labni maa toum
thickened yogurt with garlic

mujadara
savory rice and lentils

ouzy
individual phyllo pie chicken

★ Alsalam Restaurant & Meat Market

7206 5th Ave near 72nd St, Brooklyn,
718-921-1076, subway: R to Bay Ridge Ave

The chicken shwarma sandwich is the best in town—fresh cut from the homemade rotating cylinder, jammed in a pocketless pita with lettuce, tomatoes, sumac-dusted onions, and a powerful garlic sauce, with the surprise addition of split cornichons. It's then rolled in butcher paper and zapped in a Cuban-style sandwich press. This Middle Eastern lunch counter cum market—where you can get replacement supplies for your hookah, in addition to staple groceries (but no hash)—also features rotisserie chicken and vegetarian meze like spinach cooked with pine nuts and mujadara, rice tossed with lentils and frizzled onions. For uper-adventuresome diners there's a boiled brain salad that a brain-obsessed friend pronounced excellent. [¢]

Cafe Rakka

81 St. Marks Pl at 1st Ave, Manhattan, 212-982-9166, subway: 6 to Astor Pl

Attracting little attention, Cafe Rakka has been near the corner of St. Marks and First Avenue for 14 years. The rickety sign on the sidewalk, a lure to passing cabbies, advertises falafel and french fries for $2.50. Rakka is a Syrian cafe, and to sit at one of its tables with the ceiling fan lazily revolving overhead is to feel like you're in Damascus or Aleppo. The renditions of Middle Eastern peasant food are convincing and cheap—it's hard to spend more than $5 for a meal. This gets you an abundant salad platter with four choices from the list of meze. Mujadara is usually my first choice, an earthy salad of cracked wheat and lentils garnished with heavenly caramelized onions, frizzled almost dry. My second choice is moussaka, a casserole of eggplant, tomatoes, and onions, which, unlike the Greek version, contains no meat. The combination generates a sweetness greater than you'd expect from the constituents. In addition, I pick lemony stuffed grape leaves and fava beans, redolent of strong-tasting olive oil with just a hint of cumin and garlic. As if that's not enough, the platter also comes with a falafel shaped like a rubber tire and a sumac-dusted salad. [¢, vegetarian friendly]

Fatoosh Barbecue

311 Henry St near Atlantic Ave, Brooklyn,
718-596-0030, subway: 2, 3, 4, 5 to Borough Hall

In spite of its name, this Syrian cafe specializes in meze. The 13 varieties presented here are unfailingly fresh, and sharply flavored with lemon, garlic, and olive oil. My favorite is a pureed red pepper salad thickened with bread crumbs and ground walnuts. Don't miss loomi, a beverage astringent with dried lemons. [¢, vegetarian friendly]

Fountain Cafe

183 Atlantic Ave near Clinton St, Brooklyn,
718-624-6764, subway: 2, 3, 4, 5 to Borough Hall

The vittles are unfailingly fresh at this bright and spacious Middle Eastern cafe: the stuffed grape leaves homemade and served warm in a tart tomato sauce, the babaganoush airy and properly smoky tasting, the kebabs cooked from scratch with lean meat and chicken. I particularly liked the kibbeh saneeya, which is a Lebanese pie of lamb and pine nuts with a cracked-wheat crust, served with minty yogurt sauce; a friend swears their lentil soup is the best in town. [kid friendly]

Laila

440 7th Ave near 14th St, Brooklyn,
718-788-0268, F to 7th Ave

This sturdy Lebanese excels at meze like labni, a thickened yogurt laden with mint, chile powder, and garlic; smoky babaganoush; and airy falafel. The appetizer combo for two, containing all of the above, makes a perfect entree. Main courses must be selected more carefully, since items like couscous and stuffed chicken are too damn bland. Instead go with stuffed grape leaves (ask for them hot) or ouzy, a phyllo pie stuffed with everything but the kitchen sink. Or try mulokhia, a Middle Eastern vegetable with the appealing mucilagenous properties of okra. [vegetarian friendly]

Moustache

90 Bedford St near Grove St, Manhattan,
212-229-2220, subway: 1, 9 to Christopher St
265 E 10th St near Ave A, Manhattan,
212-228-2022, subway: L to 1st Ave

The specialty of these sunny restaurants owned by an Iraqi expatriate is freshly baked pita, which comes out of a pizza oven steaming and extravagantly inflated. Costing $1, the pita must be eaten within five seconds or it turns into the dry, flat variety you buy in the supermarket. Moustache uses these pitas hot out of the oven to make sandwiches, such as the one made with the cumin-laced lamb merguez. They also use the pita dough to make "pitza," their name for a pita pizza. These are about eight inches in diameter and the deep brown crust—a little more brittle and oily than regular pizza crust—is topped with cheese and tomato sauce. Optional ingredients include capers, olives, eggplant, artichokes, or mushrooms. Though no longer on the menu, the best pitza features parsley and chopped garlic. Ask for it. Now under different management, but also commendable: **Moustache Slow Food Establishment** (405 Atlantic Ave, Brooklyn, 718-852-5555).

Salam Cafe and Restaurant

104 W 13th St near 6th Ave, Manhattan,
212-741-0277, subway: F to 6th Ave; L to 14th St

In spite of the uninspired decor at this rare upscale Syrian, the lefthand side of the menu is a near-perfect collection of meze, prepared with delicacy and invention. Take the fetoush—the standard iceberg lettuce has been replaced by baby lettuces, of course, and the traditional lemon dressing has been supplemented with balsamic vinegar. There are meat meze, as well: ma-anek, a nutmeg-flavored lamb sausage that has a coarse texture that contrasts nicely with its diminutive size; and kibbeh, a torpedo-shaped pie with a cracked-wheat crust, remarkably light considering its lamb and pignoli-nut filling. A traditional Syrian meal of meze is available in vegetarian and meat versions, and is highly recommended. If Salam's meze are bebop improvisations on familiar dishes, the entrees are more like free jazz—wild flights of fancy on the part of the chef. Shrimp curry features a mushroom gravy fortified with plenty of cream, with a swarm of unexpected ingredients like pea pods and apples. It was so good that I didn't give a damn how weird it was. [$]

EGYPTIAN

Bahry Fish Market and Restaurant

484 Bay Ridge Ave near 5th Ave, Brooklyn, 718-680-8135, subway: R to Bay Ridge Ave

Egyptian specialties

milookhiya
mucilaginous vegetable

koshary
Rice-A-Roni with lentils

tawook
spice dusted chicken

Order a whole fish ($12) from the back of the menu and Mostafa Khalil will leave his cash-register pulpit, ringed with boxes of fresh-baked pastries, and go over to the front window. He'll examine the display on ice in the front window, and maybe bend over and poke a fish or two to find out which is freshest. Then he carries into the back, dusts it with sumac and a little sea salt, and rapidly grills it to blackness like a Middle Eastern Paul Prudhomme. Today the best fish is sea trout, but tomorrow it may be striped bass, mullet, or even salmon.

Your fish du jour comes with a stack of pitas, an unremarkable salad of lettuce and tomato with a tahini on the side, a choice of rice or chips. If these were chips in the English sense, you'd pick the rice. However, they turn out to be potato chips, some cut thick and some thin, fried to absolute perfection and dusted with finely powdered cumin, red pepper, and salt, and then alternating snap and squish they make as you devour them form a rhythm track to this perfect meal.

Cafe Royal

37 3rd Ave near 9th St, Manhattan, 212-253-0166, subway: L to 1st Ave; 6 to Astor Pl

Despite below-average kebabs and fumbling service, this new Egyptian cafe cum nightclub offers some excellent and fascinating dishes, the best of them vegetarian. Check out koshary—a carbohydrate and protein tour de-force presented as layered levels of rice, vermicelli, tiny green French lentils, chick peas, and onions pleasantly fried to the consistency of straw. Concealed in the middle are little nuggets of macaroni twisted like a pig's tail. A warm scent of cinnamon rises from the heaped plate. Pour on the garlic sauce for moistness, and deploy with care the blistering harissa. [¢]

Elwady

24-25 Steinway St, Queens, 718-545-7705, subway: G, R to Steinway St

Located on a shady stretch of Steinway that boasts an Egyptian coffee house, grocery, and Halal butcher, this cafe offers a pan-Middle Eastern menu with few Egyptian flourishes. From the dozen dishes we tasted, best were a plate of fava beans in a rich gravy dotted with tomatoes and streaked with tahini ("foul"), smoky kebabs of chopped lamb and onions ("kefta"), and a pita sandwich of spice-dusted chicken breast ("tawook"). Desserts are also a strong point, including a creamy rice pudding sprinkled with toasted coconut, and a grainy honey cake of Biblical antiquity served warm from the oven.

Kabab Cafe

35-12 Steinway St, Queens,
718-728-9858, subway: G, R to Steinway St

This Astorian stalwart is run by two brothers who turn out a personable collection of rural Egyptian homestyle dishes. One is a bona fide gourmet chef, and is likely to wander into the cooking of other countries as well. If his wonderful gnocchi are on the menu, which changes daily according to whim, grab 'em! Other favorites of mine are a slimy green soup made from milookhiya that would make okra jealous, and a garlicky stew of fresh fava beans.

Sahara East

184 1st Ave near 10th St, Manhattan, 212-353-9000, subway: L to 1st Ave

Right next door the mosque, this narrow eatery with its picturesque tenement garden is also one of the best places to get couscous in town, the semolina broth bathed in a broth redolent of root vegetables. It's served in a tajine, an earthenware platter with a pointed cover that keeps the good smells in, until the waitress removes it with a flourish. Another gem is moussaka, a baked preparation of eggplant, tomatoes, onions, and herbs that improves on the Greek version of the dish. [outdoor dining]

ISRAELI

D. Zion Burger

4102 18th Ave near E 3rd St, Brooklyn,
718-871-9467, Subway: F to 18th Ave

The chow at this tiny, glatt kosher cafe is from Israel, Yemen, Morocco, Eastern Europe, and other areas from which Jews have emigrated. The mainly Orthodox clientele is partly Sephardic and partly Lubavitcher, and the result is a cosmopolitan crowd speaking several modern and ancient languages and grooving on food that runs from familiar to strange. There's shakshuka ($3.50), a Moroccan dish that's a close cousin of huevos rancheros: two poached eggs

Israeli specialties

foul
stewed fava beans

Moroccan cigars
pastry flutes

schwarma
lamb or poultry gyro

shakshuka
eggs with tomato sauce

zoug
green Yemenite hot sauce

smothered in tomato sauce tasting mildly of meat broth. On the edge of the plate is a dab of pale tahini that could pass for sour cream. Mixed with smoky eggplant, this tahini serves as the basis of some of the best babaganoush I've ever tasted—supremely light and fluffy, strewn with chopped parsley. Jachnoon is a pastry cylinder composed of thick layers wound tight, damp but not sweet. Served with boiled eggs colored brown with onion skin, it's an acquired taste. Another Yemenite pastry is much easier to love: malawach. Many-layered, deep-fried, and amorphous in shape, it has a buttery taste, and is better dipped in babaganoush than in the pureed tomato that is the traditional accompaniment. Even more popular are the hearty soups, a bargain at $6. One sports an entire shank of lamb surrounded by potatoes in a dense, cumin-scented broth. [kosher]

Hapina

69-54 Main St, Queens, 718-544-6262, subway: none

The cornish hen schwarma is a wonder at this kosher Yemenite restaurant, way downstream from Flushing's Chinatown. But even better are the fries, and the ten-foot help-yourself salad bar featuring cole slaw, hot chiles, sauerkraut, crunchy turnip and beet salad, grilled bell peppers, and plenty of other roughage, in addition to the three incredible hot sauces (red, green, and mango-based yellow) that characterize the Yemenite way with condiments. Among the typical Middle Eastern offerings, the chunky, creamy, smoky baba rules, with a surprisingly tomato-rich Turkish salad a close second. Ignore the gruff service and skip the kibbeh soup. [kosher]

Hoomoos Asli

100 Kenmare St at Centre St, Manhattan,
212-966-0022, subway: 6 to Spring St

This new Sephardic-leaning Israeli grill is particularly proud of its hummus, which is fluffy and richly flavored with cumin. Have it ringed around tahini and roasted pignoli, tabbouleh, or, best of all, cradling an "Israel mixed grill"—a sauté of meat and poultry tidbits that can also contain organ meats like liver, at your request. Yemenite, Middle Eastern, Turkish, and North African dishes complete the menu, but whatever you order, make sure you get plenty of the home-made pitas. Other interesting offerings include shakshuka—a pair of poached eggs in a rough tomato-and-pepper gravy—and house malawach, a Yemenite pizza topped with feta, olives, and zattar, a spice that's a cousin of oregano and thyme. The sunny L-shaped room is relent-lessly decorated with color photos of flower beds, and the air is faintly scented with rosewater. [kosher]

Jerusalem Steak House

533 Kings Highway, Brooklyn, 718-336-5115, subway: F to Kings Highway

This lively kosher meatery poised between Midwood and Gravesend is a hang-out for Israeli immigrants, and offers some of the best charcoal-grilled meats in a neighborhood that dotes on kebabs: spicy merguez sausage, kofta made from flavorful ground lamb, and fatty veal chops—a belt-busting five per order. Best appetizer is a plate of six "Moroccan cigars," meat-stuffed pastry flutes swamped with tahini and Yemenite tomato relish. The blinding fluo-rescent light, portraits of the late Lubavitcher rebbe, and inspirational art will make you feel like you're halfway to heaven. [kosher]

Kosher Delight

**1365 Broadway near 38th St, Manhattan,
212-563-3366, subway: N, R to 34th St**

The chicken schwarma turning in the front window is divine. Cumin-dusted and moist, it's hacked off the cylinder at just the right moment and served on a pita. A paper basket on the side lets you load up with purple cabbage slaw, grilled eggplant, two kinds of peppers, pickles, onions, and baby falafel squeezed out of a scary machine that sits on the rear counter. Three sauces are available to smother the chicken: tahini, a Yemenite cilantro chutney, and, my favorite, a very tart mango dressing. Also available: kosher Chinese that's not half bad. [kosher]

Rectangles

159 2nd Ave at 10th St, Manhattan, 212-677-8410, subway: 6 to Astor Pl

Plopped down among the Jewish restaurants on the East Village's Yiddish Broadway, only gradually did Rectangles reveal its Yemenite bent. It's now a favorite hang of the Israeli restauranteurs who own many of the coffee shops and French bistros in the area. The menu, too, gradually introduced Yemenite secrets like weekend jachnoon—rolled and baked dough served with a hardboiled egg, and hamin-techelunt, a Sabbath beef stew slow-roasted overnight. But nearly everything's good here, including a homely dish of foul (fava beans) with hummus underneath and tabbouleh on top, served with an egg colored with onion skin and wedges of lemon. If you have a choice, pick the fries over the pilaf. [outdoor dining]

YEMENI

145 Luncheonette

**145 Court St near Pacific St, Brooklyn,
718-624-9325, subway: F, G to Bergen St**

Though the smeary pink interior of 145 Luncheonette is accented with fake brick like a '60s diner, a squint through the window reveals an Arabic menu at the end of the room with no English translations. Don't worry if you can't read the menu, because your host will bring you a set meal (approximately $6.50 per person, exact price revealed with your bill). It begins with a straw-colored soup, a delicate consommé of lamb that would do any French restaurant proud. In

Yemeni specialties

assid
giant dumpling with gravy

glaba
minced lamb

hulba
fenugreek emulsion

salta
bubbling brown gunk

shafota
bread and yogurt porridge

good time a salad arrives, unremarkable save for the crispness of its greens and a tangy, substantial vinaigrette.

Consistent with Arab hospitality, the food is served communally. The meat course comes on a round metal platter, bedded with sepia-stained rice marvelously aromatic of cinnamon and meat juices. At intervals around the perimeter little piles of a thick potato stew occur, but the focus is the meat. The selection is negotiable, although Yemeni favorites like kidneys, brains, and liver run out early in the day. On several visits we enjoyed pleasantly charred lamb chops, a tender roast chicken with burnished skin intact, a heap of baby lamb rib nicely salted and falling off the bone, and beef that had been thickly smeared with hawayij, a spice paste of caraway, black peppercorns, cardamom, and turmeric. [¢]

Yemen Cafe

176 Atlantic Ave near Court St, Brooklyn, 718-834-9533, subway: 2, 3, 4, 5 to Borough Hall

Need a snack? Try shafota ($3), a bowl of yogurt turned to porridge by soggy gobbets of flat-bread. Stark white, it smolders with raw garlic, cilantro, and nigella—oniony black seeds that scatter the surface. A heavier meal in the same vein is fattah ($9), a tureen crammed with strips of lamb, carrot, and bread in a tacky gravy—super comfort food, and too much for one person to finish. Yemen Cafe, in Brooklyn's Arab Quarter, vaunts a pink neon crown in the window, and photos lining the walls confirm that Yemen is spectacularly beautiful—sort of like New Mexico, but with kasbahs clinging to steep cliffs and seaside villages girdled by medieval walls.

Middle Eastern standards of lamb, chicken, hummus, and babaganoush dominate the menu, but it's the uniquely Yemeni food that fascinates. There's glaba ($9), a mince of lamb in a light sauce tweaked with cinnamon and a smattering of tomatoes, served with pilaf perfumed with cardamom. More stunning is assid ($9)—a doughy dumpling that looks like the butte Richard Dreyfuss sculpted in Close Encounters. The dumpling comes with a choice of roast lamb or chicken that arrives just as you begin to make a dent in the dome. Pick the lamb and receive four huge chunks hacked from a roast—lean, herby, bursting with flavor. The chicken is merely a rather dry roasted half.

Moroccan and Tunisan

Despite the ease of travel between North Africa and New York (a six-hour flight from Casablanca), there just aren't many Moroccans, Algerians, Tunisians, or Libyans hanging out here. Most of the Moroccan restaurants—and there are damn few—create carelessly spiced and downright bland renditions of classic dishes for diners whose impression of the country is limited to several viewings of Casablanca. Accordingly, the Moroccan restaurants below are the best of a very mediocre lot, made more so by the recent demise of Bay Ridge's Casablanca, one of only a couple of working class Moroccan eateries in town. Also note that West Village stalwart Bar Six (502 6th Ave, 212-691-1363) offers a couple of estimable Moroccan specials each evening, and does a very fine vegetable couscous at lunch on weekdays. There are virtually no Tunisian restaurants, with exception of a French place way out in Little Neck (La Baraka, 255-09 Northern Blvd, 718-428-1461) that only offers a couscous or two in a Tunisian vein, and Epices du Traiteur, which mounts a menu nearly one-quarter Tunisian. North African cooking is among the most subtly spiced and adeptly executed in the world, and even watered-down renditions have much to recommend them. Accordingly, ignore my grousing, and check out some of these places.

MOROCCAN

Cafe Fès

246 W 4th St at W 10th St, Manhattan,
212-924-7653, subway: 1, 9 to Christopher St

The tile interior with its tinkling fountain is as close as you're going to get to Morocco stateside, and the streamlined menu duplicates the piquancy of the cuisine, if not its breadth. The tajine of Cornish hen cooked with brine-pickled lemon and two kinds of olives is a perfect example of North African cooking. Also good is the tajine of lamb, artichokes, and fresh favas. Portions are not as big as they might be, so you'd better order a side of couscous to go along with the entrees.

Moroccan specialties

b'stela
phyllo pigeon pie

braewat
flaky triangular turnover

chermoula
green herb paste

couscous
semolina moistened with broth

tajine
a distinctive crockery and any stew cooked in such a dish

Chez Es Saada

42 East 1st Street near 2nd Ave, Manhattan,
212-777-5617, subway: F to 2nd Ave

Just down the block from the Catholic Worker, a mysterious and unmarked entrance is darkened except for a pair of wrought-iron lamps that allow light to escape through narrow slats. But through the iron-barred door one is surprised to find a barroom with a homey aura—if your home is Marrakech, that is. The bar itself is clad in ceramic tile with a geometric North African design; on top, a wide bowl brims with assorted olives smeared with a chile-and-herb paste so strong that one or two are enough. Inevitably you are drawn through a portal in the rear and down a winding and clammy stairway strewn with rose petals.

As is the rule in many expensive and overhyped restaurants, the appetizers are great, while the entrees are just so-so. We especially enjoyed the Marrakech salad ($9)—nine stunning disimilar mounds including spicy diced beets, carmelized onions with chickpeas and raisins, herby cukes, planked carrots with lemon, and a fluffy hummus. Braewats ($7), the national pastry of Morocco, were offered in a spinach version glued together with a fontina—atypical but not annoying. Only a mussel soup bombed—it was a cream-based vegetable chowder that derived little flavor from the bivalves. The menu offers only one tajine, Morocco's popular multi-version stew cooked over coals in a tented ceramic contraption. On one occasion, the rather daring choice of ingredients was lamb, prunes, and ginger, and the sauce was so rich that most of it got left behind. Which is probably fortunate, since few could gauge the effect of so many prunes on the human digestive system. [$]

L'Orange Bleue

430 Broome Str near Crosby St, Manhattan,
212-226-4999, subway: 6 to Spring St

A single tajine du jour heads up the menu at L'Orange Bleue, a French-Moroccan bistro. Though not served in a tajine, it was as good in its own way as Chez Es Saada's: a half chicken simply flavored with lemon zest, fennel, and a handful of black olives. As added improvements, the skin was crisp and herby, and carmelized strips of fennel kept the underlying couscous moist. A similar technique was used with cod, wherein diced beets kept the semolina damp and colored it a lurid red. The fish itself is baked in parchment with slices of lime and a smear of chermoula, a Moroccan spice paste of onions, garlic, flat-leaf parsley, cilantro, and a touch of red pepper.

Mogador

101 St Marks Pl near 1st Ave, Manhattan,
212-677-2226, subway: L to 1st Ave

Go after 5 P.M. when, to begin, they bring a lovely tray of small dishes and let you take your pick. Try the cumin-laced beet salad, the verdant tabbouleh, or the carrot salad, doused with olive oil and lemon juice. The menu at Mogador is mainly Moroccan, at a price that beats the other joints in town. The best entree choice is the tajine, a thick stew made with lamb or chicken in six variations. [outdoor dining]

TUNISAN

Epices du Traiteur

103 W 70th St near Columbus Ave,
Manhattan, 212-579-5904,
subway: 1, 2, 3, 9 to 72nd St

This French bistro has an intriguing sideline: Tunisian food, including a few specialties you won't find elsewhere. Foremost is brik, a curious fan-shaped pastry featuring canned tuna and a runny egg that remains hemmed in until you bite down and the yolk squirts all over everything. Hey, it's good! There's also a spicy onion, tomato, and red pepper bread dip called mischouia, and an abundant mixed grill matching four merguez sausages with four fork-tender baby lamb chops. Be warned: the Moroccan specialties, like the lamb-and-lemon tagine, bomb.

Tunisan specialties

brik
flaky egg and tuna pastry

merguez
spicy lamb sausage

tagine
omelet cooked in a tajine

Tunisian salad
cubed raw vegetables in vinaigrette

Persian and Afghani

Though the Turks popularized the table of mainly vegetarian snacks called meze, this style of eating is said to have originated with the Persians, who invented little dishes that went well with glasses of wine. The shish kebab itself is also probably of Persian origin, allowing the unmessy eating of grilled meat with the fingers. The kebab has proved so popular, that its range is now worldwide. But Persian food is so much more, as the national dish of fessenjen demonstrates with its wild combination of chicken, pomegranate, and walnuts. Also unique to the cuisine is the series of stews called koresh, one of which mixes spinach, kidney beans, and dried limes into a pungent and bizarrely textured stew. Afghanis share the Persian obsession with kebabs, and most eateries limit their menus to just that, with a handful of pastas thrown in. But Brooklyn's Bahar hints at the broader range of Afghani food, and their crackly pumpkin turnover is certainly among the city's hundred best dishes.

PERSIAN

Nader

**48 E 29th St near Park Ave, Manhattan,
212-683-4833, subway: 6 to 28th St**

For appetizers, skip the too-familiar hummus, baba,
and tabbouleh in favor of "dry yogurt and eggplant"
($4)—grilled slices smeared with kashk, made from
dehydrated yogurt whey, which imparts a wonderful
mushroomy flavor. Also don't miss torshi, a complicated pickle that makes even the boring pitas taste
good. It contains finely minced cauliflower, carrots,
and cabbage seasoned with nigella, dill, and coriander seed in a vinegar bath so sour it requires several
swallows of water. Powdered turmeric is responsible
for the odd orange color and pleasant muddy taste.
Save some to embellish the main course.

The heart of Iranian cooking is koresh—stews that
mix lentils, fruit, meat, and herbs to spectacular
effect. The superior choice is gheimeh ($9.45), yellow split peas and beef in a gravy tinged
with tomato and flavored with dried limes and sweet spices. For an additional 50 cents, you
can add baby eggplant to this tasty concoction. Inevitably, there are the kebabs, offered in 16
combinations ($9.90-$19.90). The best (and cheapest) are the plain brochettes of buttery
Cornish game hen and koobideh—beef ground with plenty of onions. Don't miss the rice
cooked with zereshk, a tiny native berry that's like a miniature cranberry. Known in Europe as
barberry, it is said in Thomas Culpeper's Complete Herbal (1649) to "get a man a good stomach to his victuals." I couldn't agree more.

Persian specialties

ash reshteh
vegetarian bean soup

fesenjan
walnut-and-pom egranate sauced chicken

ghourmeh sabzi
beef, kidney bean, and herb stew

jujeh
Cornish hen kebab

koobideh
minced-meat kebab

torshi
vinegar vegetable pickle

Patoug

**11 E 30th St near 5th Ave, Manhattan,
212-696-0300, subway: 6 to 28th St
220-06 Horace Harding Expwy near Springfield Blvd, Queens,
718-279-3500, subway: none**

Glowing like a saffron sun, chelo rice commands the center of the table. Served on a plate the
size of a small yacht, each glistening grain tastes individually buttered. At the East 30th St
Patoug–a new branch of the Persian favorite based in Little Neck, Queens—the rice arsenal
also includes plain basmati mingled with currants and tart barberries, and a dilled rice flecked
with tender baby limas smaller than a fingernail. The restaurant occupies a semi-subterranean
room in the rug district, and from its windows the passing foot traffic looks like a parade of
legless torsos, many carrying rolled rugs in muted browns and cerises.

Fragrant, charcoal-grilled kebabs come two to a plate with your choice of rice, a charred plum tomato, and sweet, parsley-strewn onions. The best is koobideh ($9), righteously marrying ground beef and lamb, powerfully redolent of onion. This might seem a pauper's choice, meat loaf instead of roast beef, but in these days of fatless beef and bleatless lamb, these moist wavy cylinders kick ass. A close runner-up is jujeh ($10), boneless pieces of yogurt-and-saffron-smeared Cornish hen that demand only a squeeze of lemon to attain poultry perfection. The single best dish we had, though, was ash reshteh (cup $2.50, bowl $3.50), a humble vegetarian soup crammed with wholesome ingredients—green lentils, kidney beans, chick peas, noodles, scallions, fenugreek leaves, and mint.

AFGHANI

Bahar Shishkebab House

984 Coney Island Ave, Brooklyn, 718-434-8088, subway: D to Ave H

In the middle of Coney Island Avenue's Muslim district is Bahar Shishkebab House, a solitary Afghan establishment boasting a large dining room lined with dramatic color photos of empty mountain gorges, as if a Mujahidin column were about to snake 'round the corner. Bolani kadu ($4) is a plate-size pumpkin turnover cut into strips so the scented gourd oozes at the edges. It's served with a decent herbed mayonnaise, but if you know what's good for you, order maste ($2), a homemade yogurt dotted with cukes and goosed with shallots and fresh mint.

Afghani specialties

ashi lobya
noodles with kidney beans

bolani kadu
pumpkin turnover

kalbi
carrot-and-raisin rice

maste
shallot-flecked yogurt

morgh palow
oniony chicken with rice

Influenced by noodle-rich Uzbekistan to its north, Afghan food emphasizes pastas. There's ashi lobya ($7.50), a delicious entree of broad noodles with kidney beans and yogurt accented with butter. The excellent charcoal-grilled kebabs and stews (koresh) each come with one of four different rice varieties (substitutions permitted). In chalow, each grain glistens and you'll soon find out why: an enormous gob of stewed lamb hides underneath. "Brown rice" is stained sepia by meat juices and ground sumac. Kalbi is strewn with raisins and carrots, a perfect match for the oniony roast chicken in morgh palow ($9)—a pilaf of pistachios and orange rind deploying what smells like nine dollars' worth of saffron. Topped with a generous lamb kebab in narieng palow ($9), it radiates an X-Files glow.

Although the huge portions of meat and rice have induced stupor, who could resist a dessert named gooshi feel ($3.50)? It's not a sex act, but two elephant ears of fried dough dribbled with honey and pistachios. [vegetarian friendly]

¡O¡ HELL'S AFGHANI

Manhattan has its own collection of bargain Afghanis centered on Ninth Avenue in Hell's Kitchen. Compared with similar establishments in Brooklyn and Queens, they're not that good. However, they're a convenient stopover for decent grilled shish kebabs on the way to a movie or Lincoln Center. Afghan Shish Kebab Restaurant (789 9th Ave, 212-664-0123) is my favorite, serving asheh kishida ($5.95), home-made noodles in a pleasantly lumpy yogurt sauce, and bolani, pan-fried pastries stuffed with green onion and potatoes. More famous is Afghan Kebab House (764 9th Ave, 212-307-1612), so popular that it spawned a chain (consult the Manhattan phone book for full list of addresses). Lamb, fish, and kofta kebabs rule. There are also a couple of East Side lace-curtain Afghanis that charge about double the price, like Pamir (1437 Second Ave, 212-734-3791). Perfectly OK, but nothing spectacular—time your visit to take advantage of lunch specials.

Regional American

Soul Food and American Jewish have their own sections, but here are some additional regional American stylings that have left their mark on Gotham. Some originated here, like the roast beef cuisine of Brennan and Carr (though it certainly has its antecedents in Ireland), while others, like the Cajun/Creole of Harglo's, are wholesale imports. Finally, we have the problematic barbecue places. Many prominent ones are not mentioned here, mainly because they're awful. Those recommended often compare negatively with the prototypes they're patterned after, but hey, they're all we've got.

REGIONAL AMERICAN

Brennan and Carr

**3432 Nostrand Ave at Ave U, Brooklyn,
718-769-1254, subway: D to Ave U**

Years ago families going to and from Coney Island
would get roast beef sandwiches at a series of modest stands. Rather than franks or knishes, roast beef
was the favorite lunch of beachgoers. Few of these
establishments persist today; foremost among them
is Brennan and Carr. The architecture is arresting—
a squat brick blockhouse with rifle-slit windows.
Inside an aged greeter imparts tidbits of neighborhood history. The dining room continues the bunker
theme, decorated with color paintings of Civil War
soldiers.

The menu is on a wood plaque, repeated on paper
placemats with a view of the restaurant's exterior.
Aside from some rather chalky and underclammed
clam chowder, your only opener is a cup of beef
broth, which you'll be seeing again. The rest of the menu is a dozen other incongruous items,
added in the years since the 1938 opening. The roast beef sandwich ($4.25), ordered by
three-quarters of the patrons, arrives with a side of limp fries and a cup of broth. Inside the
kaiser roll is a modest pile of gray meat. Remarkably, both the meat and the bun have been
steamed, making the bun a soggy mess of white goo. Now that I'm an aficionado, I can give
you the scoop on what to really order. The beef plate ($8.49), while pricey, is a thing of won-
der. You can ask for it rare, and the meat will come pink in the middle and pinwheeled around
the plate, oddly like a dish of Kobe beef I had at Nobu Next Door. You also get two canned
vegetables, pickles, and a pair of torpedo rolls, allowing you to make excellent sandwiches
with the ketchup, mustard, and horseradish provided. [¢, kid friendly]

Cowgirl Hall of Fame

**519 Hudson St at W 10th St, Manhattan,
212-633-1133, subway: 1, 9 to Christopher St**

The barbecue menu here is limited to brisket and beef ribs. The brisket, although copious, is a
bit dry. But the ribs are great. You get five huge ones, plenty meaty, with sides of potato salad
and coleslaw for $11.95. While this is not cheap, ribs rarely are. A couple more good things
are the honey-dipped fried chicken and fried catfish. Portions are uniformly enormous, and the
sides frequently outshine the entrees. They also offer a few weirdo dishes—like chili served in
a ripped-open bag of Fritos, said to have originated in Texas. The displays of rodeo parapher-
nalia are diverting, and help to make this one of the best eateries for kids in town. [kid friendly]

Harglo's Cafe

974 2nd Ave near 52nd St, Manhattan,
212-759-9820, subway: 6 to 51st St

This East Side bar tried to surf the popularity of Cajun food in the early '80s, serving up gumbos, étouffées, jambalayas, and blackened red fish (and, occasionally, alligator) as if they knew what they were doing. The chicken jambalaya's not half bad—made with the whole chicken and not just breast meat, rife with sausage (OK, it's Italian fennel and not andouille), pleasingly spicy and tasting of celery and onions. The seafood étouffée, however, is a train wreck, bobbing with bizarrely incongruous elements like canned baby corn, frozen peas, and other things that make it seem more like a Chinese stir fry. What really makes this place Cajun, though, is their talent at the deep fryer—the onion loaf is sweet and delicious, and identical to the kind you might find in New Orleans, where they fry nearly everything.

Mama's Food Shop

200 E 3rd St near Ave B, Manhattan,
212-777-4425, subway: F to 2nd Ave

Mama's occupies a double storefront with one side devoted to an informal dining room featuring an elegiac wall of paintings and photos of mamas—one will probably look like yours. All the food is displayed behind glass, and if your idea of a main course involves flesh, the selection is limited to ham, fish, meat loaf, and chicken. Sounds dull, right? Well, look closer. The ham is a bone-in Polish ham, the kind that was once the pride of the East Village. The fish is salmon, perfectly grilled in smallish planks. For chicken, there's a choice of two: roasted skin-on with only a dusting of paprika, and Southern-fried, dark brown and crispy. The meat loaf is ordinary meat loaf. The really amazing thing, besides the care in the selection and preparation of the ingredients, is the price: a main course with one side costs about $7. The sides, many of which can also function as mains, include two hot choices: peppery whipped potatoes with a touch of cheese, and baked macaroni and cheese with a dark upper crust. The macaroni is striking—like the Soul Food article, only creamier and with more cheeses. Selections that are served cold or at room temperature include corn tossed with tomatoes and cilantro, honey-baked yams, cukes with parmesan and red onions, fruit salad with three kinds of melon and blueberries, and a couscous salad that changes on a daily basis. The corn salad, in particular, is unforgettable—sweet kernels cut from the cob given a Mexican twist with cilantro. [¢, kid friendly]

Mississippi Bar-B-Que

201-05 Murdock Ave, Queens,
718-776-3446, subway: none

With its low frame houses and meandering lanes, this St. Albans institution might make you think you're really in Mississippi, or at least somewhere in Long Island. The pit-cooked baby-back ribs are lean, smoky, and tender, served with a mahogany sauce that's rich and not too sweet. So, too, is the chicken above average—it tastes good the next day. This storefront is an inferior successor to a shack on Baisley Boulevard that did ribs on a pair of Webers every weekend, and like the original, the banana pudding made with vanilla wafers is something to write home about. [¢]

★ Pearl Oyster Bar

18 Cornelia St near Bedford St, Manhattan,
212-691-8211, subway: A, B, C, D, E, F, Q to West 4th St

Pearl Oyster Bar is partly a throwback to the days (starting around 1820) when oyster bars were the predominant form of fast food in the city. The cheapest occupied cellars and served according to the Canal Street plan, whereby a few pennies bought raw bivalves in a seemingly endless stream—although if you overindulged, the shucker might finish you off with a bad one. This concept has been grafted onto a typical New England seafood restaurant to create Pearl's, one of my favorite restaurants in town. The menu has been kept elemental, with an emphasis on amazingly fresh oysters, clams, lobster, and one or two catches of the day. The signature Caesar salad with anchovy dressing is celebrated, while the lobster roll is a perfect reproduction of the item found in Maine's pounds, only more luxuriantly stuffed. Another triumph is an oyster po' boy that would be good enough to serve at Uglesich's in New Orleans, sided like the lobster roll with a haystack of ultraskinny fries. You can't go wrong at Pearl's, except where seating is concerned. With only one table, you must usually perch precariously at the counter while you eat.

★ Pearson's Texas Barbecue

71-04 35th Ave, Queens, 718-779-7715,
subway: E, F, G, R to Jackson Heights/Roosevelt Ave;
7 to 74th St-Broadway

What may be the city's only real barbecue is back in action—in the rear of a Jackson Heights sports bar. And the laboriously wood-smoked 'cue is as good as ever. The Texas-style pork ribs are improved, moister and tastier than before; the brisket is now a shade dry. Pulled pork is another good choice, while the hot links rule. Inexplicably, the sauces are not as hot as before, so move your choice up a notch (mild, medium, madness, and mean is the sequence). The best part—the overstuffed sandwich with your choice of meat on a Portuguese roll is still $5.95.

For those of you who don't know the history—this barbecue was founded by Robert Pearson, a gangling mop-topped guy who was once Jean Shrimpton's hairdresser in Mod London. He moved to Connecticut and got barbecue religion, making a scholarly study of Southern and Midwestern barbecuing styles, eventually coming to the conclusion, as many of us have done, that Texas is best. He made his own innovations—replacing Wonder Bread with Portuguese rolls, for example. And this alone would merit his inclusion in the Barbecue Hall of Fame (if there is one). Though he's turned the business over to a pardner, his spirit still infuses the premises. [¢]

Tad's Steaks

104 E 14th St near Irving Pl, Manhattan,
212-563-7440, subway: 4, 5, 6, L, N, R to Union Sq

My steakhouse fave is not Morton's, Ruth's Chris, Michael Jordan's, or Peter Luger, but crotchety budget steakery Tad's, so old I suspect it was named after Lincoln's consumptive son. Its dingy walls brocaded bordello red, the Union Square branch cockily resisted gentrification as even august Luchow's fell under the wrecker's ball. The irascible cook slings meat onto the grill and flames shoot hellishly hoodward, as the queue of steak-votaries pulls back in awe. The extra-cut sirloin is the way to go: about 16 ounces, it's full-flavored and tender without totally copping out. And for once the price includes everything: baked potato, tossed salad (pick the oil and vinegar dressing rather than the French, tomatoes 50¢ extra), and a thick slice of excellent, griddle-fried toast. At that price, you could eat here every day, though, on second thought, I'd rather have a skewer of adana kebab in a Turkish joint. If they ask if you want fried onions, be forewarned that they charge for them. Call Information to find the other locations, including, according to the marquee, Chicago, San Francisco, and Philadelphia.

Virgil's Real Barbecue

152 W. 42nd St. bet. 6th & 7th Aves, Manhattan,
212-921-9494, subway: 1, 2, 3, 7, 9, N, R to Times Sq

If any place deserves the name "barbecue emporium," Virgil's does. This place tries to cover all the bases, serving several regional types of barbecue, as well as Southern cooking, grilled seafood, and even raw shellfish. Dinners run in the $12.95 to $24.95 range; the sandwich platters are more affordable. I sat at the lunch counter, which looks right into the kitchen, and ordered the brisket sandwich. The platter arrived with plenty of meat on the sesame seed bun, a side of potato salad and "mustard slaw," and a half-sour pickle (weird in this context). The meat was moist and red-edged but slightly lacking in smoky flavor. (And I wish it had been sliced by hand, not by a slicing machine.) Five good sauces are provided on the table: three traditional sweet tomato sauces, a North Carolina vinegar-based sauce, and a Mexican hot sauce made in Jalisco. On another visit I tried the Memphis pork ribs platter, which included six meaty ribs, two sides of your choice, and jalapeño cornbread. The portions were so large I could have split the platter with someone else. Once again, though, they seem to have scrimped on the hardwood in the barbecuing process. In fact, this place's biggest trick is blowing smoke into the dining room so you think you're eating real barbecue. You know what? It works.

Russian
and Ukranian

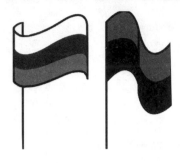

A majority of Brighton Beach's residents hail from the Ukraine, a country that was only recently separated from Mother Russia by the collapse of the Soviet Union. Yet the language that you hear spoken, except among a few fanatics, is Russian and not Ukrainian, as is the menu served at most of the eateries in this delightful seaside region, which resembles the Black Sea, as least in the minds of the residents. Like our own cuisine, Russian food is a melting pot, and many of the favorite dishes originated in far-flung parts of the empire, like the soup kharcho (from Georgia), pelmeni dumplings (from Siberia), and chicken Kiev (from the Ukraine). We concentrate below on modest establishments with minimal emphasis on bad entertainment. For a bigger blowout and hefty cover charges, check out big-budget places like National (273 Brighton Beach Ave, 718-646-1225) and Odessa (1113 Brighton Beach Ave, 718-332-3223).

RUSSIAN and UKRANIAN

Anyway Cafe Club

**34 E 2nd St near 2nd Ave, Manhattan,
212-533-3412, subway: F to 2nd Ave**

It's Brighton Beach meets the East Village at this
Russian trattoria, which fills up with Russian hipsters
every evening about nine. Many come just to drink,
smoke, and chat, but there's also a list of eats like
big doughy dumplings called pelmeni, intense
smoked herring sided with potatoes, an herbed
Russian burger with no bun, and, best of all, blintzes
oozing cheese and not even slightly sweet. Skip the
misconceived eggplant appetizer, but don't miss the
bizarre garlic-flavored vodka.

Blini Hut

**132 Nassau St at Beekman St, Manhattan,
212-233-3500, subway: 2, 3 to Fulton St**

*Russian and
Ukranian
specialties*

basturma
air-dried beef

blini
*pancakes served
with caviar*

chicken Kiev
*breast wrapped
around butter*

kasha
*steamed
buckwheat groats*

midnight in Moscow
plum sauced pork cutlet

red borscht
beet soup

vareniky
potato ravioli

To those of you who were bummed when the two
branches of Rush'n Express closed a couple of years
ago—here's the remedy. Blini Hut is backed by some of the same investors and features the
same wacky, McDonald's-style approach to Russian cooking. And the menu is three times as
long! The Siberian pelmeni ($3.97) are great, a couple dozen tiny noodle dumplings stuffed
with ground lamb and onions. The borscht is Ukrainian style, loaded with diced vegetables,
while the golubtzi (stuffed cabbage leaves) actually benefit from being frozen and long-
steamed. There are a slew of oddities not found at Rush'n Express, including donuts called
ponchekey, offered with a choice of four dips, and "Russian tea" (a gyp at $1.85), and
unpleasantly sweetened with berry preserves. [¢, kid friendly]

Cafe Paris

**3178 Coney Island Ave near Ocean View Ave, Brooklyn,
718-646-0800, subway: D, Q to Brighton Beach**

When I first spotted Cafe Paris from the elevated tracks above Brighton Beach, I figured it was
a Haitian restaurant. But then a couple of Russian friends from the neighborhood recommended it enthusiastically. Located at the terminus of Coney Island Avenue, the cafe's sign
sports a perspective-flattened Eiffel Tower wedged between the words Cafe and Paris.
Russian food is not exactly light fare—in fact, it's difficult to imagine enjoying it unless there's
a chill in the air. Take the escargots ($8.50) swamped with a garlicky mixture of white cheese
and cream, garnished with chopped fresh dill. Only slightly lighter were the vareniky, pillow-

shaped dumplings filled with potatoes and garnished with masses of mushrooms. Soups also make good starters, the best a pale borscht with more cabbage than beets. How to describe the entrees to make it sound like we weren't a little crazy to eat them? Chicken Kiev ($8.90) bears little resemblance to the puny version served at the Russian Tea Room, a giant double-breast of chicken wrapped around a stick of butter, bread-crumbed and deep-fried, with a single bone left sticking out the end. The chicken has been rolled so tight, that when you cut into it, the butter squirts out and soaks your shirt. I asked one of those Russian friends what the protruding bone was for and she replied, "To pick it up and suck the butter out."

Caffe Volna

3145 Brighton Street (the boardwalk) near 3rd St, Brooklyn, 718-332-0341, subway: D, Q to Brighton Beach

Bringing a welcome chill to the air, sunset reddens the faces of the promenaders. Wearing a sound system strapped to his chest, a sallow-faced trumpeter launches a melancholy air, sending a black poodle with red toenails scurrying. First to arrive is plums soaked in red wine ("plun in winegar," $4), each pit replaced by a whole walnut. This could be a Black Sea resort at the height of the season, only it's Brighton Beach. Caffe Volna (which means "the wave") is the southernmost of five establishments that spill their tables onto the boardwalk. "Russian pancakes with red caviar" ($6.50) is, of course, blini, six of which come neatly folded with a tiny dish of salty salmon roe. Maybe it's not the best caviar in the world, but context improves it by about 500 per cent. Basturma ($4) generates nearly as much excitement: thin slices of air-dried beef generously veined with fat, with the funk of Italian soppressata.

As the heat of the day dissipates, the heavier food becomes more appealing. Chicken tabaka ($8), a Russian standard, is an entire bird flattened through judicious removal of certain bones, coated with garlic, and deep-fried. Moist inside and glistening without, it would bring fans of Southern fried chicken to their knees. Equally admirable is sturgeon shish kebab ($13), about twelve ounces of richly textured fish served with a mound of yellow corn kernels and pom egranate syrup. But the favorite seafood, at least among Russians who hail from the Ukraine, is flounder ($10). The entire critter is lightly floured and crisply fried, and even on a Sunday evening it's stunningly fresh. [kid friendly, outdoor dining]

Pastorale

410 Brighton Beach Ave near Brighton 4th St, Brooklyn, 718-648-5484, subway: D, Q to Brighton Beach

Autumn sees the Brighton Beach dining action move indoors from the sidewalk cafes on the boardwalk to the more formal joints inland. Under the elevated D train, Pastorale is one of the more stranger-friendly—decorated with 18th-century-style French tapestries of sylvan scenes, and slinging pan-Soviet cuisine as banquetteers dance to the throbbing oratorio of Saint Casio. The cold platter of smoked and pickled fish is the compulsory starter, but don't miss the excellent red borscht. Among main courses, chicken tabaka and chicken Kiev are bugdet-wise choices; for a few dollars more there's "midnight in Moscow," a huge pork cutlet topped with plum sauce.

︎❚◯❚ UKE JOINTS

Just as successive waves of German and German-Jewish immigrants made the East Village their home base before and after 1900, respectively, the Ukrainians, fleeing Soviet domination after the collapse of the Third Reich, thronged the neighborhood in the late '40s. Many of their institutions remain, like the Ukrainian American Youth Association and the Ukrainian Orthodox Federal Credit Union, even though the community has dwindled. In fact, Ukrainian eateries used to dominate the East Village; now Polish places, boasting a similar Slavic menu, are more common. The best remaining is the Ukrainian East Village Restaurant (140 2nd Avenue, 212-529-6287), where the excellent Ukrainian borscht is a heavily and diversely vegetabled pink soup served hot with a dollop of sour cream on the side. The more familiar cold, all-beet variety is referred to as Lithuanian borscht on the menu. The sour-cream-and-paprika-laced goulash is called letcho, suggesting you should leer while eating it, while the cheese blintzes, deep-fried to make the superthin skin brown and crackly, are so good you'll remember them days later.

In the early '80s rock musicians used to hang out at Kiev (117 2nd Ave, 212-674-4040), which at that time was the only cafe in the East Village open late into the night. Every couple of years, the place would expand into another adjacent tenement storefront, making it one of the most oddly configured restaurants in the neighborhood. Its recent closing leaves Veselka (144 2nd Ave, 212-228-9682) the only breakfast hangout of East Villagers. Sit below the funky mural and watch the world wake up, as artists drift in for their first espresso of the day, then furtively head off to their day jobs. The muffins, lush and large, are among the best in town, especially the whole-wheat blueberry. Also order anything made with buttermilk, such as the well-browned waffles dusted with powdered sugar and served with a chunky raspberry puree. The cheese blintzes are fab, too; other selections that reflect the community's Ukrainian heritage include kielbasa and kasha—steamed buckwheat with a nutty flavor.

Senegalese, Ivorian, Guinean, and Malian

These countries are united by a common colonial language, by their admiration for French food, and by their use of rice, rather than mashes, as a basis for many dishes. Still, the differences between the cuisines will be apparent to anyone who tries all four, which can now readily be done in New York. The Guinean community has soared in number in the last five years, and so, consequently, has the number of its restaurants. Senegalese restaurants, by contrast, have decreased in number while those from the Ivory Coast have proliferated. Although the African restaurants in New York feature an abundance of meat, chicken, fresh seafood, and vegetables, the vast majority of people living in Africa see a piece of meat or chicken once a month or less, and eat almost nothing but rice or porridge smothered in pungent sauces, called "soups." For an idea of what some of the raw materials look like, visit the West African Grocery at 40th Street and 9th Avenue, which sells an astounding assortment of African food products—dried fish, palm oil, herbs and spices, unguents and ointment, even African beer. The smells alone are like a quick vacation to West Africa.

SENEGALESE

Africa Restaurant

**346 W 53rd St near 9th Ave, Manhattan,
212-399-7166, subway: C, E to 50th St
247 W 116th St near 8th Ave, Manhattan,
212-666-9400, subway: B, C to 116th St**

*Senegalese
specialties*

bissap
sorrel beverage

boulettes
garlicky fish balls

cheb
Senegalese fish paella

dakhine
*lamb and cow peas
in peanut sauce*

soupikandia
lamb in okra sauce

The uptown branch is the anchor of Little Africa, and is devoutly decorated with pictures of the Great Mosque at Touba. More recently opened, the downtown branch aspires to nightclub elegance, and has a devoted clientele who seem more like businesspeople than cabdrivers. One day I stumbled on a special of soupikandia, a real rarity in New York. It contained several big pieces of lamb in a chile-sharpened gravy thickened with dried okra and enriched with a couple of fragments of stockfish— the sun-dried fish used as a flavoring agent. I can never resist cheb in a Senegalese restaurant, and was pleasantly surprised at Africa Restaurant's rendition. Instead of the usual bluefish, there was a big hunk of kingfish, firm and coarse textured, stuffed with pureed parsley and garlic, a detail often neglected in New York. The cheb was subtly flavored and fragrant, the rice a deep brown with Maggi seasoning, the Swiss answer to soy sauce. A surprise inclusion was a handful of dried snails, the kind you often see in African markets threaded on sticks. There is also lamb mafé ($7)—not the usual peanut-buttery muck, but a meaty, coarse textured wonder. Like most of the entrees, it's served with rice, although vermicelli and couscous can be substituted. Beware the cheerful yellow Scotch bonnet pepper perched atop the rice. Charcoal grilling is also a particular strong point. Diby ($9.50), a generous plate of four lamb chops, is served with pickled onions that make a nice contrast with the perfectly cooked meat.

Chez GnaGna Koty's Senegal Goree Island

**530 9th Ave near 40th St, Manhattan,
212-279-1755, subway: A, C, E to 42nd St**

This tiny bistro with a big name is the first to serve Senegalese food in the Port Authority area, offering a broader selection than many similar establishments. One rarity is dahkine, a wonderful mush of rice, lamb, and tomato sauce crunchy with roasted peanuts; and boulettes, garlicky fish balls smothered with lemon-sauteed onions. The colorful dining room has attracted an international crowd, with plenty of plain grilled dishes like chicken, fish, and lamb for African-food neophytes. Since incendiary aspects have been toned down, request the excellent homemade chile paste.

Keur n' Deye

737 Fulton St near S Elliot St, Brooklyn,
718-875-4937, subway: C to Lafayette Ave

This restaurant restricts itself to "Senegalese Traditional Home Cooking," according to its business card. Senegalese cuisine is among the best in Africa, featuring fresh seafood and lots of vegetables including okra, yuca, yams, sweet potatoes, cabbage, calabaza (aka Caribbean pumpkin), eggplant, and carrots. The seafood and vegetables are essential elements of tiebou dienn, the national dish, affectionately referred to as "cheb." How it's made: chunks of fish, stuffed with garlic, green onion, and parsley, are fried in palm oil. The fish is removed and water is added to the oil remaining, in which an assortment of vegetables are then boiled. Then rice and a bit of tomato paste and hot pepper are added to the pan. When the rice—dyed a deep red by the palm oil—is done, it is heaped onto a serving platter with the vegetables and fish carefully arranged on top. The cheb here is nicely prepared, though presented nontraditionally in individual servings. This place is the longest running Senegalese restaurant in town, and a real hangout for Fort Greene bohos. Other typical Senegalese dishes include chicken or beef mafé and fish yassa. Don't miss the homemade bissap and ginger drinks.

IVORIAN

African Grill

1496 5th Ave at 120th St, Manhattan,
212-987-3836, subway: 2, 3 to 116th St

Tucked under the chin of the verdant and mountainous Marcus Garvey Park, African Grill occupies the former premises of a Harlem dive known as the Fifth Avenue Hideaway. Inside, java makers replaces the usual booze bottles— including a percolator, an espresso machine, and the redoubtable Mr. Coffee—a tip-off that the proprietors hail from the Cote D'Ivoire, where the brown brew is a ruling passion. A chalkboard broadcasts the daily bill of fare, which might be mistaken for that of a French bistro in the Village. The biggest surprise is ragout ($4), a savory lamb gravy jotted with finely ground meat and poured over hunks of creamy white yam, more filling than potato. Another delight is kidneys ($3) sauteed with plenty of garlic and onions, sided with petit pois and a gob of mayonnaise. We also enjoyed an expertly fried kingfish steak, rubbed with salt, pepper, and herbs, and served on a bed of athieke (pronounced "ah-check-aye"), the national dish of grated cassava stodge. The fish was heaped with a warm mustardy relish of onions, bell peppers, and tomatoes, a delicious accompaniment. [¢]

Ivorian specialties

athieke
cassava meal

claire viande
beef stew

dibi
grilled lamb chops

la firie
rice cooked with okra

poisson
whole fish, usually red snapper

ragout
lamb stew

But the mixture of French and African influences at several earlier meals didn't prepare us for the all-out Gallic binge of Saturday evening supper. Featured were a spiny, pan-roasted fish ($6) served with a vegetable-shot couscous, a trio of long-cooked beef ribs with vermicelli, and a massive fried lamb shank ($10) of concentrated flavor. The oddly butchered shank included two bones with a joint in between, and there was so much meat that the dish went round the table several times without being exhausted. Also excellent was the salad—ripe tomatoes, romaine, purple onions, and red cabbage carefully dressed with a thick homemade vinaigrette. You can't get more Ivorian (or French) than that.

Farfina Coffee Shop

219B W 116th St near 7th Ave, Manhattan,
212-856-8408, subway: 2, 3 to 116th St

They don't get around to making athieke at Farfina until five in the afternoon, so I was out of luck when I arrived around noon on a recent weekday. In spite of an awning that rather comically advertises hot and cold sandwiches, two hot dishes are what's usually available. One is sous, a serviceable lamb stew ($5) with a thick brown gravy that the waitress, who is from Burkina Faso, referred to rather disparagingly—maybe because its meat-intensive blandness didn't seem particularly African. Then I asked about la firie ($4), a dish advertised on a scrap of paper in the window. She nodded approvingly, lifting the lid to reveal a pot of rice cooked with dried okra, observing "Now this is really African." [¢]

Grenier

2264 8th Ave at St. Nicholas Ave, Manhattan,
212-666-0653, subway: A, B, C, D to 125th St

A mural on one wall shows a thatched granary on stilts spewing rice—hence the name Grenier. Behind the counter, a window looks into a tiled kitchen where women in colorful headscarves squat on the floor peeling cassava and plantain. Three dishes ($6) are offered each day, two usually Senegalese. Requesting something from the Ivory Coast, I was brought a lamb soup thickened with eggplant. Perfumy with Scotch bonnet peppers and musky with palm oil, it demanded to be poured over the accompanying plate of creamy rice to soften its powerful flavors. Even so, I left with my mouth on fire. [¢]

Le Worodougou

2192 8th Ave near 120th St, Manhattan,
212-864-6339, subway: B, C to 116th St

This restaurant replaces a previous Senegalese establishment that tried to go upscale with exposed-brick walls and a public relations firm. The trendy walls, at least, remain. The current Ivory Coast scarf is light years different: a plate of perfect rice topped with a choice of okra or spinach sauces, the former dotted with bits of lean lamb and properly viscous, the latter loaded with fish and beef and mellowed with palm oil. Either is only $5 for a belt-busting serving. For a dollar more, get a fried red snapper napped with African tomato salsa and strewn with onions. [¢]

GUINEAN

Kaloum

**126 W 116th St near 6th Ave, Manhattan,
212-864-2845, subway: B, C to 116th St**

Kaloum's extensively refurbished interior is a
symphony of Formica, dominated by contoured cream
benches and maroon tables. There's also a delightful
mural of a West African village with chickens and
goats in the foreground and citizens staring toward an
empty village square as if awaiting the arrival of fast-
food franchises. The menu has been expanded to
include Senegalese as well as Guinean fare, a cuisine
remarkable for its leaf-based sauces. Typical is sauce de feuilles ($5), a stew of beef thick-
ened with potato leaves that generate a deep-green sludge with the faint tang of oxalates.
Served in a soup bowl, this transcendent selection accompanies a huge plate of rice that lets
you know that the meal is fundamentally rice with a little sauce on the side, rather than the
other way around. Kaloum's version of Senegalese cheb, which features bluefish, cabbage,
carrots, and eggplant over brownish rice, was perfectly adequate, but not the knockout the
sauce de feuilles was. As we looked around, we noticed that most of the diners—all male and
dressed in either black leather jackets or three-piece suits—were eating delicious-looking
whole roasted chickens, presented on a bed of salad. Take that, Colonel Sanders! [¢]

Guinean specialties

epinards
*spinach-and-peanut
sauce*

sauce de feuilles
sweet-potato-leaf sauce

soup
*any sauce that goes
over rice*

Kaloum Star

**Classon Ave and Park Pl, Brooklyn,
718-857-4541, subway: 2, 3 to Grand Army Plaza**

Though Guinean, this Prospect Heights micro-cafe also concocts Senegalese and Ivorian
mainstays to please the pan-West African constituency double-parked right outside the door.
The sauce de feuilles is a good bet, deep green and leafy, flavored with smidgens of fish and
meat, delicious over the plate of Uncle Ben's. Ditto the chicken in a mild peanut sauce, made
better as far as I'm concerned by the toughness of the bird. There's also a wonderfully slimy
okra sauce. Sit at a communal table and eat with a big spoon as the black-velvet painting of
Nefertiti beams down on you. [¢]

Mont Loura

**525 Franklin Ave near Fulton St, Brooklyn,
718-398-6002, subway: A, C, S to Franklin Ave**

Named after the tallest mountain in Guinea, this new coffee shop offers a limited range of specialties from the Ivory Coast as well as Guinea. From the former comes athieke and fish, a
snapper fried crisp and flopped on a bed of cassava meal textured like couscous, only denser.

🍽 HARLEM'S LITTLE AFRICA

West 116th Street is the original African outpost in town, spawned by the presence of the Malcolm Shabazz Mosque and a Halal butcher shop. The famous African market has been moved to a newer, fancier premises between 5th and 6th Avenues. It remains to be seen if the tourists will come to this new location, or whether the market will whither, as Africans become wealthy and move to the suburbs. A slew of eateries—10 at last count—still exist on the two blocks west of 6th Avenue and on the adjoining avenues, with new ones springing up to replace those going out of business. The proprietors tend to be inexperienced restauranteurs who don't go in for a lot of the niceties that attract outside patrons and keep them coming back. The African presence on 116th is not limited to eateries, however. A couple of doors east of Africa Restaurant Is Touba Khassayitt (243 W 116th St, 212-280-0827), a store that sells Senegalese religious articles and curlos. The smell of incense wafts out the door, and the prerecorded chant of the muezzin calls the faithful to prayer. There are also hair braiding salons, convenience stores selling African products, and a real Ivory Coast coffee shop. We leave it to your peregrinations to discover the latest mix of African businesses on the block.

An undressed salad of tomato, cucumber, and onion accompanies both (call for the French dressing). Typically Guinean is sauce de feuilles, a dark green slurry of sweet potato leaves dotted with lamb and dried stockfish, with a wonderful okra-like slime provided by the leaves. The proprietors are among the most gracious in the city, but bring your French dictionary. [¢]

MALIAN

Mali-Bo

218 W 116th St near 6th Ave, Manhattan, 212-665-4481, subway: 2, 3 to 116th St

Recently, the street got its first taste of Malian food. Carvings and travel posters decorate the spare interior of Mali-Bo, the most prominent depicting the Grande Mosquee at Djenné, a magnificent adobe structure whose protruding beams keep the mud in

Malian specialties

aloko
fried plantain

tô
millet porridge

place. An ostrich egg tops each of the soaring towers. There is no printed menu, but the waitress gladly recites the offerings in English, French, or Bambara. We asked for tô ($6), a millet porridge eaten in many Sahel countries. Mali-Bo's version substitutes the readily available corn meal for millet. Steamed and unmolded onto the plate from an aluminum takeout container, it makes a handsome display. The "soup" that goes with it features big chunks of beef in a thin tomato and palm-oil sauce. Eat it the traditional way by using your right hand to dip clods of corn pone in the sauce. Floating atop the soup is a wonderful fishy puree of okra flavored with sun-dried stockfish—watch out for the bones.

Another satisfying choice is the whole fish ($7), a two-pounder of the dory family rubbed with salt and perfectly fried. The sweet, flaky flesh is divine if you're not deterred by the scary spines that protrude along its backbone. The entree comes with an abundant salad of tomatoes, lettuce, and onions dressed with a colonial vinaigrette, and a mound of aloko—rounds of sweet fried plantain that are a West African staple. On the edge of the plate is a pool of homemade red sauce, a concoction of tomato paste and habanero peppers that is among the hottest I've ever tasted. [¢]

Soul Food

What we call soul food or, sometimes, Southern cooking, is one of America's proudest inventions, a compilation of African and Native American elements, with some French and Spanish thrown in. The quintessential dishes are so tasty and cost effective that they've made their way into the mainstream American cuisine, after being carried northward by countless individuals over the last century-and-a-half. Maybe brought by the Portuguese to the west coast of Africa, Southern fried chicken is a thing of genius, and who can deny the universal appeal of red beans and cornbread, or collards dotted with smoked meat? The list below is heavy on old-time places that have remained virtually unchanged since Carolina and Georgia immigrants first arrived in Harlem nearly one hundred years ago.

SOUL FOOD

Charles Southern Style Kitchen

2839 8th Ave near 152nd St, Manhattan, 212-926-4313, subway: A, C to 155th St

This double storefront—one side carryout, the other all-you-can eat cafe—is the successor to Charles Mobile Soulfood Kitchen, a van that made stops all over Harlem with the best traditional African-American cooking around. Some say the carryout side is better, but in the cafe there's nothing like eating your fill of turkey-dotted collards, vinegary barbecue ribs, moist and crunchy fried chicken, and macaroni and cheese made fluffy with a bit of egg. The $9.99 tariff ($6.99 at lunch, half price for kids) includes beverage and a slice of melon for dessert.

Soul Food specialties

chitterlings or chitlins
pork small intestines

collard greens
dark leafy vegetable of the cabbage family

salmon croquettes
canned-fish fritters

trotters
pig feet

M & G Diner

383 West 125th Street near 8th Ave, Manhattan, 212-864-7326, subway: A, B, C, D to 125th St

This Harlem old-timer will put almost anything between two slices of white bread. Try the short rib sandwich: four huge hunks of cow in a rich brown gravy with only a few bones to get in the way. The specialty of the house is Southern fried chicken, cooked fresh throughout the day with just a trace of breading on the crunchy skin, and moist throughout. Like it says on the neon sign out front, "Old Fashion But Good." Breakfast served till 1:00 p.m., and don't miss the salmon croquettes.

Majester's

378 Lenox Ave near 130th St, Manhattan, 212-860-9875, subway: 2, 3 to 135th St

It's not much to look at, but this Harlem seafood specialist produces some of the best fish and chips in the city. The delicate flounder filets are lightly battered and crisply fried as you watch, and you get a paper boat piled high with them. The shrimp are not nearly as good, but even better are the crabs, steamed with an agreeable spice mixture and outlandishly cheap at 75 cents each. Bring your own wooden mallet to extract the thin slivers of flesh—you'll see why lump crabmeat is so expensive. [¢]

🍴 GEORGIA SAUSAGE

It all started out when I dropped by Smoke's Seafood and Soul Food Haven at 114th and Fred Douglass, one of my favorite Harlem hangs. I expected to cop their specialty, Georgia sausage, a blistering hot and large-circumference weenie that's plopped on a piece of white bread and extravagantly smeared with mustard. The smoky taste and grainy texture are unforgettable. One day I had asked if it really came from Georgia, and the guy behind the counter fished around in the trash and came up with a plastic wrapper that proved it. Unfortunately, Smoke's now seemed to be permanently closed.

Then I discovered a new place to get Georgia sausage—Umoja's (543 Lenox Ave, 212-495-9413) a meat market that pushes a grill into the street in the afternoon and does hamburgers, Philly cheese steaks, and the sausage ($2.50), which the griller claimed they had been supplying to the doomed Smoke's Haven. On sunny days, Umoja's is not the only place to proffer this Southern treat—freelancers up and down the avenue push makeshift grills out onto the sidewalk, hoping to cop a little business from the nearby Harlem Hospital. Just the thing after your triple bypass!

Margie's Red Rose

**267 West 144th St near 8th Ave, Manhattan,
212-862-8110, subway: A, B, C, D to 145th St**

Located midblock, this ancient Harlem eatery has been overlooked by all but the neighborhood regulars. The very good fried chicken, lightly coated with flour, salt, and pepper, is upstaged by the spectacular collard greens. Tart and sweet, ungreasy, and slow-cooked with a good quantity of chile pepper, they may be the best in town. Whiting was another hit at our table, four filets to an order and sided with potato salad and cole slaw. Only the biscuits were disappointing. Look for your favorite '60s and '70s soul and disco hits on the jukebox.

Pink Tea Cup

**42 Grove St near Bleecker St, Manhattan,
212-807-6755, subway: 1, 9 to Christopher St**

This longtime favorite bills itself as the "foremost soul food restaurant in the Village"—it's the only one as far as I know, although Greenwich Village has been a center of African-American culture since before the Civil War. In our own time, this neighborhood is home to prominent black writers like bell hooks, Stanley Crouch, and Walter Mosley, among others. The four-course lunch special is an unbelievable deal at less than $10, but I'm more likely to make the scene at breakfast for their salmon croquettes, spicy sausage, and unassailable biscuits.

Sherman's Bar-B-Q

2509 7th Ave near 145th St, Manhattan,
212-283-9290, subway: 2, 3 to 145th St

As well as any of the big ticket places like Sylvia's and Copeland's, this modest carryout embodies culinary history. It's not Texas-style hardwood barbecue, but the tangy oven-style that originated in the Carolinas and became Harlem's signature. Choices are limited to savory and mildly smoky pork ribs, chicken that's a bit too rubbery, and pig's trotters that form a gelatinous mass on the plate—an acquired taste, to be sure. As sides, the mustardy potato salad and crunchy coleslaw make durable choices, but more interesting is the spaghetti, served with a Creole meat sauce dotted with onions and green peppers. The antique decor is reason enough to visit this place. [¢]

Singleton's Bar-BQ

525 Lenox Avenue near 136th St, Manhattan,
212-694-9442, subway: 2, 3 to 135th St

Leafing through back issues of the Amsterdam News at the Schomburg Library, I stumbled on a restaurant advertising section dated January 26, 1946. Many intriguing display ads evoked a bygone Harlem—the Swanky Bar and Grill, Braddock Inn ("Laughs—Cocktails and Excellent Food"), and Randolph's Shangri-La ("The Glamour Spot on the Hill"). Sadly, now are all gone. Yet just north of the library lurks a narrow cafe which is certainly as old. Singleton's has a window plastered with emphatic plastic signs offering deals on breakfast, lunch, and Thanksgiving dinner. Inside is a cramped lunch counter with five stools that never seem to be occupied, and a carry-out window that sees most of the action. In the rear dining room, purple-shrouded tables and mirrors stenciled with crazy red squiggles lend a shabby elegance.

Singleton's offers the unreconstructed fare of the Deep South, including plenty that won't find favor with modern nutritionists—pig tail stew, chitterlings, hog maws, and a rollicking combo of pig ears and feet—legacy of the recipes once invented to turn porcine scraps into culinary gold. The amazing $3.95 lunch rarely features any of these, but offers a good selection of soul food's greatest hits. The Carolina-style "chopped bar-bq pork" mothers amorphous chunks in a delicious vinegary glaze. After trying both fried and smothered chicken ($6.95), I'm unable to decide between them—the former sporting the lightest possible dusting of flour and fried to order, the latter drenched in a mellow gravy that's not too salty. Also commendable, surprisingly, is a dense meatloaf nearly blackened from long cooking—it nearly stole the show. [¢]

Soul Fixin's

371 W 34th St near 9th Ave, Manhattan,
212-736-1345, subway: A, C, E to 34th St

Chicken is king at this soul food hang, whether you order it baked, barbecued, or deep-fried (my pick). Or you can make do with just the wings—served Buffalo style. Other mainstays include decent barbecued pork ribs and wonderful whiting, cornmeal-coated and fried to order with skin intact and a few spiny things sticking out here and there. Sides in order of preference: candied yams with a touch of nutmeg, vinegary collard greens, corn off the cob, and macaroni and cheese. Only open weekdays until 7 P.M.

A Taste of Seafood

50 E 125th St at Madison Avenue, Manhattan,
212-831-5584, subway: 4, 5, 6 to 125th St

If you've ever wondered what it feels like to be a sardine, drop by the corner of Madison and 125th. Occupying a prime location still unclaimed by Starbucks, Ben & Jerry's, or The Body Shop, the timeworn storefront enigmatically proclaims "Servants of God" and "A Taste of Seafood." A line snakes out the front door on a sunny winter afternoon, dominating nearly all the floor space inside the narrow premises. Behind the counter, an aproned chef presides over a bank of four bubbling fry-o-lators. Deftly dredging four filets at a time, he keeps the production line going, tossing whiting into the first fryer. This has been Harlem's favorite fish for decades, and at least a dozen places specialize in white bread sandwiches swabbed with artar and Tabasco. The fish is preternaturally fresh, and the chef is careful to watch the temperature and age of the oil, so there is no greasy or rancid taste. A close cousin of hake, whiting—or merluccius bilinearis—is a member of the cod family. Most specimens weigh in at a pound or less, and it has traditionally been a fish of little commercial potential, since the flesh is soft and flaky and best when eaten soon after being caught. The fried shrimp and chicken wings are also emphatically recommended.

Unfortunately, the french fries are nothing special. They're frozen and precut and don't get the chance to develop the brown sheen preferred by fry enthusiasts. Instead, side your fish or wings with the standard Harlem sides, which incorporate Southern and Caribbean faves. The mac and cheese is supreme, each pasta morsel coated with liquid cheese, and with a crusty coating on top that's once again doled out by the employees with an almost eligious equanimity. [¢]

Spanish and Portuguese

Though tapas had been around the city a half-century or more, a fad for them arrived in New York a few years ago and never left, and tapas bars continue to open at the rate of one every three months or so. Some stay close to the Spanish formula; some diddle it by introducing a range of international small dishes. Is sushi tapas? Not if you crave the garlicky and salty kick that true tapas deliver accompanying lusty Spanish reds and toasty sherries. The tapas bars mentioned below stick to the original formula. Most of the restaurants, too, are old-fashioned in style and cuisine. Why are so many, like Sevilla (62 Charles St, 212-929-3189) and El Faro (823 Greenwich St, 212-9298210) located in the West Village? I think it's because of the romance Spanish revolution had for the bohos who once lived there.

New York has only a handful of Portuguese restaurants, perhaps because language isolates Portuguese immigrants in communities like Ironbound in Newark, New Jersey. Accordingly, I've included a couple of places from there, easily attainable by riding the PATH train to its Newark terminus and walking a few blocks down Ferry Street. And don't forget to hang out in one of the great pastry shops (there are about 10) after your meal.

SPANISH

ñ

**33 Crosby St near Broome St, Manhattan,
212-219-8856, subway: 6 to Spring St**

ñ (pronounced "enya"), narrow as a pencil, sports
two copper-topped bars and little additional seating.
After a steady diet of Spanish reds and headache-
inducing sangria at other tapas bars, you'll welcome
the list of 24 sherries. The companion vittles are
admirably suited to the small size of the establishment. I like the little empanadas of tuna, toasts
smeared with olive puree and pimiento, and an
incredible plate of spinach sauteed with ground
almonds that has an exotic North African flavor.

*Spanish
specialties*

bacalao
salt cod

chorizo
wine-flavored sausage

empanada
turnover or pie

paella
*yellow rice cooked with
meat and seafood*

sangria
wine punch

tapas
bar snacks

★ Meigas

**350 Hudson St at King St, Manhattan,
212-627-5800, subway: 1,9 to Houston St**

This elegant newcomer offers Spanish food of superior delicacy and flavor, using traditional
imported ingredients but hiking the presentation (and price) to cooking-school levels. Expect to
pay in the neighborhood of $40 per person for food such as a wonderful tower of artichoke
hearts, crisply fried Serrano ham, and smoky Idiazábal cheese; a stew of tender veal tripe and
cubes of chorizo in a brick-red sauce; and arroz marinero estillo Vasco, a greenish near-paella
of rice cooked with garlic, shallots, parsley oil and several kinds of seafood. The wine list,
composed exclusively of Spanish vintages, is impressive. [$]

Pintxos

**510 Greenwich St near Spring St, Manhattan,
212-343-9924, subway: 1, 9 to Canal St**

Sporting a grotto-like brick dining room decorated with hand-painted wood and antique photos, it's the homey Basque eatery you always dreamed of—well, almost. Though the appetizers are perfect—delicious pickled sardine filets heaped with garlic and parsley, cheesy stuffed
mussels, and a plain salad garnished with white asparagus and artichokes—the entrees are
sometimes bizarrely undergarnished. Baby squid in a savory ink sauce tastes great, but,
served with no vegetables, rice, potato, or side dish of any sort, it's an unsatisfying anticlimax
to the meal.

★ Rio Mar

**7 9th Ave at Little West 12th St, Manhattan,
212-243-9015, subway: A, C, E to 14th St**

This Spanish dowager, located directly across the street from Pastis, is a holdover from the days when the West Village was dominated by Iberian eateries and its location in the meat district had a lot to do with the bargain prices on its heavy chops and steaks. But even better tasting is their seafood: try the transcendent hot octopus appetizer (then save the rest of the sauce for glue), the bacalao stewed with potatoes, or queen of the menu, broiled lobster strewn with mussels, clams, and shrimp. It's a bargain if you split it between two—it's either that, or you'll be taking most of it home. The rough-and-tumble crowd in the downstairs bar used to be your guarantee of authenticity, now fight the suits and ties for floor space at peak hours. The tapas and sangria are worth it.

Spain

**113 W 13th St near 6th Ave, Manhattan,
212-929-9580, subway: F to 14th St; L to 6th Ave**

Wipe off the dusty glass case out front and be rewarded with the sight of yellowed reviews 30 years old, featuring great names from the past like Martin Burden and Craig Claiborne. Then make the journey into the past by commuting down the dark sunken hallway past the bar, past a tiny afterthought of a dining room, past the kitchen, and into the skylit rear room, festooned with paintings ancient and modern—meaning from 1960 or so. Sunflowers by Van Gogh has pride of place, but the eye-socking cadmium yellows have long since withered to dark browns, helped along by decades of atomized grease that comes from the kitchen like fog off the Okefenokee.

The pungent food is just as you remember it—a massive paella with more volume devoted to shrimp, clams, chicken, chorizo, and lobster tail than to rice; a simple salad with dressing like bottled chile sauce; a bowl of mussels steamed in white wine with garlic; and—the perpetual amuse gueule—short ribs cooked to the texture of stiff rope, and brushed with a tarry sauce that makes Worcestershire seem bland.

Xunta

174 1st Ave near 11th St, Manhattan, 212-614-0620, subway: L to 1st Ave

The East Village's favorite tapas bar got off to a slow start when it opened in the former Pete's Spice, but now it's jumping. A bit of luck gets us a table after a 20-minute wait. The 32 selections, priced from $1.50 to $11, are pleasantly doctrinaire except for a few Galician twists, like tasty empanadas of tuna and salt cod cooked as massive pies instead of turnovers. Some of the simplest tapas are the best, like a slightly charred chorizo or a plate of dry-cured ham. More ambitious but equally delicious is a stew of scallops and white asparagus accented with wine and served in a big shell. A flaming bowl of mushrooms is brought to the table by a waiter who, we couldn't help but notice, had all the hair singed off his arm.

PORTUGUESE

Luzia's

**429 Amersterdam Ave near 81st St,
Manhattan, 212-595-2000,
subway: 1, 9 to 79th St**

Why aren't there any really cheap Portuguese
places in town? Portugal, vying with Ireland and
Spain as poorest country in Western Europe, might be
expected to spawn budget eateries. Luzia's, unfortunately, is not cheap, but the food is well worth the
splurge. If Portuguese fish stew is available—grab
it! Also get anything made with shellfish, especially
the dish of pork, clams, potatoes, and chorizo that's
characteristic of the meat/ shellfish combos of
southern Portugal. Desserts also recommended,
especially when they come right out of the oven in
the afternoon.

Portuguese specialties

broa
dark cornmeal loaf

caldo verde
kale soup

**carne de porco
a alentejana**
pork and shellfish stew

linguica
thick garlic sausage

piri-piri
hot sauce

★ O Padeiro

**614 6th Ave near 20th St, Manhattan,
212-414-9661, subway: F to 23rd St**

Situated on a stretch of 6th Avenue once known as the Ladies Mile, O Padeiro ("The Baker")
was spawned by a Newark bakery that delivers excellent Portuguese bread to New York groceries. Overflowing baskets of bread hang from the ceiling, while gorgeous hand-painted tiles
show peasants harvesting and baking. Miniature tables scatter the L-shaped dining area;
there's also seating at the bar, over which plate-glass hexagons cantilever to hold drinks and
plates. It's the sort of cosmopolitan place you encounter in Lisbon, where patrons linger for
hours over coffee and a sandwich.

O Padeiro ties everything to bread. Broa, a loaf compounded of white cornmeal and rye,
stars in the fresh sardine sandwich ($5.50). Its moisture and sweetness provide the perfect
context for the briny grilled fish, which is lightly mashed with lemon mayonnaise and
broad-leaf parsley. At dinner the menu shifts from sandwiches, salads, and soups to what
the restaurant calls Portuguese tapas. There is no tapas tradition in Portugal, but every
corner bar puts a chalkboard out front offering two or three earthy dishes every evening at
modest prices, and from this class of food O Padeiro takes its crepuscular inspiration.
There's a rib-sticking casserole of white beans, sausage, and presunto ham, and an even
better bake of salt cod, potatoes, and onions served in an earthenware pot. Also typical is a
cauldron of baby clams under so much garlic that even fanatics will wipe most of it away.
But most remarkable is açorda, a dish that begins with a peppery shellfish broth to which

the improvising cook adds fresh shrimp, cilantro, garlic, and plenty of olive oil. Gobbets of stale bread and whipped eggs are then tossed into the bubbling mixture, creating a puddingish texture that's at once soupy, solid, gooey, and wonderful.

Pão

322 Spring St at Greenwich St, Manhattan,
212-334-5464, subway: 1, 9 to Canal St

The room is warm and compact. White-clothed tables by tall windows face out on Greenwich and Spring. This desolate corner recalls Soho and Lo-Bro in their heyday, before the mercantile hoards made their assault. The limited menu at Pão offers a pleasing overview of regional Portuguese cooking. From the Alentejo in the south comes carne de porco a alentejana, a novel combination of pork chunks and small clams. An appetizer enjoyed all over Portugal is a length of linguica flamed in brandy. The incineration of this thick garlic sausage takes place tableside in a ceramic barbecue shaped like a pig. Native to the Algarve region is a seafood combo steamed in white wine and garlic in a cataplana, a hinged pot that looks like a Valkyrie's brassiere. It was OK the night we tried it, although the copper vessel contained only two types of seafood, cockles and shrimp. This paucity stands in contrast to the Portuguese passion for all forms of crustaceans—even barnacles are considered a great delicacy.

Pic-Nic

233 Ferry St near Wilson Ave, Newark, New Jersey,
973-589-4630, subway: PATH to Newark

At this Portuguese barbecue, the main room is dominated by a broad counter behind which stand two guys, a cashier and a full-time pitmeister. The latter presides over two coffin-shaped brick pits pushed against the wall. Suspended over one grill is a score of splayed chickens on a hand-cranked rotisserie. To a quarter of the birds he administers a dense red piri-piri sauce that mostly slides off into the fire. Every once in a while he picks up a bag of charcoal briquettes and dribbles them into the pit to keep the smoke going. I ordered a half chicken and a half order of pork ribs, which the cashier extracted from a holding area, cut up expertly, and dumped into a huge aluminum carryout tray. He filled the balance of the space with a volume of french fries sufficient to feed three people by itself, then crimped foil over the top, with a few holes punched to allow steam to escape. [¢]

Seabras Marrisquiera

87 Madison St, Newark, New Jersey,
201-465-1250, subway: PATH to downtown Newark

Founded in 1989, this is Newark's only Portuguese seafood restaurant. Sure, every Ferry Street chow shack serves a substantial number of dragged-from-the-ocean specialties, but Seabras is typical of a style of Portuguese eatery that hasn't migrated here. In the rear is a formal dining room with white cotton tablecloths and a menu sporting dozens of pricy selections; in the front is a beautiful tiled bar serving a handful of bargain-priced, seasonal specialties prepared with tons of garlic. Tops on a recent visit was a plate of sardines ($8) which, astonishingly, included six large fish flamed so the skin was blackened in spots, ringed with boiled potatoes and sided with a small salad. I also had a cauldron of cockles, cooked with scads of garlic, cilantro, and olive oil, making a very thick and fragrant broth. Soon after we went for a seafood stew that came thick with rice like risotto. A giant grilled shrimp cavorted on top, and the dish contained small and large chunks of more kinds of fish than I could identify, but certainly including dorade, sword, cod, and flounder. We also had a plate of excellent chorizo, tangy with wine, sliced and sauteed and served with rice and salad; and a dish of beef Lavrador style ($10), cooked in an incredibly concentrated tomato sauce. [kid friendly]

Thai

Until recently, Gotham's Thai food lovers had a difficult choice: hang their heads in shame or move to California. Then Sripraphai appeared, and we had at least one place to brag about. Now, more great Thai eateries are accumulating in Queens, like Kway Tiow, joining the few good places—mainly working-class joints catering to office workers—in Manhattan. And don't forget the plethora of places sired by Thai Cafe and popularized by its most famous offspring, Planeat Thailand, itself no longer recommened since it turned into a sushi lounge and cocktail bar. What are the elements of great Thai food? An emphasis on sharp, emphatic flavors like galangal, lemongrass, cilantro, and holy basil (a smaller cousin of the Italian leaf with more pungency), and a menu that runs from homely noodle dishes that use the everything-but-the-kitchen-sink approach, to soupy curries with plenty of burn, to savory stuffed omelets, to barely sauced stir fries that depend on garlic, fish sauce, and a handful of basil leaves for flavor.

THAI

Amarin

**617 Manhattan Ave near Driggs Ave,
Brooklyn, 718-349-2788,
subway: G to Nassau Ave**

A renegade staffer from Planeat Thailand established this joint in Polish Greenpoint, and the food
has some of the same sparkling qualities. "Naked
shrimp salad" features six perfectly grilled crustaceans ringing baby lettuces with a light chile
dressing; even the house salad is a revelation, decorated with lattice potato chips and bathed in a
peanut sauce not even slightly sweet. Look to the
specials list, though, for the best choices, such as a
delightful red curry of rubbery homemade fish cake
with green beans and eggplant. Surprisingly, some
of the dishes poach on Italian territory.

Thai specialties

bu du
fish-flavored sauce

jungle curry
*soupy pork and
eggplant curry*

mee grob
shrimp-and-noodle salad

nems
pork sausage

pla chu chee
fish in peanut sauce

tom yum
sour shrimp soup

Bangkok Cafe

**27 E 20th St near Broadway, Manhattan,
212-228-7681, subway: N, R to 23rd St**

A particularly fine concoction is crispy duck salad ($7.95)—boneless pieces of crunchy-
skinned mallard with red and green onions, cashews, baby lettuces, roasted chiles, and fresh
pineapple dressed with lime juice. It works, believe it or not. Any dish on the menu with the
first word "basil" is also topnotch. At most Thai eateries, the holy basil leaves are tossed in
with the stir-fry, so their pungency is enjoyed only when you chomp down on the actual leaf.
At Bangkok Cafe the leaves are chopped fine and fried in the oil before other ingredients are
added, resulting in a basil-y flavor that permeates the entire dish. Basil fried rice and basil
noodles (both $6.95) are particularly good showcases for this technique. Also recommended is
anything made with the green curry paste, which packs a much greater wallop than usual.

Bua Thai

**50 West St near Rector St, Manhattan,
212-514-8118, subway: 1, 9 to Rector St**

The scent of holy basil fills the air as you plunge into this downscale crowd-pleaser at the
mouth of the Brooklyn-Battery Tunnel. Skip the appetizers, since the entrees are huge—try
spicy rice noodle, wok'ed with green pepper, dried red chiles, and plenty of garlic and pork.
Also recommended is the vegetarian Thai salad loaded with tofu, a cornucopia of vegetables,

and fine bean-thread noodles in a chile-and-lime dressing. Watch the steam table for daily specials, like an anisey stew of pork and boiled eggs in sweet dark sauce. [¢]

Cheers

**612 Metropolitan Ave near Lorimer St, Brooklyn,
718-599-4311, subway: L to Lorimer St**

This unfortunately named cafe takes over from the mothership of Moondog, the local ice cream chain that overextended itself, then vanished overnight. The current occupant offers Siamese with a few Malaysian twists, and bohos fleeing the tourist crush of Planeat Thailand have filtered in. Appetizers of steamed mussels and mee grob, a sweet salad of fried noodles and shrimp, are excellent, especially if you spoon on the homemade hot sauce which tastes like Hong Kong XO. And while pad thai flounders, the green and red curries are delicious, served with plenty of rice-soaking gravy. [¢]

Jai-Ya

**396 3rd Ave near 29th St, Manhattan, 212-889-1330, subway: 6 to 28th St
81-11 Broadway, Elmhurst, Queens,718-651-1330, subway: G, R to Elmhurst Ave**

If you can't make it to the original, the Manhattan offspring will have to do. You can't go wrong ordering shrimp: start with the provocatively-named naked shrimp, barely cooked and tossed with lemongrass and green onion in a sharp lemon dressing, then proceed to an entree of shrimp with ground pepper and garlic—six jumbos deep-fried with a coating that's mainly garlic. Although the Thai food reaches a consistently high level, crowded tables and frantic service discourage frequent visits to the Manhattan location, while the Queens original is often half-empty. The weekday lunch specials are a particularly good deal at both places.

★ Kway Tiow

**83-47 Dongan Ave near Broadway, Queens,
718-476-6743, subway: G, R to Elmhurst Ave**

This modest storefront on a side street off Elmhurst's humming Broadway is decorated with tons of carved wood and Buddhist iconography, the walls peppered with antique sepia-toned photos, including a water buffalo pulling a sledge, headdressed royal children, and a pair of handsome elephants threatening to swamp a thatched houseboat. Watercraft are a key motif at Kway Tiow; the elegantly simple appetizer of fried beancurd lands in a ceramic sampan garnished amid ships with carved vegetables, a sweet chile sauce stowed aft. Also afloat is the ethereal peek-gai yat sai ($5.25), a brace of outsize chicken wings stuffed with mushrooms and delicate bean-thread vermicelli. It's worth the price just to see how it's done. Salads make great starters, too, especially the wonderfully spicy toss of bamboo-shoots and purple onions in a woozy fish-sauce dressing.

An acid test passed with flying colors is tom yum ($3.50). If you like tart, this soup will make you swoon. In it float lime leaves and slender reeds of lemongrass, the sourness further amplified by lime juice and astringent green chiles. At the bottom lurks a thick plug of galangal, a woody, ginger-like rhizome imparting a perfume that orchestrates the other bold flavors. The large size ($5.95) is so shrimp-rich and chile-potent that it can bathe a tableful of diners in sweat. Turn to the xeroxed specials at the rear of the menu to find unusual dishes like luad moo ($6.95), a pig offal soup featuring liver, heart, and intestines flavored with blood. Another time we tried a wonderful dish of shucked mussels fried into an eggy pancake, the orange-lipped shellfish making a dramatic color contrast against the yellow egg. [¢, kid friendly]

Royal Siam

240 8th Ave near 21st St, Manhattan,
212-741-1732, 10011, subway: C, E to 23rd St

The "royal" cuisine of Thailand was a 19th century invention of a gourmet king. This is one of my favorite places to enjoy it, with a broad range of carefully prepared dishes accented with ginger, garlic, and holy basil, and swimming in rich coconut milk. Check out the ethereal duck salad—nuggets of crunchy-skinned Daffy tossed with purple onion, roasted cashews, orange sections, red peppers, and tempeh in a tangy tamarind dressing. Or pick any of the whole-fish preparations like pla chu chee—sea bass smothered in a unique curried peanut sauce that will leave you licking the plate after the last morsel is gone.

★ Sripraphai

6413 39th Ave near Roosevelt Ave, Queens,
718-899-9599, subway: 7 to Woodside-61st St

The decor is so plain here that the high points are a pair of large television monitors. The proprietor flashes a crooked smile and warns us that jungle curry ($7.50) is way hot, putting us on notice that he doesn't intend to pull his punches. Entering in a clay pot, it bobs with tiny Thai eggplants streaked red and green, pork strips, lime leaves, string beans, bamboo, and basil, with plenty of liquid to soak the accompanying plate of rice. The awesome and lingering hotness comes from both red and black pepper competing to singe your membranes, with a tiny dish of fresh green chiles in vinegar offering a third vector for the seriously deranged.

But there are plenty of blander options: pan-fried egg with ground pork ($6), a crisp omelet stuffed with green onions and meat that's a favorite Siamese luncheon dish; and "saute noodle with meat chili, basil leave" ($6.50), matching broad rice noodles and strips of red pepper whose sweetness contrasts nicely with the basil's bite. Our favorite not-hot selection, however, is rice with mixed vegetables and bu-du sauce—a spunky, fish-flavored dressing. Pour it over the layered bean sprouts, cucumber matchsticks, sprigs of cilantro, and rice dusted with shrimp flakes, toss like a salad, inhale it, then tell me: how do they do that bu-du so well? Highly recommended, and also unusual, is crispy catfish in spicy sauce ($9). The flesh has been pounded into a lattice and then fried, producing a texture like loofah or cruller. Served with plenty of vegetables in a hot and tart sauce, the fish magically retains its feathery texture in the face of the liquid onslaught.

Thai Cafe

925 Manhattan Ave at Kent St, Brooklyn,
718-383-3562, subway: G to Greenpoint Ave

This cafe in Polish Greenpoint was progenitor of Planeat Thailand (141 N 7th St, 718-599-5758), the wildly popular Williamsburg eatery that recent expanded into a giant L-shaped premises, becoming more bar and sushi bar than Thai restaurant. Make the hike and hang with the parent.

The squid salad appetizer—tender squid mixed with shredded iceberg lettuce, cilantro, cucumber, tomato, scallions, onions, and julienned carrots in a fiery-sweet chile dressing—is large enough for lunch. Pad thai ($5.25) is a mixture of rice stick noodles, grilled shrimp, green onions, and tiny chunks of dried bean curd film with an agreeable heap of bean sprouts on top. Sliced chicken with bamboo shoots and basil in coconut curry sauce is exactly what it says, but this doesn't hint at the transcendent orange color of the sauce in the serving bowl. With a similar concern for display, a grilled shrimp salad containing tomato, onion, green onion, and cucumber is flanked by a haystack of grated purple cabbage. The beef with zucchini in a dark peanut sauce is set off by a precise array of cucumber slices. Nearly all of the 50 menu items are priced in the $5 to $10 range. [¢]

Yum

129 W 44th St near 6th Ave, Manhattan,
212-819-0554, subway: B, D, F, Q to 42nd St

You'll be disappointed if you expect carved vegetable garnishes or ethnographic geegaws at this no-frills, weekdays-only lunch counter—but the food is more surely and subtly spiced than the city's more pretentious Thai eateries. Best summer choice is yum ped, nuggets of crunchy duck tossed with apple, orange, pineapple, and tempeh in a delicious tart dressing. We also fought over a pad thai that was not the usual circus of discarded meat and seafood, but a barely dressed heap of noodles and big shrimp with clear, sharp flavors. The place could use more ventilation, so you may want to take the food to Bryant Park. [¢]

Trinidadian, Guyanese, and Surinamese

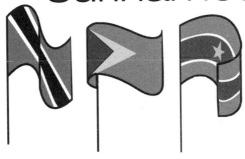

You probably already know that a roti is a Caribbean sandwich made by folding an Indian flatbread called dal poori around a variety of ingredients, usually curried. Rotis are enjoyed in Jamaica, Trinidad, Guyana, and Surinam, the latter two of which, even though they're technically not in the Caribbean, have more in common with the West Indies than with South America. All four countries have East Indian populations who make big contributions to the local chow. The sandwich-style roti, so called because you can pick it up and eat it like a sandwich if it isn't too soupy, seems to have originated in Trinidad, where multiple variations have evolved, including "bust up shot," a version made with a flatbread called pharatha that's served separately and "busts up" when unrolled. Another variation is called doubles—a pair of mini-flatbreads with stewed chickpeas in between, usually eaten on weekends, and maybe created in direct emulation of Lord Sandwich's creation. In spite of the fact that Trinidad is the world leader in rotis, folks in the States are more familiar with Jamaican rotis, which are much easier to score. Of course, they're delicious wherever you find 'em. Guyanese joints in Brooklyn often serve rotis in order to satisfy a pan-Caribbean clientele, but according to a Guyanese acquaintance, this is rare in Guyana.

Like a lock of hair on the forehead of Brazil, Surinam clings to the northeast coast of South America. The food of this former Dutch colony, 90 per cent roadless rain forest, is among the most diverse in the world, reflecting an amazing ethnic mix of Amerindians, East Indians, Javanese, Chinese, Europeans, and Africans, among whom are the Bushnegroes—descendants of 18th century slaves who disappeared into the outback, only to return in the 1980s as a revolutionary movement called Jungle Commando. Another surprising component is the Indonesians, who came to South America as indentured plantation workers in the late 19th century and still retain many of their folkways, including gamelan music and a love of street-food vendors called warungs.

TRINIDADIAN

★ A & R West Indian Restaurant and Roti Shop

2345 8th Ave near 126th St, Manhattan, 212-749-8758, subway: A, B, C, D to 125th St

To enter A & R, navigate a narrow hallway past a Plexiglas-boxed shoe repair shop that looks like a diorama in the Natural History Museum. Behind is a tiny dining room, with a still tinier kitchen. Kitchenward, a man with a stately carriage meanders around checking the metal receptacles scattered around the room. His face is Indian, but his dress is Caribbean. In the doorway is a padded folding chair for takeout customers to sit on while their orders are being prepared. The bill of fare features rotis but also includes curries over rice, beef patties, Jamaican soups, and a section called "American Favorites" that includes cheeseburgers, beef sausages, shwarma, and something called Steak 'n Take. All meat is Halal, since many Trinidadians are Muslims. [¢, halal]

Ali's Trinidad Roti Shop

1267 Fulton St near Nostrand Ave, Brooklyn, 718-783-0316, subway: A, C to Nostrand Ave

There's a line out the door at this popular Bed-Stuy roti shack, where the marquee invites "Hurry, Hurry, Come for Curry." Of the rotis, my fave is conch—a plenitude of tender gastropod vying with potato for domination of the brown, thyme-inflected gravy. Or pick from curries of shrimp, goat, oxtail, and beef, any of which can also be poured over peas and rice. A particular favorite is the vegetarian corn chowder, mobbed with okra, taro, carrots, and microdumplings, and thickened Chinese-style with cornstarch. Note that the sweet and frothy peanut punch is much better as a dessert. [¢, halal]

Glenda's Home Cooking

854 St. John's Pl near Nostrand Ave, Brooklyn, 718-778-1997, subway: 3 to Nostrand Ave

The yellow awning that promised more dishes than I can list dragged me in, even though the view through the window was eclipsed by a forest of potted cacti. Paneled rec-room style, the interior is lined with carefree pictures of life in the islands. The stew fish is wonderful—a big slab of fried kingfish smeared with tangy tomato gravy and plumped down on a bed of well-oiled rice and peas. Also fantastic is the goat roti, crammed with Halal meat and curried potatoes, so carefully constructed—as one regular pointed out to me—that you can pick it up and eat it like a sandwich. If you dare, wash it down with mauby, a beverage that tastes like a cross between bubble gum and quinine. [¢, halal]

Molly's Bakery

820 Nostrand Ave at Lincoln Ave, Brooklyn,
718-773-8691, subway: 3 to Nostrand Ave

Catty-corner from Glenda's Home Cooking is Molly's Bakery, a modest establishment with a couple of very cluttered counters and a few stools looking out the smeary picture window. The pay phone, in constant use, is the center of the establishment, and Molly herself seemed to always be on it. They make great cheap rotis here—chicken, vegetarian, oxtail, and goat. The dahl poorie wrapper is a little thicker and less yielding than most, but the potato filler is particularly savory and dense. The counterguy, who has a dish-towel wrapped haphazardly around his noggin (not a religious turban, just a dish-towel), ladles on lots of chickpeas. The cost: three or four dollars for a whopper. [¢]

Terry's Gourmet

575 6th Ave at 16th St, Manhattan,
212-571-3733, subway: F, L to 14th St/6th Ave

Terry's Gourmet is a carryout deli with gleaming fixtures and extensive glass cases displaying a profusion of cosmetically perfect prepared dishes. Normally I would run in the opposite direction, only I happen to know that the proprietors and crew are from Trinidad, and if you look behind the counter you will see a tiny steamtable where rotis are prepared. There are only three choices—goat, chicken, and vegetable ($4-$6). They use good, fresh dahl poori. The potato filling is punctuated with chickpeas, and the goat curry that goes with it has a mild taste. There are bones in some of the goat pieces, so watch out! Ditto with the chicken. The counterman will ask if you want the roti wrapped around the filling or with the ingredients separated (although he didn't refer to the latter as a "bust up shot," it was). I prefer the wrapped-up form, although eating around the bones requires some concentration (like one of those barbecued rib and Wonder Bread sandwiches Down South). Make sure you ask for some of the Trinidadian hot sauce, which they keep in a paper cup, served out with a plastic spoon. [¢]

GUYANESE

Flavored With One Love

1941 Madison Ave near 125th St, Manhattan,
212-426-4446, subway: 4, 5, 6 to 125th St

Like it says on the menu: "Dishes bursting with flavor served in a warm and delightful atmosphere." This modest East Harlem Guyanese cooks up a wonderful chicken soup, laced with oregano and powerfully fortified with potatoes and starchy finger dumplings. Any of several savory stews and curries (think oxtail, goat, chicken, or vegetable) can be loaded into a dahl poorie to make a roti, or served with a more fragile Indian flatbread to make a "bust-up-shot". The rice and peas are also fab, especially with a little beef gravy poured on. Just the thing for a cold winter's afternoon. [¢]

Guyana Roti House

3021 Church Ave near Nostrand Ave, Brooklyn,
718-940-9413, subway: 2, 5 to Church Ave

This modest Flatbush lunch counter cum bakery has a roti selection that always includes shrimp, chickpeas, chicken, goat, and beef. Also check out the Guyanese snacks, like the East-Indian-inspired mittai and crummer—little fingers of fried dough—or the more familiar cod cakes and tamarind balls, all priced at $1 per package. Beverage selection includes Caribbean standards of mauby, sea moss, and ginger beer even though Guyana, of course, is located on the South American continent. [¢]

SURINAMESE

Sorrento Bakery

88-17 Jamaica Ave, Queens,
718-846-0313, subway: J, Z to Woodhaven Blvd

Don't be fooled by the Italian name: although it's also still a bakery, Sorrento is the city's sole Surinamese eatery. Glass cases filled with biscotti, cream puffs, and sfogliatelle dominate a room whose decor is limited to a framed Lord's Prayer and a pair of ebony cranes, whose heads incline toward the ceiling as if looking for a speck in the spotless interior. The expansive menu offers West Indian standards you'd expect to find in Jamaica, Trinidad, or Guyana, like roti. The turkey version ($5.50) features big gobbets of bony poultry with potatoes and chickpeas in a thick curry gravy, so soupy it must be eaten by breaking off little bits of the bread and dipping it in the sauce. The menu also includes Hispano-Caribbean favorites like arroz con pollo and pernil. A version of nassi goreng ($5.50), Indonesian fried rice, comes topped with an appealing stewed chicken tasting of palm sugar, soy sauce, and garlic. Briny cucumber pickles on one side support a fiery homemade relish of shredded habanero peppers. Also Javanese is sauto ($2.50), a variation on Mom's chicken soup featuring a triple starch whammy: noodles, rice, and matchsticks of fried potato. In a distinctly African vein is telo, jagged yuca chunks french-fried till the interior is pillowy soft, then inundated with a funky dried-fish gravy. [¢]

Turkish

Turkish cuisine is like a mule and a horse yoked together and pulling in opposite directions. The mule is the vegetarian side of the menu, said to have been inspired by the Persians, but adopted by the Turks and force-fed to their conquerees from Eastern Europe to the Middle East. Many nations now claim babaganoush and hummus as their own, but you'll often find the best versions in Turkish joints. The horse, of course, is the meat, though only in France and perhaps Turkey itself will you literally find it coming from a horse. Instead, the favored flesh is lamb, and the Turks have dozens of ways to butcher it, mince up, mix it, and grill it. Over the last few years, many places have begun to substitute chicken or even Cornish hen or turkey in their kebabs, but this seems to be more an economic measure than a knee-jerk to the laughable health consciousness of our sorry age. At any rate, not only will any Turkish restaurant satisfy your vegetarian friends, it will allow non-vegetarians to simultaneously indulge in some of the most toothsome meat around. By the way, all the places below merit the vegetarian friendly notation, but I've reserved it for those with a particularly long and diverse choice of meze.

TURKISH

Bay Shish Kebab

**2255 Emmons Ave near E 23rd St,
Brooklyn, 718-769-5396,
subway: D, Q to Sheepshead Bay**

An expanded appetizer list features five eggplant
choices alone, ranging from the too-familiar
babaganoush ($3) to the more obscure soslu patli-
can ($3.50)—the Barney-like vegetable cubed and
stewed with tomatoes, green chiles, and chunky
garlic. The olive-oil ooze was quickly staunched with
freshly made pide bread flecked with nigella and
sesame seeds. The pide also goes great with the
busier-than-usual cacik—a dipping sauce of homemade yogurt dominated by garlic despite the best
efforts of dill and mint. The menu also offers
obscure kebabs like calf liver, garlicky and peppery
beyti, and the criminal's nemesis, cop shish
($9.75)—chunklets of baby lamb. All were distin-
guished by moist, tasty meat and plenty of smoke.

*Turkish
specialties*

adana kebab
*lamb or beef chopped
with peppers*

barbunya
kidney bean stew

doner
twirling mystery meat

iman bayildi
*stuffed and braised
eggplant*

kisir
bulgur salad

piyaz
white bean salad

shepherd's salad
diced raw salad

But there are also a handful of Uzbek dishes on the menu. The reason: there's a large Turkish
population in that former Soviet republic; in fact, one of the restaurant's cooks grew up there.
Mantu dumplings ($3 the pair) are massive doughy pouches more flavorful than their simple
filling of lamb, parsley, and onions suggests. Samsa loads a similar filling into a pastry crust—
like Indian samosa, baked rather than fried. The best choice, however, is the national dish:
palav ($6), a deliriously oily entree of rice simmered with carrots, onions, chickpeas, and lamb.
As it cooks, rice anneals to the bottom of the pan; scraped off and strewn on top, it forms a
crunch barrier.

★ Bereket

**187 E Houston St at Orchard St, Manhattan,
212-475-7700, subway: F to 2nd Ave**

This round-the-clock Turkish fast food, within striking distance of most East Village rock clubs,
has recently undergone an earth-shaking expansion that's left it twice as large as before, with
a gleaming premises that looks like a strip-mall restaurant on the moon. I'm happy to report
that the food, however, is even better than before. If the weather outside is sweltering, go for
the cold appetizer plate ($7.50), your choice of four from eight displayed in the unsmudgy
refrigerator counter. If the baba rocks, then so does the kisir, a cracked wheat concoction
leaking red oil like a damaged spaceship. There's also a red-bean stew with plenty of chunky

vegetables (definitely not the frozen kind) and a floppy toss of roasted eggplant sweetened with tomatoes and peppers. The kebabs, too, are now exemplary, and you'll pardon me if, as is nearly always the case, I prefer the adana (on a platter, $7 for one, $9 for two). [¢, vegetarian friendly]

Beyti Kebab

4105 Park Ave at Pathmark St, Union City, NJ,
201-865-6281, subway: none

When 20 of us celebrated a birthday here, our ravenous party ate plate after plate of meze and mixed kebabs piled high on platters, and drank glass after glass of raki for a bargain price of less than $20 per person. The hummus was one of the best I've ever tasted, coarsely textured but light, with a restrained touch to the garlic. It's served with fine Turkish bread, a round, yeasty loaf with a wrinkled brown crust. Someone with a more moderate appetite is likely to get by for $12 or so. Chicken shish kebabs, marinated in yogurt and moister than most, are especially good. Don't miss kisir, a salad of bulgur with a thick, peppery tomato dressing.

Gyroland

351 2nd Ave near 21st St, Manhattan,
212-254-3200, subway: 6 to 23rd St

A new theme park specializing in physics? No, a new Turkish restaurant in a neighborhood where several similar establishments have failed in recent years. The adana kebab of chopped lamb is appropriately peppery and oniony, but even better is the Alexander kebab, slices of moist beef gyro doused with tomato sauce and layered over pita fragments; a cloud of thick yogurt accompanies. Among starters the Mediterranean salad heaped with feta and the smoky babaganoush were preferred. The lighting in the spacious dining room is so dazzling, you'd better bring sunglasses.

Kazan Turkish Cuisine

95-36 Queens Blvd, Queens,
718-897-1509, subway: G, R to 63rd Dr

The eight-item vegetarian appetizer plate at this Rego Park restaurant is spectacular, including smoky hummus, lebni—thickened yogurt zapped with garlic and walnuts—a sweet and savory stew of eggplant and tomatoes called patlican soslu, and a bulging grape leaf stuffed with rice and pine nuts. Sigara bureka, thin pastry flutes stuffed with dilled cheese, is also fab. With starters like these, the more predictable kebabs come as a slight disappointment. My fave is kasarli kofte, little grilled cheeseburgers with the feta cheese inside. Another plus: the staff is particularly friendly and accommodating. [vegetarian friendly]

★ Sahara

2337 Coney Island Ave near Ave U, Brooklyn,
718-376-8594, D, F to Ave U

Disregard the location along Desolation Row. Even if the food wasn't first-rate, the fact that Sahara bakes its own bread would be enough to make you check it out. That bread is a flat oblong loaf generously sprinkled with yellow and black sesame, well-browned and crusty. The interior is white, porous, resilient—perfect bread, fit to be compared with any bread on earth—especially good with the excellent meze. Arnavut cigeri ($7) is cubes of baby calf liver lightly dusted with flour and sauteed in paprika-laced oil. The version of patlican salatasi ($4) varies the usual plainish puree of eggplant and garlic with fragments of tomato and sweet red pepper. King of the entrees on the recently expanded menu is the mixed grill ($16.95), with four different preparations of lamb: doner kebab, shish kebab, lamb chops, and adana kebab. Ask to substitute beyti kebab for adana, because it contains hot red chiles and ots more garlic. Both are a matter of pride for Turkish restaurants, since preparing them requires a special technique in which two sharp swords are wielded simultaneously, one in each hand. Watch out!

Late on a hot summer evening, the vine-festooned rear garden is one of the best places to hang in Brooklyn—you won't believe you're only a hundred feet from Coney Island Avenue. [outdoor dining]

Sahara Grill

558 7th Ave at 40th St, Manhattan,
212-391-6554, subway: 1, 2, 3, 9 to Times Sq

The gang from the late lamented Ali Baba has made a dramatic return in this corner-located shoebox in the Garment Center, open 24 hours. Gyros of chicken or lamb are the preferred flesh, with the poultry so fresh it almost jumps off the cylinder and into the sandwich. Pick the yogurt sauce over the tahini, and ask for an additional dab of chile sauce. Among meze, the babaganoush is best, with enough raw garlic to blow the top of your head off. Also look for a pot of non-menu provender bubbling on the burner—it's often what the staff are making for themselves. On a recent afternoon, it was a scramble of eggs and long green chiles. Though it's mainly carryout, there are a handful of tables where you can sit and ponder why a Turkish place is named Sahara Grill. [¢]

Turkish Grill

193 Bleecker St near MacDougal St, Manhattan,
212-674-8833, subway: A, B, C, D, E, F, Q to W 4th St

If you want a price break on your Ottoman nosh, head down to Turkish Grill, the carryout branch of the pricey **Turkish Kitchen** (386 3rd Ave, 212-679-1810), which brought a new sophistication to Ottoman menus several years ago with ingredients like tripe, quail, and octopus, while other East Side Turks still limited themselves to kebabs and pilaf. The decor is a garish cut above that of the neighborhood falafel shacks, with professionally designed graphics and plexiglas pilasters lit with pink and blue neon. I would return for the bread alone—a homemade pide flecked with black sesame seeds. Use it to scoop cacik—yogurt, garlic, and fresh mint, much better for you than cream cheese. Adana kebab and swordfish are the best grilled items, although the latter is available only as a platter, rather than the preferable sandwich format. [¢]

Yatagan

104 MacDougal St near Bleecker St, Manhattan,
212-677-0952, subway: A, B, C, D, E, F, Q to W 4th St

If you crave doner kebab, that amalgam of twirling mystery meat known to the Greeks as gyro and Middle Easterners as schwarma, go to Yatagan, a long-running Turkish stand that serves the best in town. Ask for both the yogurt and hot sauce on your overstuffed sandwich, and check out the interesting range of Turkish soft beverages, like sour cherry. There is a pint-sized dining room, but most folks step up to the window.

Vietnamese and Cambodian

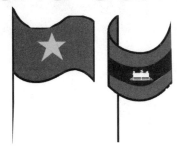

When the last edition this book was published, Vietnamese food was a hot ticket in Chinatown. Now its importance has faded, eclipsed by a profusion of Malaysian and Fuzhou joints that sell cheaper to the Asian immigrant community. Meanwhile, Vietnamese fare has been assimilated into the Pacific Rim eateries that dot more affluent neighborhoods, places that often have cutesy names like Rain and River. Things are still hopping though in Little Vietnam, the two blocks north of Canal between Bowery and Chrystie, and that's where you'll find Pho Cong Ly, which I consider the best Vietnamese eatery in town. Stroll the neighborhood and find video stores, groceries, fish markets, and vendors that sell banh mi, the sandwich that blends East and West by piling cold cuts, pickled vegetables, fish sauce, and cilantro on French bread. Cambodian food presents an interesting twist on the flavors you'll recognize from other Southeast Asian cuisines—lemongrass, galangal, garlic, cilantro, and sweet spices. Unfortunately, there's only one restaurant that serves it, a very friendly Fort Greene spot that lards the menu with other countries' cooking, just to confuse you. Don't miss chicken ahmok, a light mousse sparkling with tart flavors.

VIETNAMESE

Gia Lam

**5402 8th Ave near 54th St, Brooklyn,
718-854-8818, subway: N, R to 53rd St**

At the southern end of Sunset Park's Chinatown, this
Vietnamese restaurant is often thronged with
Vietnamese families eating spring rolls and big bowls
of soup. One such soup is pho dac biet ($5),
described on the menu as "special rice noodles soup
w. beef, brisket, navel, flank and tendon." To the
uninitiated, these various forms of beef are indistin-
guishable. But each has a unique character and they
are mixed and matched in eight different soups,
which are made with a thin but flavorful meat broth
and contain flat rice noodles and a sprinkling of
chopped green onions. Each is served with a plate of
sprouts and basil leaves. The unusually large spring
rolls contain ground pork and vermicelli in a
superthin wrapper. A small plate with romaine lettuce leaves and fresh mint comes on the
side. I always thought you were supposed to wrap each roll in a lettuce with some mint before
downing it, but Vietnamese diners nearby wolfed them down straight and reserved the lettuce
for bites between mouthfuls of soup. One of the best things here is goi tom can tay ($6), a
delicious and plentiful cold salad of shrimp and crisp celery dressed with vinegar and crushed
roasted peanuts. It leaves you wondering how they can afford to give you so many shrimp at
that price. [¢, kid friendly]

Vietnamese specialties

banh cuon
Vietnamese crepes

bo la nho
*beef charred in
grape leaves*

goi tom cang
*shrimp and
cucumber salad*

nuoc cham
clear dipping sauce

nuoc mam
fermented fish sauce

pho
beef and noodle soup

Little Saigon Cafe

**374 W 46th St near 9th Ave, Manhattan,
212-956-0639, subway: A, C, E to 42nd St**

When they say little, they mean little. This cafe in the theater district's Restaurant Row has
only 12 seats at four tables and a kitchen so small that you couldn't lie down in it. But the dining room is cheerful, and the food is a bargain: no dish is over $8.25, and most of the noodle
soup and over-rice selections are priced around $5.25. Quantities are generous: Vietnamese-
style beef noodle soup is a full quart of noodles and thinly sliced beef in a substantial broth
seasoned with onions, lemongrass, and fresh whole mint leaves. Vietnamese-style fried rice is
oily, red, and slightly spicy, with pieces of shrimp and chicken. The highlight of the meal is the
chef's special kim-ting shrimp ($7.25); six good-sized shrimp are wrapped in rice paper and
stuffed with vermicelli and ground pork—it's like a shrimp shoved into a spring roll. End you
meal with "French black condensed milk coffee" or one of the other slow-dripping varieties
made at your table. During the summer, the cafe puts a couple of tables out on the sidewalk.
[outdoor dining]

Miss Saigon

473 Columbus Ave near 82nd St, Manhattan,
212-595-8919, subway: 1, 9 to 79th St
1425 3rd Ave near 80th St, Manhattan,
212-988-8828, subway: 6 to 77th St

In an era when many restaurants are festooned with kitsch, the functionality of the interior at Miss Saigon is one of its chief attractions, and the cheap prices don't hurt either. High points of a recent meal included a wonderful salad of grilled beef and green papaya in an astringent dressing, and barbecued pork chops marinated in lemongrass and garlic—the volume of meat so abundant, it nearly fed three. Conversely, a Chinese-style plate of spareribs was rather dull and fatty. This is a real cheap dining resource for these neighborhoods, but not to be confused with much better places in Chinatown. Not to be confused with the Broadway musical of the same name, either.

New Pasteur

85 Baxter St near White St, Manhattan,
212-608-3656, subway: J, M, N, R, Z, 6 to Canal St

Com xuon bi cha is one great plate of food: a mesa of rice topped with a charcoal-grilled pork chop, a dusty julienne of gelatinous pork skin, and a mysterious vermicelli omelet—yellow on top, brown below, with a faint taste of crab. With the usual Vietnamese garnish of cucumber and mint leaves, and a pour-over sauce containing vinegar, sugar, carrots, and the funky Vietnamese fish sauce, nuoc mam, the plate is enormous for the money ($6), and can't be called boring. The pork chop in particular is unforgettable—sliced razor thin, with a sweet glaze that complements the smoky flavor. New Pasteur is named after one of Saigon's main drags and was first restaurant in New York to serve Vietnamese food. It has long been a lunchtime favorite of the jury duty crowd. Nearly any over-rice selection can be recommended, especially chicken with chili and lemongrass or the same dish made with squid. The modest sounding "shrimp with little salt and pepper" turns out to be a beautiful oblong plate with beaucoup shrimp, faintly tasting of ginger, onions, and green pepper. In the "casseroles" section of the menu, you'll find tom satee, a ceramic pot of shrimp and finely chopped peanuts in an oily red sauce flavored with lemongrass. [¢]

Nhu Y

35 Lispenard St near Church St, Manhattan,
212-431-0986, subway: J, M, N, R, Z, 6 to Canal St

This Vietnamese spot can afford to be way off the beaten track, poised between Chinatown and TriBeCa: it has such an interesting menu. I heard about it on the Internet from a member of a Chinese business fraternity, who said it was a favorite haunt. We especially like an entree of baby clams in coconut curry, with the clam broth adding an extra dimension to the flavor of the sauce, and another of sauteed pigeon done to a turn and garnished with green onion and lemongrass. Also worth trying is a crab and bamboo-shoot soup, as long as you mix in the condiments of lemon, chili sauce, and spice powder.

★ Pho Cong Ly

**124 Hester St near Chrystie St, Manhattan,
212-343-1111, subway: B, D, Q to Grand St**

Cong Ly offers a less ambitious bill of fare than some of its Little Vietnam neighbors, catering to working-class Vietnamese—cabbies pull up to the front door and get handed their pho without leaving their cars. The food is spicier, with no concessions to make it more acceptable to Western tastes. Despite its modest menu, Cong Ly boasts a couple of unique dishes that by themselves would justify a visit. Banh cuon ($4) is colorless rice-starch crepes, stuffed with ground pork and cloud-ear fungus. When the dish arrives at your table you won't see the crepes at first, since they're covered with slices of the rubbery pork roll much favored by the Vietnamese. Flanking this are copious quantities of lettuce, sprouts, cucumber, and mint, with crunchy brown onions strewn over all. Another great dish is chao long, a rice soup that the waitress, the soul of hospitality, warned me away from. How could I resist? It turned out to contain pig intestines, organ meats, delicious rounds of very French sausage studded with

¡O¡ VIETNAMESE SANDWICH

When cultures clash, new cuisines are formed. Sometimes a dish stands at the battle line, with one foot in each camp. One such is banh mi, the Vietnamese sandwich. Check out the version at the Tan Phong Supermarket (85 Bowery, Manhattan, no phone). Once inside, you'll find that it's not a supermarket in the normal sense of the term, but a Super Market—a hall of stalls where the shopkeepers vie with one another to present the most popular goods—bras, beauty supplies, cassette tapes, and cheap shoes. Just as you enter, on your right is a narrow space that sells cigarettes, gum, notions, juices, and sandwiches. A neon sign in the window in ideograms and also in the Roman alphabet says, "Vietnam Sandwich French Sandwich." The name of the stall is Banh Mi So 1, and behind the counter is a toaster oven that is being used as a display case for a pile of baguettes already smeared with mayonnaise and stuffed with an assortment of meats: smoked pork (like bacon), rubbery chicken roll, and Chinese-style roast pork with a fibrous texture. When you order a sandwich ($2.25), the counterman pulls one out of the toaster oven, and warms it in a microwave for a minute. Then he piles on raw cucumber and a julienne of sweet preserved carrot, and carefully selects a sprig of cilantro that is just the length of the sandwich. Finally, a squirt of hot pepper sauce and another of nuoc mam. The baguette seems especially made for the purpose—ultra crusty, and more flattened than usual, with diagonal slashes across the top. Wash it down with a can of pennyroyal drink or young green coconut milk.

peppercorns, and crisp dried shrimp. Every bite was heavenly. The pho at Cong Ly also deserves special mention. It comes with a couple of unexpected vegetables: fresh Asian basil leaves with a licorice bite and tiny rings of fresh hot chile. [¢]

Pho Viet Huong

75 Mulberry St near Bayard St, Manhattan,
212-233-8988, subway: J, M, N, R, Z, 6 to Canal St

The bewildering 250-item menu makes this the most overreaching Vietnamese restaurant in town, but luckily, many things are good, and the menu length justifies a handful of really worthwhile Vietnamese oddities. For instance, this is one of the few places to serve bo 7 mon co tieng. A secret military protocol? No, a traditional seven-course meal in which beef is deployed in every course, beginning with beef grilled tableside, and ending with a beef congee. Another example—bo la nho, lozenges of beef wrapped in grape leaves and grilled till the greenery is charred and the meat assumes an astringent quality. There's a big family scene in the large dining room on weekends. [kid friendly]

CAMBODIAN

★ South East Asian Cuisine

87 S Elliot Pl near Fulton St, Brooklyn,
718-858-3262, subway: C to Lafayette St

Cambodian specialties

chicken ahmok
poultry-and-coconut mousse

nataing
ground-meat vegetable dip

samlor mchoo srae
sour fish soup

tchruok spey koaob
mixed vegetable pickle

In Phnom Penh when people go out to eat, the choices are mainly French and Chinese, which means that Khmer chefs do most of their cooking at home. This convention has continued in this country, with many Cambodian immigrants in Los Angeles and New York preferring to eat Chinese, which is plentiful, cheap, and familiar. But New York has one Cambodian restaurant—South East Asian Cuisine. Its slogan: "Less fat—better than Chinese food." S.E.A. Cuisine (as it says on the window) is located on a sunny square in Fort Greene. The dining room is strikingly utilitarian, with no embellishment except the obligatory Heimlich maneuver poster. The first thing to order is the first thing on the menu, tchruok spey koaob (95¢), a lovely dish of sweet-and-sour pickled vegetables good for nibbling. The generous serving is a warning against over-ordering. Next get chicken ahmok ($6.50), surely one of the strangest and most delicious dishes available in a New York restaurant. It arrives looking like a small white Frisbee with a fluted edge, perched on a kale island in a dense broth strongly flavored with lemongrass. The ahmok is decorated with spokes of red pepper with shredded leaves in the center, a musty tasting herb called lamb leaf. The mousse-like texture is achieved by beating raw chicken breast with coconut milk. Other estimable selections include mekong fish ($12.95), a two-pound tilapia served crisp in a subtle chile sauce; and samlor mchoo srae ($6.95), reminiscent of the Thai soup tom yum, but with a much thicker broth. Cambodian meals often begin like an American cocktail party, with chips and dips, only instead of chips they use slices of French bread or slivers of raw vegetable. There are a couple of typical dips on the S.E.A. menu, including "hot and spicy ground beef appetizer" ($2), which is a small bowl of fiery ground meat. Admired by everyone at the table, it inspired a test of dexterity to see who could scoop up the most on a carrot slice.

Brooklyn

MIDTOWN EAST & BELOW

Ansuya's Caribbean Cafe
(International) 100
Chikubu (Japanese) 123
Chola (Indian) 90
Curry in a Hurry (Indian) 91
Dai Jia Lou (Dai) 38
Genki Sushi (Japanese) 123
Gyroland (Turkish) 211
Harglo's Cafe
(Regional American)173
Indonesian Mission to the
United Nations (Indonesian) 144
Jai-Ya (Thai) 200
Jubilee (French) 19
Katsuhama (Japanese) 125
Kuruma Sushi (Japanese) 127
Menchanko-Tei (Japanese) 125
Mexico Lindo (Mexican) 151
Mezze (International) 102
Nader (Persian) 168
New Madras Palace (Indian) 92
Patoug (Persian) 168
Restaurant Nippon (Japanese) 126
Rolf's (German) 72
Turkish Kitchen (Turkish) 212
Vatan (Indian) 93
Wu Liang Ye (Sichuan/Hunan) 45

MIDTOWN WEST

Ahp Ku Jung (Korean) 134
B. Frites (Belgian) 16
Bali Nusa Indah (Indonesian) 143
Bay Leaf (Indian) 89
Bêco Azul (Brazilian) 23
Cabana Carioca (Brazilian) 23
Chez GnaGna Koty's Senegal
Goree Island (Senegalese) 181
Chimichurri Grill (Argentine) 10
Chinar (Indian) 89
Cho Dang Gal (Korean) 134
Dalquis Restaurant (Dominican) 50
Diamond Dairy Restaurant
(Jewish) 131
Ishihama (Korean) 136
Jams (Jamaican) 116
Kosher Delight (Israeli) 162
La Crêpe de Bretagne (French) 21
Little Saigon Cafe (Vietnamese) 215

Los Dos Rancheros Mexicanos
(Mexican) 148
Mandoo (Korean) 136
Menchanko-Tei (Japanese) 125
New York Kom Tang Soot
Bull House(Korean) 136
Nick's Place (Greek) 82
Pomaire (Chilean) 13
Sahara Grill (Turkish) 212
Sapporo (Japanese) 125
Soul Fixin's (Soul Food) 191
Soup Kitchen International
(International) 103
Tacocina (Mexican) 153
Taprobane (Sri Lankan)98
Terminal House (Korean) 138
Veronica Ristorante
Italiano (Italian) 112
Virgil's Real Barbecue
(Regional American) 175
Wu Liang Ye (Sichuan/Hunan) 45
Yum (Thai) 202

SOHO & VICINITY

416 B.C. (Bulgarian) 58
Ghenet (Ethiopian)69
Honmura An (Japanese) 126
Hoomoos Asli (Israeli) 161
L'Orange Bleue (Moroccan) 166
La Poême (French) 20
Lahore Deli (Pakistani) 96
Le Pain Quotidien (Belgian) 15
ñ (Spanish) 193
Nhu Y (Vietnamese) 216
Palacinka (French) 21
Rice (International) 104
Snack (Greek) 82

UNION SQUARE /
FLATIRON DISTRICT

Bangkok Cafe (Thai) 199
Havana Pies (International) 101
La Pizza Fresca (Italian) 111
O Padeiro (Portuguese) 195
Republic (International) 103
Ribollita (Italian) 11
Silver Swan (German) 74
Tad's Steaks
(Regional American) 175

UPPER EAST SIDE

Cafe Guy Pascal (French) 17
El Pollo (Peruvian) 66
Galil (Jewish) 132
Halal Indo-Pak Restaurant
  (Pakistani) 95
Heidelberg (German) 72
Le Pain Quotidien (Belgian) 15
Miss Saigon (Vietnamese) 216
Mocca Hungarian (Hungarian) 58
Pamir (Afghani) 170
Pastrami Queen (Jewish) 133
Wu Liang Ye (Sichuan/Hunan) 45

UPPER WEST SIDE

Ansuya's Caribbean Cafe
  (International) 100
Barney Greengrass (Jewish) 131
Epices du Traiteur (Tunisian) 166
Gabriela's (Mexican) 149
Haru (Japanese) 124
Krik Krak (Haitian) 85
Los Paisas (Mexican) 152
Luzia's (Portuguese) 195
Miss Saigon (Vietnamese) 216
Pampa (Argentine) 12
Tibet Shambala (Tibetan) 98

Queens

ASTORIA

Bascarsija (Bosnian/Croatian) 56
Christos Hasapo-Taverna (Greek) 81
Churrascaria Girassol (Brazilian) 24
Istria Sports Club
  (Bosnian/Croatian) 56
Kabab Cafe (Egyptian) 160
S'Agapo (Greek) 82
Samba & Sabor (Brazilian) 24
Uncle George's Greek Tavern
  (Greek) 82
Zenon (Greek) 83
Zlatá Praha (Czech/Slovak) 57
Zodiac (Greek) 83

BAYSIDE

Akida (Japanese) 123

CORONA

Don Pepe (Ecuadorian) 61
El Gauchito (Argentine) 11
La Esquina Criolla (Argentine) 10
Green Field (Brazilian) 24
Rincon Colombiano (Colombian) 25

FOREST HILLS

Bombay Kitchen (Indian) 89

FLUSHING

ABC American Cooking
  (Hong Kong) 42
Dosa Hutt (Indian) 91
Haejo (Korean) 135
Hapina (Israeli) 161
Hong Kong Seafood (Hong Kong) 41
Joe's Shanghai (Shanghai) 43
Kazan Turkish Cuisine (Turkish) 211
Laifood (Taiwanese)46
Laterna (Greek) 81
Master Grill (Brazilian) 24
Niederstein's (German) 73
Patoug (Persian) 168
Satay Hut (Malaysian) 142
Shin Jung (Korean) 137
Taste Good (Malaysian) 142
Warteg Fortuna (Indonesian) 144
Zum Stammtisch (German) 74

JACKSON HEIGHTS

Jackson Diner (Indian) 92
La Fusta (Argentine) 10
La Picada Azuaya (Ecuadorian)62
La Porteña (Argentine) 12
Malaysian Rasa Sayang
  (Malaysian) 141
Olympic Garden (Korean) 137
Pearson's Texas Barbecue
  (Regional American) 174
Pio Pio (Peruvian) 65
Tabaq 74 (Pakistani) 97

JAMAICA

El Comal Pupuseria (Salvadoran) 28
Norman's Jerk Chicken
   Restaurant (Jamaican) 119
Sorrento Bakery (Surinamese) 207
Xelaju (Guatemalan) 28

LITTLE NECK

La Baraka (Moroccan) 164

LONG ISLAND CITY

Al Dewan (Lebanese/Syrian) 156
Costal Colombiana (Colombian) 25
Elwady (Egyptian) 159
5 Stars Punjabi Indian Cuisine
   (Pakistani)94
La Espiga II (Mexican) 149
Yerevan (Armenian) 31

QUEENS VILLAGE

Dee's West Indian Bakery
   (Jamaican) 117

REGO PARK

Registan (Uzbek) 33

RIDGEWOOD AND ELMHURST

Captain King (Cantonese) 36
David's Taiwanese Gourmet
   (Taiwanese) 46
El Arrayan (Chilean) 13
Inti Raymi (Peruvian) 65
Jai-Ya (Thai) 200
Kway Tiow (Thai) 200
My Uncle's (Argentine) 11
Salut (Uzbek) 34

ST. ALBANS

Mississippi Bar-B-Que
   (Regional American) 173

WOODSIDE

Darul Kabab (Bangladeshi) 97
Izalco (Salvadoran) 29
Sripraphai (Thai) 201

Staten Island

Killmeyer's Old Bavarian Inn
   (German) 73
West Brighton Italian Grocery
   (Italian) 113

New Jersey

Beyti Kebab (Turkish) 211
Chowpatty (Indian) 90
Pic-Nic (Portuguese) 196
Restaurant Oaxaqueño #2
   (Mexican) 153
Seabras Marrisquiera
   (Portuguese) 196
Yaohan Plaza (Japanese) 129

About the Author

Robert Sietsema writes a pair of columns, Counter Culture and Chow Choices, for the *Village Voice*, and contributes to *Gourmet*, *Biography Magazine*, *Travel & Leisure*, *i-D* magazine, and *Salon*. He is also the publisher of *Down the Hatch*, the world's first foodzine. Robert lives in Greenwich Village with his wife and daughter.

Listed here are some additional titles from City & Company. Like New York itself, our guides are smart and sassy— exploring subjects of interest to our fellow New Yorkers and their visitors.

Whether you're setting off solo, with a friend, as a couple or with the family, they are valuable references for the culturally adventurous. Add them to your home library, office bookshelf or carry them with you as you discover the crème de la crème of where to go, what to see and do. Filled with on-and off-the-beaten-path destinations, tested resources, tips and inside information, all of them are one-of-a-kind manuals to real life in New York.

You can find these books at your local bookstore, through booksellers on the web, or by contacting City & Company.

City & Company
22 West 23rd Street   New York, NY 10010
tel: 212.366.1988 fax: 212.242.0415
e-mail: cityco@mindspring.com www.cityandcompany.com